Life in Post-War Britain

Life in Post-War Britain

"Toils and Efforts Ahead"

Anton Rippon and Nicola Rippon

First published in Great Britain in 2023 by
Pen & Sword History
An imprint of
Pen & Sword Books Ltd
Yorkshire – Philadelphia

Copyright © Anton Rippon and Nicola Rippon 2023

ISBN 978 1 39906 475 0

The rights of Anton Rippon and Nicola Rippon to be identified as Authors of this work has been asserted by them in accordance with the Copyright, Designs and Patents Act 1988.

A CIP catalogue record for this book is available from the British Library.

All rights reserved. No part of this book may be reproduced or transmitted in any form or by any means, electronic or mechanical including photocopying, recording or by any information storage and retrieval system, without permission from the Publisher in writing.

Typeset by Mac Style
Printed in the UK by CPI Group (UK) Ltd, Croydon, CR0 4YY.

Pen & Sword Books Limited incorporates the imprints of Atlas, Archaeology, Aviation, Discovery, Family History, Fiction, History, Maritime, Military, Military Classics, Politics, Select, Transport, True Crime, Air World, Frontline Publishing, Leo Cooper, Remember When, Seaforth Publishing, The Praetorian Press, Wharncliffe Local History, Wharncliffe Transport, Wharncliffe True Crime, White Owl and After the Battle.

For a complete list of Pen & Sword titles please contact

PEN & SWORD BOOKS LIMITED
47 Church Street, Barnsley, South Yorkshire, S70 2AS, England
E-mail: enquiries@pen-and-sword.co.uk
Website: www.pen-and-sword.co.uk

Or

PEN AND SWORD BOOKS
1950 Lawrence Rd, Havertown, PA 19083, USA
E-mail: Uspen-and-sword@casematepublishers.com
Website: www.penandswordbooks.com

Contents

Introduction		vii
Prelude		viii
Chapter 1	A New Year Dawns	1
Chapter 2	A Savage Winter	7
Chapter 3	The Final Insult	16
Chapter 4	Learning to Live Together	26
Chapter 5	The Petticoat Pilgrims	34
Chapter 6	Mutiny in the RAF	42
Chapter 7	Public Ownership is the Answer	50
Chapter 8	From the Cradle to the Grave	56
Chapter 9	Lessons Learned	62
Chapter 10	A Betrayal of British Values?	67
Chapter 11	Good, Thrifty, Hard-working People	76
Chapter 12	No Dogs, No Blacks, No Irish	83
Chapter 13	Murders Most Foul	90
Chapter 14	A Perfect Orgy of Crime	98
Chapter 15	If They Win the Cup, We Don't Mind Feeding Them	110
Chapter 16	Austerity Olympics – A Glorious Reality	119
Chapter 17	That's Entertainment	123

Chapter 18	Fashion on the Ration to the New Look	131
Chapter 19	Britain Can Make It – But Britain Can't Have It	137
Chapter 20	Two Foreign Office Men are Missing	144
Chapter 21	By The Skin of Their Teeth	150
Chapter 22	Britain in Colour	157
Chapter 23	Joyous Event … Greatest Sorrow	168
Chapter 24	A Crowning Glory	178
Acknowledgements		181
Index		183

Introduction

In November 1945 my paternal grandmother sent me birthday greetings from her home in the Lincolnshire fenland town of Spalding. Whether she was pre-empting a delay in the postal service in those difficult times, or whether she simply got the date wrong, I don't know, but the card arrived a month early. I still have it, although it isn't a birthday card in the traditional sense. It is simply a postcard showing a cartoon of a small boy and his dog and it carries a quote from Winston Churchill. Announcing to Parliament, six months earlier, the German surrender, Britain's wartime prime minister warned, 'Let us not forget the toils and efforts that lie ahead.' It isn't the sort of sentiment you would normally send anyone on their birthday, let alone a one-year-old. But, then again, life in post-war Britain was going to be tough. So why wrap it up?

Growing up in the years after the Second World War was, indeed, to experience 'austerity'. Our playgrounds were bombsites, and food was rationed. 'Be careful with that butter, it's got to last all week,' was a mantra that my mother trotted out each teatime. It wasn't that we couldn't afford to buy any more; we just weren't allowed to do so.

For our parents and grandparents, of course, this was not normal, even if, compared to today's choice of food, clothing and household goods – not to mention holidays – life before the war had also been far from luxurious. True, there were no more nights spent in an air-raid shelter, but now even bread was rationed.

As Winston Churchill had promised, there were toils and efforts ahead.

Anton Rippon

Prelude

A revolution takes place in Britain by ballots instead of bullets. The English genius for compromise will probably be at work and a middle course will develop.

Detroit Free Press

On 26 July 1945 the British people learned that they had a new government. Eight weeks earlier, following the Allies' victory in Europe, the coalition that Winston Churchill set up in 1940 had been dissolved. The Labour Party, now anxious to fight a general election for the first time in a decade, had withdrawn its support. Since 1935 there had been a huge change in the public's outlook. The *Beveridge Report*, published in 1942, recommended a comprehensive welfare system that included a national health service. Throughout the country, William Beveridge's plans enjoyed widespread support, but not from Churchill and the Conservative Party whose reaction was, at best, lukewarm. With Germany defeated, the Labour leader, Clement Attlee, wanted to put the new left-leaning agenda to the ultimate test.

The new prime minister was an unprepossessing figure whose modesty saw opponents poke fun at him. One story going the rounds was that during a train journey to Fulton, Missouri, in March 1946, when President Harry Truman told Churchill, 'Clement Attlee came to see me the other day. He struck me as a very modest man,' the former prime minister replied, 'He has much to be modest about.' Another story has Churchill saying that 'an empty taxi pulled up in Downing Street, and Clement Attlee got out'. There is no evidence for this, either. The quip was first used in 1879 to describe the slender French actress Sarah Bernhardt: 'An empty carriage drove up … and Sarah Bernhardt alighted from it.'

But Attlee was indeed a modest figure, and while the left wing of British politics has seen plenty of charismatic characters, he was not one of them. Born in Putney, the son of a solicitor and the seventh of eight children, after gaining a Bachelor of Arts degree with second-class honours in modern history at University College, Oxford, Attlee was called to the Bar in 1906. The poverty that he saw while working as a volunteer with boys from the East End slums converted him to full-on socialism. He had abandoned his legal career and was lecturing at the London School of Economics when the First World War began. Although then 31, he volunteered to join the army and was commissioned, with the rank of captain, in the South Lancashire Regiment. He fought in the ill-fated Gallipoli campaign that had such severe political repercussions for its main sponsor, Winston Churchill, who was demoted from First Lord of the Admiralty as a result. In contrast, Attlee's older brother, Tom, was a conscientious objector who was imprisoned, first in Wormwood Scrubs and later in Wandsworth Gaol, from January 1917 to April 1919.

Mayor of Stepney in 1919, Clement Attlee had entered the House of Commons in 1922 as the member for Limehouse. Two years later he was appointed Parliamentary Under Secretary of State for War in Ramsay MacDonald's short-lived Labour government. In MacDonald's second minority government, from 1929 to 1931, he was promoted to the Cabinet. Attlee became Labour leader in October 1935 and, although initially opposing re-armament, had been a critic of Neville Chamberlain's appeasement of Hitler and Mussolini. In 1940 he had taken Labour into Churchill's coalition government, first as Lord Privy Seal and, from 1942 as Deputy Prime Minister. In late May 1940, as Allied troops prepared to evacuate Dunkirk, when Foreign Secretary Lord Halifax challenged Churchill's approach, advocating instead that, through the good offices of the (barely) still-neutral Mussolini, it would be possible to negotiate a settlement with Hitler, it was the support of Attlee and the Cabinet's other Labour member, the more voluble Arthur Greenwood, as well as that of the Liberal leader, Sir Archibald Sinclair, which helped save the day. Throughout the war, Attlee remained Churchill's staunch ally. Now, in peacetime, he was Winston's steadfast opponent.

Churchill had wanted to wait until the war in the Pacific was won before calling the election, but when Attlee walked away, he had no choice but to go to the country. Election day was 5 July. The results were announced three weeks later, to allow servicemen and women stationed overseas to vote. Churchill had banked on his popularity as the nation's wartime leader – 'Vote National – Help Him Finish The Job' was the slogan – but in a speech on 4 June he attacked the Labour Party in a way that astonished even his own supporters: 'No socialist government conducting the entire life and industry of the country could afford to allow free, sharp, or violently-worded expressions of public discontent. They would have to fall back on some form of Gestapo, no doubt very humanely directed in the first instance.'

The word 'Gestapo' leapt out, and Attlee seized upon it:

> Make no mistake, it has only been through the power of the State, given to it by Parliament, that the general public has been protected against the greed of ruthless profit-makers and property owners. The Conservative Party remains, as always, a class party. In twenty-three years in the House of Commons, I cannot recall more than half a dozen from the ranks of the wage earners. It represents today, as in the past, the forces of property and privilege.

Attlee reminded voters that Churchill, their wartime leader, was now simply Churchill, the leader of the Conservative Party, and 'I thank him for having disillusioned them so thoroughly'.

On election day, the *Daily Mirror*, the most popular newspaper with servicemen, published on its front page a powerful cartoon by Philip Zec. It showed a bandaged and battered soldier standing in a ruined landscape and holding out an olive branch and a piece of paper on which was written, 'Victory and Peace in Europe'. The caption read, 'Here you are – don't lose it again!'. The cartoon had first been published in the paper on VE Day. Now it appeared alongside an editorial urging people:

> Vote on behalf of the men who won victory for you. You failed to do so in 1918. The result is known to all. The 'land fit for heroes' did not come into existence. The dole did. Short-lived prosperity gave way to long, tragic years of poverty and unemployment. Make sure that history does not repeat itself … . Move forward to happier times. The call of the men who have gone comes to you. Pay heed to it. Vote for THEM.

Despite opinion polls showing Labour six points ahead of the Tories, there was only guarded optimism in Labour ranks. When the early results came in, they gave cause for hope that the pollsters had been correct. Leo Amery and Brendan Bracken, two of Churchill's most loyal supporters, had lost their seats, Amery to Labour's Percy Shumer at Birmingham Sparkbrook. That was perhaps no great surprise: during the war, Amery's elder son, John, had made propaganda broadcasts for the Nazis and encouraged British prisoners-of-war to join the British Free Corps, a unit of the Waffen SS. John Amery would be hanged for treason at Wandsworth prison in December 1945. But the political demise of Bracken, Britain's wartime Minister of Information, was altogether unexpected. He lost his seat to Labour's Sir Frank Noel Mason-MacFarlane, who had been governor of Gibraltar during the war.

There were many more shocks to come, and when everything had been added up, Labour had a Commons majority of 146 seats with 47.8 per cent of the vote and an 11.8 swing in their favour. The number of Conservative MPs had dropped from 387 to 197. The Liberals – Sir Archibald Sinclair lost his seat in a tight three-way contest in Caithness and Sutherland, the Tories winning it from Labour by six votes – were reduced to twelve MPs. Churchill was reported to be astounded, but the man who had led Britain through a world war was not seen as the man to lead Britain in peacetime. He had refused to embrace the *Beveridge Report*, and many returning members of the armed forces had voted Labour in the hope of a better life at home in the years to come. In 1935 there had been 31.3 million eligible voters, 21.9 million of whom cast their vote. In 1945 some 25 million out of 33.2 million voted. In those ten years Labour's aggregate popular vote had grown by 10 per cent. Tens of thousands of first-time voters had had their say. There were several successful fringe candidates, and, taking political leanings more generally, the *Birmingham Daily Post* reckoned that if one counted in Liberals, Independent Labour Party, Commonwealth, Communist and Independents against the Tories, National Liberals and Nationals, then the Left had a majority of 210. Whichever way one chose to interpret it, voters in the 1945 General Election had delivered a crushing blow to Winston Churchill.

There was sympathy for him, but also a sense of realism, even across the Atlantic. One Washington correspondent cabled:

> The silencing of the voice which, in the dark hours of near defeat inspired ten million Americans with faith and hope in the cause of free people, has shocked and saddened Americans of all shades of political opinion … but most Americans I have spoken to in

all walks of life declared, 'We are sorry for Mr Churchill, but it is probably a good thing'.'

The *New York Times* commented:

> It is perhaps the natural reaction of a nation sick of war and moved by a desire for change .... If the Labour government functions on a broad basis of popular support as it takes on an unfinished war and the tasks of reconstruction at home and abroad, Britain may play in peace an even greater role than she has played in war.

The *Washington Post* thought that 'there is no more gratitude in electorate than in princes'.

Australia's former Liberal prime minister Robert Menzies, now the country's opposition leader, felt that the disappearance of Churchill and Anthony Eden, the Foreign Secretary, at this crucial moment was 'tragic', but New Zealand's Labour prime minister, Peter Fraser, declined to comment. The *Cape Times*, voice of South Africa's ruling United Party, said that 'the results of the experiment will be watched with some sympathy but with some anxiety'. The defeat of Leo Amery, the Secretary of State for India, was generally acclaimed by all political parties on the sub-continent, and most of the French Press welcomed Labour's victory. In Moscow a radio commentator thought that 'the fact that in ten years about seven million young people, whose sentiments the parties have ignored, had come of age may have had something to do with the British election results'.

Hugh Gaitskell, Harold Wilson, James Callaghan, Michael Foot, Barbara Castle and Denis Healey were among the Labour faces entering Parliament for the first time, but, before the Commons could meet, four by-elections had to be organised. Only one day after the election results were announced, Alfred Dobbs, the Labour member for Smethwick, was killed on the Great North Road near Doncaster when the car he was driving was in collision with a military vehicle after he swerved to avoid a child. His passenger, Mrs Elsie Marshall, died later in hospital. Two other MPs – Bromley's Sir Edward Campbell and Monmouth's Leslie Pym – had died on the same day, 17 July, while the appointment of Ashton-under-Lyne MP Sir William Jowitt as Lord Chancellor created yet another immediate vacancy. Harold Macmillan, who had lost his

Stockton seat in the General Election, won Bromley to begin his third term as a Conservative MP.

On 15 August 1945 Britain celebrated VJ Day. Officially the war still had a few days to run because the Japanese would not surrender with a signed document until 2 September, but the dropping of two atomic bombs on their country had signalled the end. Celebrations were muted because many families still did not know the fate of loved ones who had been fighting in the Far East. The new prime minister had some sobering words, too. Peace heralded, not days of plenty, but even greater austerity. In August 1945 the US government's abrupt and unexpected ending of Lend-Lease, the programme whereby the Americans provided food, raw materials including oil, medical supplies and clothing, not to mention warships, warplanes and weapons, to its Allies, meant major cuts in imports, while goods meant for home consumption would now have to be exported. Britain had been the biggest recipient of Lend-Lease, accepting $31 billion-worth since 1941.

The war had all but ruined the country economically. Since 1939 Britain had spent annually more than 40 per cent of GDP on defence, a figure that had reached 52 per cent of GDP in 1945, by which time UK government debt peaked at around 270 per cent of GDP. Lend-Lease might have kept Britain going, but it had done so at a massive cost, both in terms of huge borrowing and in having to sell overseas assets. When Lend-Lease ended, the stock retained was sold to Britain at a knockdown price of around ten cents to the dollar. But that was still a huge sum of money. In the autumn of 1945, John Maynard Keynes – Lord Keynes – the world's most eminent economist, went to the United States to beg for financial aid. Keynes, gravely ill and in the last few months of his life, was disappointed with the Americans' offer: a loan of $586 million (about £145 million at 1945 exchange rates) to pay for the retained stock, and a further loan of $3.75 billion (about £930 million) at an interest rate of two per cent, payable in dollars over fifty years starting in 1950. In 1946 the British government would also agree a US$1.19 billion line of credit loan from Canada.

The Americans also insisted on the complete abandonment of the so-called 'imperial preferences'. That would now make life difficult for Britain's colonies when it came to them trading outside the Commonwealth. The entire arrangement caused resentment in both Britain and the US. The British could not understand how, in their wartime ally's greatest hour of need, the Americans could be so ungenerous. The Americans thought the British were ingrates who felt that they were entitled to special treatment.

The American press led a growing anti-British campaign. In November 1945, 57 per cent of US principal newspapers still supported the loan. By New Year's Eve, that number had dropped to 37 per cent. Writing in the *Daily Herald*, journalist Michael Foot, who had won the Plymouth Devonport constituency for Labour in their landslide victory, said, 'Press opinions are no index of American opinion and American action ... but even those newspapers who have given a consistently fair record of Britain's war effort appear to have given little or no report of serious British misgivings about some terms of the settlement.' The *Chicago Tribune* published a cartoon of John Bull standing at America's back door saying, 'Spare a morsel for a weak, starving man, but make it sirloin medium rare, and if it isn't done just right, I won't eat it, and there's no use begging me.' In the *New York Daily News* a cartoon showed John Bull emerging from a pawnshop, saying, 'Even when I don't pay it back, I don't like it.'

In December 1945 the *Yorkshire Post* said:

Americans are shocked at the British reaction to the Anglo-United States loan agreement. That is plain from the dispatch from our New York correspondent, Mr M.R. Werner, which we publish today. People in this country will reply that they themselves felt at least an equal shock when the terms of the loan plan were announced. The explosion of feeling which followed was involuntary and if the American public appreciate how sincere and unpremeditated it was, they will probably make allowances for any asperity that may have crept into the tone of the press.

The *Washington Evening Star* said:

It is not encouraging to find such a respected British publication as the *Economist* proposing reluctant acceptance of the cruelly hard American conditions. Possibly, as the inevitable economic pressure beats down more heavily upon the British people, they will have to come, as they have before, to blame the United States for their plight, and to regard the annual payments on the loan as nothing more than further exactions by 'Uncle Shylock'.

Earlier, the Conservative MP for Canterbury, Major John Baker White, had summed up the majority feeling. At a meeting at the Foresters' Hall in Canterbury he said:

> To the American people I say this. Your battle for your freedom, your security, for the American way of life, was first fought out in the skies above Kent. The cliffs and beaches of this island were at one time the only barrier that stood in the path of the black flood of evil. If we had not stood alone and won through, if we had been defeated in 1940, the Nazi flag would be flying over the capital in Washington today.
>
> We have not gone to the Americans as poor relations begging from a rich uncle, but his partners in total victory. It wasn't a Pekinese we sent to Washington but the old British bulldog himself. He is a bit grey about the muscle and scarred about the eyes; and there is precious little flesh on his ribs, but his heart is a sound as a bell. And he has got some fine strong offspring strong around the world and ready to help him. I believe I am interpreting the sentiments of the British people when I say that our proposition to America today is this: 'Will you work with us as equal partners to bring back prosperity to the world?' If the American reply is 'No' – that they can only deal with us as master and servant, our reply must be: 'No, we will go on alone with such help as the Empire can give us. We will take the long hard uphill road. We will continue to travel the road of toil and sweat that we have travelled for six long years. And we will triumph in the end. Britain always has and always will.'

Major Baker White said that the end of Lend-Lease was an event which affected the lives of all. It had been called Britain's economic Dunkirk – but that was a defeat and he preferred economic Alamein, 'the day when we started to attack post-war problems in the long battle to victory in prosperity'. He said that the Americans were surprised at the way Britain had reacted to the end of Lend-Lease 'because they did not recognise the British war record'. 'Not a single civilian in America's 136 million population was ever wounded by a German air-raid.' He emphasised that 60,585 of Britain's 47 million population were killed and another 86,000 severely wounded. Four and a half million houses were destroyed or damaged. Britain had a far stricter rationing system and industrial mobilization, conscription of women, 100 per cent austerity, and the blackout. His remarks were greeted with sustained applause. Major Baker White was a colourful, some would say eccentric, character who, before the war, had served as director of the Economic League, a privately funded anti-Communist pressure group. In the late 1930s he had spent time in Germany as a spy, and so well did he convince the Nazis that he was invited to the 1937 Nuremberg Rally. He managed to slip out of the country in April 1939, after exposing Nazi propaganda and fifth column activity. During the war he had worked for Section D of the Secret Intelligent Service. Now he seemed to speak for the people.

Seven months earlier, announcing to Parliament the German surrender, Winston Churchill had said, 'Let us not forget the toils and efforts that lie ahead.' So, the British people faced hard times, but there were also a few chinks of light. On New Year's Eve 1945 the first shipment of bananas arrived in Britain since 1940. Within an hour, dockers at Avonmouth had unloaded 3,370 stems from the Jamaican ship. Then seven special trains with a total of 380 wagons took the still green fruit to warehouses throughout the South-West, South Wales and the Midlands. It would be two weeks before it went on sale to the general public, and then for unders-18s only. In Nottingham, greengrocers were advised that their allocation cards could be obtained from Messrs W.H. Hinton and Son at the city's wholesale market, at a charge of one shilling per grade which was the retailers' contribution towards the cost of the scheme for the distribution of all imported fruits. There would be long queues.

On Christmas morning 1945, 16-year-old Jim Phelps went to his local Methodist Church in Derby where there were some German prisoners of war in the congregation. They sat shoulder-to-shoulder with their fellow worshippers, and together they sang *Silent Night*. Jim said, 'My mind went back to that September day when war was declared, and I thought about all the horror, the hurt and heartache. And then I wondered what we had learned, and what tomorrow would bring.'

Chapter One

A New Year Dawns

The people of Britain ... enter 1946 resolved to make their wish come true.
Daily Herald

The clock struck twelve midnight at the Spa Royal Hall in Bridlington, and the final year of the Second World War made its exit to a chorus of boos and catcalls. The large crowd that had spent the evening dancing to the music of John Sharman's London Orchestra then applauded the arrival of the first full year of peace. A small handful of partygoers were distracted, however. The last day of the old year had ended in a blanket of fog, and the eight trawlers that had left for the fishing grounds of the North Sea before dawn were being guided back to haven by the fog signal at the end of the North Pier. The fishermen arrived home just in time to hear the church bells of Bridlington ring out a merry peal to welcome in 1946. Word reached the dance hall. Then everyone could relax.

One hundred and seventy-eight miles away, as the proverbial crow flies, Londoners welcomed 1946 in their carefree thousands. The *Daily Herald* reported: 'They crowded into Piccadilly Circus and danced around the boarded plinth of exiled Eros in a singing "crocodile" of young people.'

They were joined by GIs from Rainbow Corner, the American Red Cross club where off-duty troops relaxed. 'Midnight was still an hour away when thunder-flashes shook the Circus and revellers wearing paper hats and blowing squeakers and tin whistles and brandishing coloured paper whips, streamed into the Circus.'

As midnight drew near, the crowds grew more boisterous. Private cars and taxis were stopped and rocked to and fro, while merrymakers held out their hands to wish the occupants 'Happy New Year!' The roof of one taxi was torn apart by a group of men and girls. Servicemen and women of all nationalities were out in force, and an American military police jeep, in which sat three American Red Cross girls, was mobbed by GIs. The celebrations extended along Coventry Street into Leicester Square.

Trumpeters of the Welsh Guards heralded the New Year at the Savoy Hotel, but, on the steps of St Paul's at five minutes past midnight, servicemen stood strangely quiet as civilians nearby danced, sang and swung football rattles. Among them was a Canadian flight lieutenant, there to keep a vow to meet fellow officers. Three years earlier, in a German prisoner-of-war camp, he had befriended two Scandinavians, Lieutenant Haldor Elsplid of Norway and Lieutenant Thompson of Copenhagen. They were separated but agreed to meet at St Paul's on the first New Year's Eve after the war. The Canadian waited and waited, but his friends did not appear. Lieutenant Elsplid had been shot by the Gestapo after escaping; Lieutenant Thompson did manage to escape and made it home, but the Nazis reported that he was later drowned trying to cross from his German-occupied homeland to neutral Sweden.

In Edinburgh thousands welcomed in the New Year around the Tron Kirk. *The Scotsman* reported that men and women, many in uniform, some of the men from the American and Canadian forces, joined in the dancing wearing carnival headdresses: 'At twelve o'clock, cheering arose proclaiming the birth of another year; greetings and good wishes were exchanged all round; and groups broke into singing *A Guid New Year*, with zest and with heart, if not in perfect tune.'

In Belfast thousands gathered around the Albert Clock to see in the New Year for the first time since the outbreak of war. The *Northern Whig* reported:

> Long before the hour-hand of the Albert reached midnight, the surrounding thoroughfares were packed with a solid mass of singing, laughing humanity – men and women, boys and girls, and youngsters, well sprinkled with men in khaki and navy blue – that overflowed along Victoria Street and High Street. The last hour of the Old Year was whiled away in community singing or, where servicemen were gathered together, with reminiscences of similar celebrations on one or other of the war fronts .... The sirens of ships on the dockside chorused in harmony, and coloured rockets, bursting high in the air, floated down towards the sea of upturned faces. Then the crowd slowly dispersed. High Street – the main exit – being a moving mass of people for almost fifteen minutes afterwards.'

In Cardiff, where most public dance halls had been granted extensions from midnight until 1.00am, people danced the Old Year out and the New Year in. Because of staffing difficulties there were few hotel dances in Cardiff, but, at the Drill Hall in Dumfries Place, officers of the Welch Regiment held an invitation dinner dance, the proceeds of which were for the regimental memorial in Llandaff Cathedral. At a NAAFI club in Plymouth, a performance of Reginald Beckwith's comedy *A Soldier For Christmas* was given by a company of servicemen and servicewomen under the auspices of United Services Entertainment, after which 'an informal New Year's Eve dance was held'.

The *Birmingham Daily Gazette* was in less joyous mood, 'The prospect of continued austerity in 1946 cast a shadow over Birmingham's celebration of its first peacetime New Year's Eve for six years, and, for most people, it was definitely a "fireside festival".' The paper, however, did go on to report: 'But despite fears, happily falsified, of a repetition of Sunday night's fog blackout, there were packed houses at the pantomimes and other places of entertainment. Befitting revelry was …enjoyed at many festival dances, which in some cases continued long after the singing of *Auld Lang Syne* at midnight.' There was, though, bad news for drinkers: 'The last of the holiday licensing extensions followed what had been one of Birmingham's "driest" weekends since the summer. Many houses, particularly in suburban areas, greeted customers with "Sold Out" notices, and only those able to get special New Year's Eve deliveries were able to stay open until 11pm.'

An unknown and unannounced BBC engineer was the first person to broadcast on the wireless in 1946. The chimes of Big Ben hardly died away when he was heard to say, 'Okay'.

It had been a foggy end to 1945 everywhere. On the morning of New Year's Eve, three people were killed and three seriously injured when a train travelling from Baker Street to Aylesbury was in collision on the Metropolitan Line at Northwood Hills in Middlesex with a train proceeding to Watford. Two coaches of the Watford train were telescoped and the centre compartments burned out. Cars and buses in towns, cities and on country roads everywhere had been driven at a snail's pace, with visibility at times down to less than 50 yards. At Folkestone 1,500 troops, coming home on leave or looking forward to being demobbed, disembarked from the steamer *Canterbury* after being delayed in Calais by twenty-four hours because of dense fog in the English Channel. Food had been in short supply on the *Canterbury* and a tug sent out from the French port to deliver supplies to the leave boat was unable to find it.

Unlike during the war, when the publication of weather forecasts had been banned for fear of helping the enemy, at least when they awoke on 1 January 1946, Britons knew what to expect that day. Newspapers reported that a large anti-cyclone over Scandinavia meant that, although the fog had cleared, cold weather would continue over Great Britain. During the night there had been air frosts throughout South-East England and the Midlands. At Lympne in Kent the temperature had dropped to 26F. Horse racing at Cheltenham was abandoned for New Year's Day and the day after.

The New Year's Honours List was the biggest ever announced, running to 165 pages of the *London Gazette*. The main story was that Winston Churchill had been awarded the Order of Merit. It was apparently the only honour that Britain's wartime prime minister, who had been so roundly rejected as its peacetime leader, would take. King George VI had asked him to accept the Order of the Garter, the highest order of British chivalry, but he chose to remain plain 'Mr Churchill'. There were viscountcies for the men who had led Britain to victory – Alexander, Montgomery, Cunningham, Portal and Alanbrooke – and Marshal of the Royal Air Force Arthur Tedder was given a baronetcy. The English actress Edith Evans, who had entertained troops in Gibraltar during the war, became a Dame Commander of the British Empire. It was really a Victory Honours List by which the nation could officially recognise the immense war service of at least some of those who had borne the heaviest burden since 1939. There were, of course, tens of thousands of others, ordinary citizens who had done more than their bit. But not everyone could have a medal.

All in all, 1946 was going to present some major challenges for Clement Attlee's government. Yet the London correspondent of the *Gloucester Citizen* saw some light on the horizon:

> Britain enters 1946 still limping rather badly but in better health, from a point of view of moral stamina, than during any of the immediate pre-war years, when, though there was an abundance in the shops, there were signs that all was not well with the nation. The

call of arms tightened the moral fibre and showed that the doubts and the conflicts and the cynicism were not proof against patriotism. Today we have a national unity, a sense of brotherhood which will remain in the foreground of our thoughts so long as we recognise that division would mean failure. The emergency of war is over, but the aftermath of war is still very much with us. It cannot be dissipated without tremendous concerted effort. Until it is, the workshops will be at half pressure, the shops will be scantily stocked, the homes we need will not be built. The year just begun will be critical. During the coming twelve months we can lay the foundations of prosperity. But opportunity lost during 1946 may be lost for ever … . Tired as we are after the war, we are not tired out … .

The *Hull Daily Mail* reminded its readers that the first blessing was the end of 'the mental dread we at home suffered of receiving bad news from the headquarters of the various Services'. In the coming months, the paper said,

although men would be returning in their thousands, many of them would be in no hurry to return to work, and although most industries were already desperately short of workers, the men who had fought the war needed time to adjust. Once their demob leave was over, however, with it would end their pay and allowances, and when they returned to their old jobs that would mean a greater flow of household goods, of boots, clothing, curtains, linen and the like, before many months have passed.

The Hull newspaper, however, was worried about industrial action:

The great danger to the return of prosperity is a sporadic outbreak of strikes. Happily, there is peace in industry as a whole just now, and if this can be maintained then progress in 1946 is certain. The bugbear is that, in so many callings, black-coated and manual, there are always people prepared to foment trouble, and kick against the elected leaders of the guilds or trades unions. Glib-tongued, and perhaps forceful in character, they are apt to carry men away with their rhetoric … the only result is misery and want in the homes of the workers deprived, voluntary or not, of their employment. If only disputes can be met fairly and squarely by both masters and men in a conference room between representatives appointed by recognised methods, then there is no reason why, next December, we should not be looking back on 1946 as a year of all-round improvement and, indeed, one of great blessing.

There was, however, good news for dock workers. An agreement between port employers and unions meant that dockers would now be paid the new national minimum wage of 19 shillings (95p) per day. Backdated to 26 November – the previous rate had been 16 shillings (80p) a day – it meant a New Year's nest egg for workers who were also guaranteed one week's annual holiday with pay at the standard time rate of 44 hours. A regular port worker would now earn £4 2s 6d, (£4.13p), less income tax of course.

The *Daily Mail* summed up:

> It would be folly to deny that the atomic bomb overshadows the world as it enters 1946, or that such problems as Russian relations with Persia and Turkey give cause for acute anxiety, yet it would be equal folly to allow our attention to be unduly distracted, or energy dissipated on these matters. As a nation we shall need all your strength for the urgent task which must have first priority – that is to put Britain on her feet, to make this country once more a going concern. It is to set the wheels rolling, to get trade started, to give our people constructive use for peaceful work. In the next twelve months we must have more houses, more clothes, more food, more household goods, more motorcars, more shoes for the children, better transport. We must move surely and speedily towards that abundance of the civilised amenities which we once enjoyed, and more also. Our slogan must not be 'back to 1939' but 'forward to 1950'.

The *Daily Herald* has its sights set on the immediate future: 'Let the pessimists jeer if they wish. They have the people against them. For in 1945, the people of Britain ranged themselves decisively on the side of the optimists, and they enter 1946 resolved to make their wish come true.'

Chapter Two

A Savage Winter

But some of us may at least have the satisfaction in the years to come of sitting back and telling our grandchildren, 'Ah, you don't get winters now like that of 1947.'

Pontypridd Observer

In December 1946 the *Derby Evening Telegraph* warned its readers that the chances of buying a pair of children's wellingtons was 'about 200 to 1'. The situation was just as bad when it came to obtaining a pair of women's sheepskin boots. Which was unfortunate in the extreme because Britain was about to experience its worst winter in living memory.

As if that was not bad enough, the effects of the icy weather would soon be compounded by a shortage of fuel. On 5 December 1946 the first national power cuts took place. At that stage it was not a complete breakdown in power supplies, simply a reduction known as an 'economy cut'. There were several of these as the government wrestled with a problem that seemed to have no solution: the weather was cold, the temperature hovered around freezing, so the demand for power soared – but coal stocks were low and thus power stations became increasingly unable to cope with that demand. Eventually, the answer seemed to be to ease the strain by cutting power completely at certain times, lowering consumption the rest of the time, and attempting to spread demand rather than have peak times of consumption.

Early December 1946 was cold and foggy – a fog turned into a 'smog' by thousands of domestic coal fires spewing smoke over towns and cities throughout the country. The air tasted of it, and on very bad days people coughed up soot. The number of respiratory illnesses soared, and conditions were about as unpleasant as could be imagined.

There was little to cheer up the country. In Parliament, an amendment to the Civic Restaurants Bill prohibiting the sale of alcohol in these state-run enterprises was carried by 53 votes to 22 with two abstentions. One

MP told the House that permitting the sale of drink in civic restaurants would 'encourage young people to start tippling in circumstances which would make them believe that it was not such a bad thing after all'. He painted a picture of young people coming out of cinemas shivering in the cold with no alternative but the pub between the end of the show and catching the last bus home.

Four days before Christmas there was ten degrees of frost across most of the UK, and now the whole of Europe was locked in an icy grip. Near Dusseldorf in occupied Germany, coal in railway wagons was frozen so hard that it could not be unloaded, and Paris, besides being at a virtual standstill because of the freeze-up, was also covered in sickly yellow fog. On Saturday 21 December, Air Ministry weather experts forecast that the weather would turn milder but that most inland areas could expect heavy fog followed by rain, and there would be gales in many places.

As the holiday drew nearer still there was more bad news over the power situation. Total power cuts were short in duration but became more frequent. They would be preceded by a warning broadcast over the wireless. There had already been an announcement that further drastic cuts in electricity were needed. Now it appeared that the gas supply was also under threat. As coal stocks dwindled, gas mains were under enormous strain, in many instances greatly overloaded as local gas undertakings reduced pressure. Only half the normal supply of coal was being delivered, which meant that reserve stocks had to be drawn upon.

But the gas and electricity companies were not the only ones suffering from a coal shortage. It affected almost every home because coal fires were an essential means of heating. Now it seemed that many people might be without coal by Christmas Day. One coal merchant said, 'As fast as a wagon comes into the sidings, we empty it. We're doing our best to give everybody a bit of what we're getting but we're receiving very small quantities.' Derby Co-operative Society was working 'from hand to mouth' to get what coal it could to customers. In desperation, people began queuing at their local gas works and trundling bags of coke back home aboard prams and pushchairs.

The run up to the New Year was foggy, very cold and windy, but there was some cheer for the nation's miners when their industry was nationalised. There was, however, no time for celebrations, not when the nation's coal stocks were so low that miners were being urged to work all out. At the weekend there were ceremonial unveilings of name-boards at colliery entrances and the unfurling of the National Coal Board flag, but that was about the extent of it. And there was still trouble. On New Year's Day itself, 600 miners at the Powell Duffryn Power Collieries at Hirwaun in Glamorgan walked out against the advice of their union officials because the management wanted to change the type of lamps that they carried underground.

The Minister of Fuel and Power, Emanuel Shinwell, told miners at Durham, 'The nation and the world is watching us.' Although, following nationalisation, Shinwell was popular with the miners, he was becoming increasingly unpopular with the public. He had reduced the consumption of coal by cutting the electricity supply to industry and introducing a nationwide reduction of the domestic supply to 19 hours a day. All over the country thousands were thrown out of work as the fuel shortage closed factories. Cadbury's announced that their Bournville works near Birmingham would be shut for ten days, laying off 8,000 workers. Another Birmingham factory, Dunlop Rubber Company, stood down 3,000 workers because coal supplies had not arrived. In Blackburn, twenty-seven textile factories closed, with 4,000 operatives out of work, and at the Lower Darwen Royal Ordnance Factory 1,700 workers were laid off for two days. Across the country, up to four million people claimed unemployment benefit. After Shinwell received a bomb threat, a police guard was stationed at his house in Tooting.

Even the bad winter of 1940, the first of the war, would pale by comparison with what Britons were about to endure. In the early hours of Monday 6 January, snow began to fall over almost the whole of the country and, as dawn broke, the people looked up to see thick flakes curling out of a leaden sky. By 2.00pm most of the UK was covered in a thick mantle of snow. To compound people's misery there were the first power cuts since before Christmas – and this on a day when the temperature was just under 28 degrees Fahrenheit (minus 2.22 Celsius). It had been the coldest night since 15 December.

If the lead story on the front pages of the nation's newspapers told one gloomy story – 'Snow Delays Trains, Buries Sheep – Warning Of Power Cuts Tonight' – the second lead wasn't far behind in terms of bad news, '5,000 Lorry Men On Strike – Threat To Nation's Food Supply'.

East London lorry drivers had been joined by 500 heavy transport drivers and carriers at London's Smithfield Meat Market in an unofficial strike which 'is likely to spread and affect supplies for the whole country, including food, newsprint, wines, spirits and tobacco'. The men, dissatisfied with proposals of the Road Haulage Central Wages Board on claims for better wages and conditions, complained that negotiations had been going on for nine months without any prospect of an agreement.

One striker said:

> Transport drivers' expenses are three or four times higher than those of people working in factories and offices. The highest wage is £5 10s (£5.50) and sometimes as much as £2 10s (£2.50) goes on expenses in a week. We are the worst-paid men on the road, and our daughters can laugh at us. Some of them earn more money than we do.

The strike lasted for ten days before the nation breathed a collective sigh of relief when it was called off.

Throughout January the weather held its grip. When a thaw came, it was quickly followed by fog and frost, and on 10 January conditions were described as 'slippery' before the mercury again dropped below freezing and a dense, lung-searching fog reduced visibility to a few yards. Five days later parts of England enjoyed their warmest day of the year so far, a relatively balmy 51 degrees Fahrenheit (10.55 Celsius), but it was a temporary respite. On 20 January the Board of Trade announced that the next six weeks would be critical for British fuel supplies. The weather was about to test them again, and even more severely so this time.

The main case this time was an anti-cyclone that sat over Scandinavia, forcing depressions across the Atlantic towards the south of the United Kingdom. By 30 January, even the Isles of Scilly were under 7 inches (17.7 cm) of snow. That day the biggest power cut to date, a reduction in gas pressure and a continuance of the biting cold which froze up water pipes, drove people to improvise. Shops used candles for light and heat, housewives made the early-morning tea with the contents of overnight hot-water bottles and used their meagre coal reserves to melt snow for a morning wash. Parts of the Midlands had 15 degrees Fahrenheit (minus 9.44 Celsius) of frost during the night of 29/30 January and there was no sign of a let up. RAF meteorological experts at Cardington in Bedfordshire could not even take readings because the doors to the instrument shed had frozen solid.

On 31 January, the thermometer at Cheltenham showed 20 degrees Fahrenheit (minus 6.66 Celsius) of frost and at the RAF station at Moreton-in-Marsh it dropped to zero – 32 Fahrenheit (17.77 Celsius) degrees of frost. The busiest people were plumbers as water pipes, and even water mains, burst. LMS trains from the north were arriving in Cheltenham two hours late and GWR services from London were suffering similar delays.

In Bodmin, one pub landlord had to gently thaw out bottles of beer before he could sell them. In Canterbury, a grocer opened in the morning to discover that his shop was covered in frozen foam from bottles of fizzy drinks that had exploded during the night, and women queuing outside a baker's shop in the historic city fainted from the intense cold.

It seemed like the dawn of a new Ice Age was gripping the whole of Europe. In Paris, people jammed cinemas heated by black-market coal. In Germany, still devastated by the war, dynamite was used to blast clear frozen rivers and canals.

Almost everyone seemed to be suffering with a cold. Anyone with a sore throat or runny nose was advised to 'Give Your Cold a Cephos Reception For Quick Relief'. It was 'sold everywhere in tablet or powder form' and cost 'twopence [less than 1p] a dose including purchase tax'. The advertisement added, reassuringly, 'Cephos Does Not Affect The Heart'.

On the last day of January there was a rise in temperature to just above freezing, but this only brought more misery as thousands of hitherto frozen water pipes burst. Homes were flooded and plumbers were kept busy round the clock. By the time even half the pipes had been repaired, the temperature had dropped to well below freezing again and those people unlucky enough not to have been visited by a plumber probably now considered themselves the lucky ones; they could just wait for the next thaw and pay only once.

On 4 February three busl4oads of people travelling home to Hull after visiting a pantomime in Leeds were trapped when blizzards swept northern England. They included women in their seventies, an expectant mother and several children, and for twelve hours they had no food. Villagers from North Newbald in the East Riding battled across fields with two buckets of coffee. They cut a narrow passage three-quarters of a mile long through head-high snow and helped the half-frozen women back to the village where the local fish and chip shop opened in the afternoon to give the women their first meal in twelve hours. Another bus taking twenty-eight women and children to Whitby after the panto was trapped all night before German prisoners of war helped clear a passage to safety.

During the night of 6/7 February, the UK was almost blotted out by another widespread snowstorm. Only Wales and parts of the South-West escaped. Valiant efforts had managed to re-open Derbyshire's 'lifeline' – the A6, the main traffic artery which ran through Derby, Matlock, Bakewell and Buxton to Manchester – but then the snow returned, and troops of the Manchester Regiment were rushed to Buxton to help weary council snow-clearers who battled against heavy odds as the blizzard raged on. They were eventually reinforced by 2,000 Polish troops who had to dig themselves out of their camp at Blackshaw Moor near Leek – today it is the site of a caravan and motorhome park – before going to the aid of beleaguered Buxton.

Milk was being fed to animals because the snow had prevented churns being collected and delivered to dairies, and there were no fresh vegetables because supplies could not be brought through. That great British institution, Sunday lunch, was also in danger. Meat supplies were limited, potatoes were in short supply – and if the ingredients were available there was a good chance that a power cut would ruin the meal anyway.

On Saturday 8 February came the crunch. It was announced that there would be two days of nationwide power cuts in a last-ditch attempt to conserve Britain's dwindling coal stocks. There was some confusion over what became known as the 'Shinwell Shutdown' and many firms had already announced that they would be unable to open on the following Monday. Tens of thousands of people were expected to be idle. Ministry of Labour staff worked throughout the weekend and extra staff were engaged to cope with the expected flood of applications for unemployment benefit.

Britain faced what one newspaper called 'grave news'. And, with one exception, the press was unanimous in placing the blame for the crisis squarely on the Labour government. Even one of its traditional allies, the *Daily Herald*, said, 'Frankly, we think that several Ministers deceive themselves … they believe that however trying and irksome our present problems may be, the average man will blissfully murmur, "Attlee's in

10 Downing Street, all's right with the world." That is a treacherous delusion.'

The *Daily Mail* said:

> Now the news tells the story – and it is a shock. This week Britain is in real trouble ... . We do not absolve the Government for failing to provide against it [the bad weather] but we should be less than patriotic if we did not do everything in our power to meet and overcome it.

The *Daily Telegraph*, 'The Government have behaved like a general who ignores the actions of his enemy. Warned by his intelligence of a menace on their flank they have thrust on with their own grand schemes till the threat has become a disastrous reality.'

The *News Chronicle*, 'Unless the Government realises that the coal industry and the reconditioning of power stations must be given priority now, we shall be in an even worse mess next winter.'

The *Daily Graphic*, 'If the disastrous muddle and ineptitude which have brought our present plight continues ... the shadow of national bankruptcy will begin to fall darkly across the land ... .'

Only the Communist *Daily Worker* could find a reason to attach the blame elsewhere: 'It is the Tories who are fundamentally to blame for this situation.'

On Monday 10 February, the BBC said that to save power it was shutting down the Third Programme and the television programme for the duration of the emergency. The latter affected few people; in 1946 only 7,000 sets had been sold. On 11 February there were warnings of a reduction in the bread ration as the power cuts and shortages affected bakers. When housewives tried to make their own bread, supplies of yeast eventually ran out. As the severe cold continued, newspapers pledged to reduce the number of pages and there were threats of longer power cuts.

On 17 February there was better news. Coal ships had begun docking in British ports and, for the first time in weeks, coal was collected from the pit heads and distribution resumed. Although the end of the severe weather was not yet in sight, there were the first signs that the fuel crisis might be easing. On 19 February, though, with the nation's coal stocks slowly being replenished, there were fresh heavy snowfalls. Even the fishing industry was affected as trawlers could not leave port.

On 26 February, as blizzards again swept in, it was announced that night-shift working would be a feature of industrial life for at least three years, as it would take at least that long to manufacture the new electricity-generating plants needed to cope with the enormous burden on the country's power supply. Spreading the load was the only option. It was estimated that some 7 million workers – 2.3 million of them women – would be required to work at least one week of nights every three or four weeks, making the total number of people on nights at any one time at around 2.25 million. The entire pattern of working life was about to change, although, of course, night shifts had been a prominent feature of the war years.

According to records, snow had fallen somewhere in the United Kingdom for fifty-five consecutive days and, because the temperatures had rarely exceeded freezing, most of it had settled. The appalling conditions caused all manner of accidents throughout the British Isles. In the Worcestershire village of Kemerton, children tobogganing down a hill collided with a horse and cart, causing the horse to take fright, and a cart wheel to run over the driver's foot and hand. In Kimmage, a suburb of Dublin, there was tragedy when 16-year-old Anthony Burke, 13-year-old Christopher Byrne and 8-year-old Edward O'Toole died in the freezing water of a quarry after ice broke under the weight of twenty children playing hockey.

The good news was that at 1.00pm on 17 March, the temperature reached 51 degrees (10.55 Celsius), the highest recorded so far in 1947.

But the warmer weather brought rain, and thousands of square miles of southern England lay under floodwater. The worst hit areas were the Thames Valley – where the River Thames was three miles wide in places, causing the Windsor borough engineer, Geoffrey Barker, to say, 'We could cope only if we had a spare Thames or two' – and the fens of East Anglia where the entire Royal Engineers resources of Eastern Command were mobilised in the battle against the floods. 'It has been a terrible sight,' the Duke of Gloucester told farmers as he ended a tour of the flooded fens. The National Farmers' Union called it 'the greatest food production tragedy Britain has ever known'.

On Wednesday 24 March came the headlines that everyone had been waiting for, 'Rivers Fall – Floods Recede,' and 'Weather Will Get Better'. At long last the awful winter was coming to an end. Power cuts would still be in operation all summer, according to a government announcement, and food and clothing rationing would also be a feature of life for some time to come. But weather-weary Britain was in for some brighter days; indeed, the summer that year was one of the best on record with scorching temperatures and long cloudless days. But, while it had lasted, the winter of 1947 had brought as much, if not more, misery than did many periods of the Second World War. It had brought death and destruction, discomfort and inconvenience, disruption and shortages.

But there was hope. On 30 March *The People*'s 'Man of the People' wrote:

> Crocus and daffodil are in bloom again, and the lilac is in bud. The savagery of an incredible winter is spent. Across the waste of subsiding waters, the breath of Spring is borne on the warm current of national fellowship ... the country is recovering from a great shock. Given the right tonic, it will soon be fighting fit.

Chapter Three

The Final Insult

The most hated measure ever to have been presented to the people of this country

Daily Mail

On 8 January 1940 the British government had introduced food rationing. The newly established Ministry of Food had already issued every person in Britain with a ration book, and the holders of those books, or, most often, the housewife on behalf of her entire family, had to register with nominated retailers. The Ministry explained its reasons for the introduction of rationing: half the nation's meat and most of its bacon, butter and sugar came from overseas and it was unreasonable to ask sailors to risk their lives to bring in unnecessary cargoes.

Six years later, the war now over, merchant seamen were no longer threatened by U-boats, and there was perhaps room for optimism. With the release of more shipping space there would presumably be an increase in the varieties of food, even though it was taken for granted that rationing of both essentials and luxuries would continue for some time, which, according to the *Hull Daily Mail* in January 1946 was 'a plain justice over which no one can grumble and in the end it will be better for all that we return to normal by gradual steps rather than in one jump'.

In fact, food rationing was about to become even more strict. On the morning of Monday 1 July 1946, a crowd gathered outside Leopold's baker's shop in the Strand in Cheltenham. In the window was a notice that read, 'Bread Rationing Protest Meeting at Town Hall, 6pm'. Below the notice were pinned display packets of the daily bread, cake and flour rations for the seven sections of the community proposed under the scheme. Some of the allowances exhibited were (one ounce [1oz] is the equivalent of 28.3495 grammes): Children under one year, ½ thick slice of bread (1oz), ½oz of flour and ½oz of cake; Children aged 5 to 11, 8oz of flour or 3 slices of bread, 2oz of cake, 3oz of flour; Adolescents, 12oz of flour approximating to 4 slices of bread, 3½oz of cake and the rest in flour. A few days earlier, the *Manchester Guardian* had declared it a 'complicated system' and a 'profound irony that it should be in the year of peace and recovery that we have to accept this new hardship'.

The shop's proprietor, Mr F.B. Leopold, said that people did not realise that the ration would be inadequate, particularly for manual labourers who had to take lunch out. That was why he had set out the examples in his shop window, to bring home to his customers exactly on what they would be forced to manage. He said that he would be staging the exhibition at the Town Hall meeting that evening, when members of the Master Bakers' Association, and the Housewives' League, planned to protest at the proposed legislation. Even in wartime, bread had never been rationed. Now peace had been restored but the British people were having further restrictions imposed upon them. 'Disgusting,' 'Impossible,' and 'Totally inadequate,' were some of the comments of both men and women gathered in front of Leopold's window. Someone posted a poem there:

> Many a gallant air crew
> Bombed and bombed for all they knew
> To Kill the Hun!
> But what's the fun of having won
> When our daily bread we must shun
> To feed the Hun.

The bread shortage was being linked to the food crisis in occupied Germany, where the daily ration set by the Supreme Headquarters Allied Expeditionary Force (SHAEF) was 2,600 calories but was, on average, around only 1,200 calories because the Allies had severely underestimated the damage to German infrastructure and overestimated a defeated nation's ability to grow its own food. In late July the *Daily Mail* would send one of its senior writers to find out the truth. Andrew Clifford reported: 'Slowly, quietly, hygienically, the Germans are moving towards death. If anything can be done to avoid it, even to the extent of British bread rationing, it is worth doing.' The *Daily Herald* congratulated the rival newspaper for publishing 'a message which so dramatically exposes the shallowness of its campaign against bread rationing and against the Government's food policy in general'.

It was the conquerors' responsibility to ensure that Germans had enough to eat and so, instead of helping to maintain the weight of loaves that British housewives were buying, a percentage of Canadian wheat was being diverted to the British occupied zone, hence the ditty displayed in the window of Leopold's shop on 1 July.

That same day, the National Union of Railwaymen's conference received a telegram from an emergency meeting, at Nottingham, of the National Union of Small Shopkeepers, appealing to the NUR to use its influence to prevent bread rationing: 'We are fed up with attacks on our liberty and freedom. Shopkeepers are confident that if more regulations are put into effect, bread will be wasted and not saved. A victory for the black market will be the obvious outcome.'

The previous day, the president of the London Masters Bakers' Association, Mr A.F. Tompkins, had issued a statement:

> We regard bread rationing as detrimental to the public interest. Administratively there are difficulties which the Food Minister cannot have foreseen. Unless he has more information than we have, we are not convinced that rationing is necessary. The difficulties concern spoiled and stale loaves. We want to know what bakers can do in these circumstances. Can confectionery be sold in single units? If people cannot buy less than half a pound of cake, many will not get much. Another point is the price of 9oz of bread. The price is fixed for 14oz and 28oz loaves. A person living alone and entitled to 9oz presents a problem which the Minister has not yet settled.

The food minister in question, John Strachey, a journalist by profession who had served in the war as an RAF officer in a planning and public relations role before being re-elected to parliament in 1945, was already an unpopular figure. But then, overseeing the nation's food at such a time was always going to be a proverbial poisoned chalice. His predecessor, Sir Ben Smith, had soon discovered that. Smith, a driver of one of London's first taxi cabs, and national organiser of the Transport and General Workers Union from its formation in 1922, had been given the thankless task after the Labour landslide. In February 1946, he found his reputation at a new low when he announced that domestic food rationing was being reduced to levels that were unknown even when the U-boat war against British shipping was at its height, resulting in a critical shortage of staple food items. The day after Smith's announcement, demonstrators gathered outside the Whitehall headquarters of the Ministry of Food, waving placards bearing the words 'Starve with Smith'. Smith was a rather avuncular figure, which made the slogan even more telling. There was disquiet throughout Britain. Sir Ben's office received a telegram which declared bluntly, 'Women of Liverpool to demonstrate against ration cuts'. The first of the demonstrations was to be held the following day, at the Pavilion in the Childwall district of the city.

Smith had no option, though. An example was dried egg, no delicacy but a staple of Britons' diet throughout the war. Most of it was imported from the United States at a cost of almost $10 million dollars a year. Smith said that such imports now had to cease: 'I simply don't know how I can lay my hands on the money,' the *Daily Mirror* quoted him as saying. Replying to a question in the House of Commons, Sir Ben said that he could not add any dried eggs imported from the Dominions to the domestic ration in preference to catering establishments, otherwise 'there would be no cakes or pastries for anyone in the country'. However, during 1946, he said, shell eggs worth $CAD18.5 million would be imported from Canada.

Clearly, Sir Ben, now 67, and hitherto a popular moderate with a sharp wit, was under enormous pressure. In May 1946 he resigned:

> I am very tired. I asked Mr Attlee to allow me to relinquish office on 5 April, and I am glad he is now able to grant my wish. I am sorry I was unable to do more to improve our diet and I hope my successor will have better fortune.

The *Daily Express* political correspondent said that for some time Sir Ben had been angry and restive about the storms of criticism over his work at the Ministry of Food, but the last straw was believed to have come when it was the deputy prime minister, Herbert Morrison, who was chosen to fly to Washington to discuss the worsening world food crisis with President Truman. According to the *Express*, Sir Ben said he regarded it as a public slight and hotly resented it. When Morrison made his statement, about his mission, to the Commons, Sir Ben had not taken his usual place on the front bench. A Conservative member called out, 'Where is Ben Smith?' A Labour MP replied, 'He is not far away.' He would soon be far, far away, however. The *Daily Mail* said it understood that Sir Ben had three times tried to resign from the £5,000-a-year post: 'Inside and outside the House of Commons he was frequently attacked. He seems sensitive to criticism in the House and his replies were sometimes considered abrupt.'

What had ended Sir Ben's days as Minister of Food was the decision to reduce the size of a 2lb-loaf (907 grammes) to 1lb 12 oz (793.78 grammes) with no reduction in price. The 1lb-loaf (453.92 grammes) would lose 2oz (56.69 grammes), again with no reduction in price. If the Ministry of Food thought that housewives would not notice the missing couple of slices, it was mistaken.

While Smith became chairman of the newly created West Midlands Coal Board, Strachey picked up the baton as Minister of Food. Local food offices began to receive copies of the Bread Rationing Order that was expected to operate for one year. The issue was due to be debated in the Commons on 18 July, but the outcome was already assured.

The *Derby Evening Telegraph's* 'Derby and Joan' columnist said that the feeling experienced by mothers with whom they had spoken on the subject of bread rationing was one of 'utter weariness'. 'I will write to the Derby MPs and give them a piece of my mind,' one mother had told the paper. Another said, 'I will take all the bread ration and make the kids eat it.' Another said, 'My kids won't get enough, so I will have to give up some of mine.'

Yet another mother, whose family was almost grown up, felt that 'this is the final insult given to mothers – at least I hope it's final'. She continued:

> We have tried so hard to keep the wheels of our homes running smoothly during a terrible war, always dreading that something would happen to our children or our husbands, and forgetting that if it happened to us, then the centre of family life would disappear. We have queued and worked and contrived to keep our children as well fed and dressed as possible, and we have been grateful for the words of encouragement our husbands and our women friends have said to us. These words have helped us carry on even when we felt as if nothing mattered. We have had words of encouragement from Governments, too, but they have always been followed by cuts in rations or points value, and that has made us a bit cynical – not our usual state of mind.

Asked how bread rationing would affect her household, she replied:

Probably very little, if at all. That is the point. I maintain that the mothers of this country have been insulted. They have been told that they have been naughty children for not saving scraps of bread, and now they have got to pay for their naughtiness by a fresh outburst of restriction and bureaucracy. The trouble about it is that once bread rationing has been established it is going to be very difficult to get rid of it and the salaried staffs needed to keep it going. We have won the war and now we are being treated as though we hadn't. I am not surprised when I read that many young men and women hope to emigrate some day.'

On 3 July the *Daily Mail* said that bread rationing was 'the most hated measure ever to have been presented to the people of this country'. Not everyone held the same view. A letter writer to *The Scotsman* argued that, far from queues for bread being longer still, as opponents of the scheme claimed, 'on the contrary, queues are never so long in shops like grocers, where your food is rationed, and where you are assured of your ration, whether you call for it early or late ... it is the unrationed bread which may be sold out before queues gather'. Nonetheless, in Bristol, housewives announced that they would hold a mass protest meeting on Durdham Down on the following Sunday evening. All over the city local groups were forming to take up the matter with their MPs. It would all be to no avail.

C.H. Storey, acting secretary of the Greenwood Labour Association in Hull, was, inevitably perhaps, firmly on the side of the government:

> The grumbling has started again ... I would like to ask the grumblers two things: (1) How much bread have I wasted? (2) Would any government have rationed bread if it could have avoided it? ... If the USA and the scientists were to experiment on the food question instead of seeing how many they can wipe out with atom bombs, there would be more satisfaction in this country. I have every sympathy for the woman shopper but let us face facts.

There was greater sympathy from farther afield. Waterside workers in New Zealand threatened to refuse to load a freighter with 10 million pounds of butter bound for the United States if their government did not give a satisfactory explanation of why the consignment was not bound for Britain. There were 1.5 million people on New Zealand's two main islands, and in April and May they had surrendered no fewer than 1.6 million meal coupons and 90,000 butter coupons so that their rations could be sent to Britain.

Reporting on the Commons debate, the *Nottingham Evening Post*'s 'Echoes from the Town' columnist felt that John Strachey's speech 'left behind the feeling that our [food] lifeline with America is as much in peril as if the Battle of the Atlantic were still on'. The writer continued:

> Our reserves are at such a low ebb that, in the opinion of the food experts, some form of rationing is inescapable. The Minister marshalled his facts with a skill that greatly delighted the rather glum Government benches. Later, the debate developed into a somewhat party wrangle, and there were some heated passages between Mr Strachey and Mr Hudson that threw the chamber into turmoil.

The Tory MP Robert Spear Hudson had held the post of Minister of Agriculture and Fisheries during the war; in 1939, when he was Secretary for Overseas Trade, Hudson had 'offered' Germany a loan of hundreds of millions of pounds, payable only if they did not invade Poland. That ended in humiliation. Neville Chamberlain told the Commons that Hudson was speaking for himself, and no such loan had ever been considered. Now Hudson was telling Strachey that, apart from Germany and Austria, Britain was 'about to become the about the worst fed white nation in the world'. Socialists chorused 'Withdraw!' After some minutes, the Deputy Speaker asked the House to allow Hudson to continue. Bessie Braddock, the MP for Liverpool Exchange, said, 'I will not let him continue. I will not be quiet.' It was only by sheer persistence that Hudson was able to finish his speech before he sat down to a swelling chorus of boos from the Government benches. The Liberals voted with the Government, and the stormy debate ended in the defeat – by 343 votes to 178 – of the token censure motion against introducing bread rationing. When Blackburn MP Barbara Castle declared that it 'is the time to put heart and encouragement into our people', a voice from the Conservative benches called out, 'And bread into their stomachs'.

Winston Churchill had already described Strachey's announcement as 'one of the gravest I have ever heard in time of peace'. Britain's wartime leader demanded that figures of stocks and movements of cereals should be produced by the Government to justify 'this extreme measure'. Anthony Eden told the Commons that the Government's major error had been not to inform 'the House, the country and the world' about the facts. Strachey said that bread would now be regarded as one of three restaurant courses allowed, but that during the season he was exempting herrings from being regarded as a main course. The *Nottingham Evening Post* responded:

> It is rather hard on patrons for the fish and meat portions now served with a five-shilling 'austerity meal' have become so diminutive that with bread appetites are scarcely satisfied ... waiters have clearly had instructions to serve no bread at all unless it is expressly asked for – a rule hitherto observed only in the case of butter. Sweets, moreover, hardly afford a satisfactory extra. For what seemed an interminable time we were served with stewed rhubarb which calls for lashings of sugar to be palatable.

Bread rationing came into force on 21 July 1946 and, as the *Manchester Guardian* had forecast, it was the most complicated system that Britain's rationing schemes had ever imposed. The bread units for each week were the same figures as the daily ration in ounces. Thus, the ordinary adult could have 9 ounces (255 grammes) of bread a day, and their bread units per week were also nine, which they spent using coupons of varying values from their ordinary ration book. The scheme provided for seven different categories of consumers whose bread unit coupons would have to cover bread, flour, cakes, buns and scones – in fact all flour products not already covered by the points system.

Allowances to catering establishments would be restricted, but there would be special provision for industrial canteens and for the packed-meal schemes for workers on heavy manual jobs. Agricultural workers receiving the extra cheese ration would be able to get extra coupons.

John Strachey promised that bread rationing might end when the 'immediate squeeze' was over. In fact, bread rationing remained in force for two years, ending in July 1948. According to the historian Dr Christopher Knowles, 'bread rationing turned out to be completely ineffective in reducing the level of consumption in the UK, and most historians agree it was probably unnecessary'.

Other foods that had been on ration since the dark days of 1940 would continue to be so through the post-war years, indeed right up until 1954, when meat became one of the last items to come off ration. Ending rationing had been a central plank of the Conservatives' successful 1951 general election manifesto, but while it lasted it was always a headache for shopkeepers who were at the front line of any complaints. In June 1948 members of Burton and District Butchers' Association heard Mr G.H. Swindell of the National Federation executive tell them that, during the years of food rationing, butchers had lost a lot of their liberty and had become the buffer between bureaucracy and the customers. They always had to bear the first shock of the customers' disappointment, and a surfeit of regulations which required almost a legal mind to know and appreciate them. He said, 'Whatever one can say about the butcher, no one can put him in the 'spiv' class.'

Clothes rationing ended in 1949 and soap rationing and petrol rationing in 1950, because, of course, food was not the only commodity that remained on ration after the war. In June 1948 the Motor Spirit (Regulation) Act ordered some petrol to be dyed red, and that 'red petrol' could be used only in commercial vehicles. A petrol station found to have sold red petrol to a private car driver could be shut down, and if red petrol was found in a private car, then the driver could lose their licence. In fact, commercial petrol was defined as that having diphenylamine, and the red dye was only to assist motorists and garages to ensure that the correct fuel was being dispensed. Red petrol without diphenylamine was legal. So, as the *Bradford Observer* reported: 'Mystery Chemical Aids Police'. A second, unnamed chemical was being added to enable police to carry out a simple roadside test. The same month, motorists would be allowed 'standard' petrol for pleasure, enough for 90 miles per month, which worked out at one-third of the former basis rate.

Coal rationing, meanwhile, did not end until as recently as 1958, even though Britain was a coal-producing nation. Industry needed coal, but so did ordinary people. Domestic heating came from coal fires, hot water was produced by coal-fired coppers and boilers and some people still cooked on coal-fired kitchen ranges. And if coal being rationed – the allowance was two and a half tons per household per year – was not bad enough, there was anger at the quality of the stuff that was being tipped down the nation's grates and shovelled into its coalhouses. The dreadful winter of 1946-47 made matters even worse. Writing to the *Sunderland Echo and Shipping Gazette* in January 1946, 'Cold Wearsider' really let go:

Sir, It is possible the majority of householders manage on the ration allowed by the Ministry of Fuel, provided, of course, they are really supplied with coal. I received my ten hundredweight at the beginning of December last. This was finished nineteen days later. Since then, I have managed on coal saved in the summer months, but this is now exhausted, and I can only have a fire when some kind neighbour will loan a bucket or two, which, of course, will have to be replaced out of my next ten hundredweight.

My last ration was made up of 50 to 60 per cent of slag, 20 per cent of dirt and whitewash, and the balance poor quality coal, and this, mark you, at nearly £3 per ton and living on top of a mine. Who is to blame? The miner must be filling this rubbish, the management cannot clean the coal as it is passed over the conveyors, so it is passed on to the consumer who is left holding the baby – and a very expensive baby it is. My last ration worked out at approximately £7 per ton. If we have to be rationed, for goodness' sake let's have coal and then we might pull through. But it is impossible with 70 per cent waste matter.

There was some good news concerning clothing and footwear, however. On 29 January 1946, the *Daily Herald* reported, 'It will pay to save your coupons for the boots and shoes, particularly women's and children's, expected to soon be in good supply.' Manufacturers had endorsed the forecast of Major F.J. Stratton, the nation's Footwear Controller, who said that production had reached a peak during October and November 1945 and optimism was therefore justified. Experts agreed, explaining that the bottleneck had been solved by the release from the services of pre-war footwear factory employees. There was more good news about the lifting of austerity restrictions on certain classes of hosiery and knitwear. The goods affected were socks, stockings, three-quarter hose, knitted jumpers, cardigans, pullovers, slipovers and jerseys, men's, youths' and boys' knitted vests, infants', and children's knitted clothing other than those made from knitted fabric, and scarves of any material. A spokesman for the Board of Trade warned that supplies might not be immediately available owing to the delay in manufacture and distribution.

And then there was bread rationing, rubbish coal and even the sweet ration halved by John Strachey – 1946 still offered little hope of better days to come.

Chapter Four

Learning to Live Together

I think all working families should be able to have these sorts of homes.
Isabel Innes of Hull

In January 1946 Britain's big need, said the *Hull Daily Mail*, was for housing. Unless this was given priority, the results would be not only distress among young people but 'very real trouble'. The odd building was being erected here and there, but it had to 'come in on a big scale, and that before the passing of many months'.

By 1945, many people in Britain had nowhere permanent to live. The damage and destruction of tens of thousands of properties by German air raids had made worse a pre-war shortage of affordable housing. In Hull, for instance, it was estimated that 91 per cent of the city's housing stock was damaged in some way or other, and over 152,000 people were rendered homeless. Some 5,300 houses had been destroyed and a further 3,000 severely damaged. In 2017 it was reckoned that 1,213 high explosives, 101 anti-personnel devices and 70 incendiary explosives were still buried under the streets, gardens, and allotments of arguably the most heavily bombed British town or city of the Second World War.

Even in a place like Derby, which had suffered relatively little damage during the Blitz – despite its Rolls Royce works manufacturing the Merlin engines that powered the Spitfires and Hurricanes that won the Battle of Britain, and the Avro Lancasters that bombed Germany – there was still a significant housing shortage. Recently demobbed servicemen returned home to find their wives and children living in two rooms of a shared house. One solution, which had been adopted in several towns, was the conversion of disused military camps into temporary residential use.

In Derby the most obvious location for such a settlement was the sprawling public open space of Markeaton Park, on the outskirts of the town, that had been home to a hutted military camp during the war. It was decided that ex-servicemen and their families would be given priority. Once the army moved out, and the conversion was sanctioned by the Ministry of Health, in 1946 work began on the temporary housing estate that would provide emergency accommodation for local families

The *Derby Evening Telegraph* called it 'Derby's new garden city settlement' and, on the face of it, it certainly boasted decent facilities. There was a canteen and a concert hall, a dance hall, a gymnasium and two messes, indoor space for children to play in rainy weather, and ready-made allotments that had been established by the troops.

It was estimated that the former camp would be required for no more than two years, after which it could revert to being a public park. While the camp had housed 1,200 troops, it was expected to cater for only 200 families. According to the *Derby Evening Telegraph*, 'Some of the troops' huts could be converted into two homes, and there are Nissen huts which would be suitable for one family.'

The borough council believed that residents, aware that their stay was only temporary, would be prepared to share many amenities. Group Captain Clifford Wilcock, one of Derby's two Labour MPs, noted, 'The housewives will have to use tact and forbearance and, like their menfolk in the services, will have to learn to live together ... in a spirit of understanding. They may find that the time they spend there will be a very happy period of their lives.'

To ensure that only those given priority used the huts, there was a caveat: anyone who decided to move in without permission, and effectively squat, would not be considered for the tenancy of any council house; their names would be struck off the waiting list. The first 'Markeaton Hut Homes' were ready for occupation in September 1946, and the first fifty families moved in during mid-October, with approximately ten more homes being occupied each week. Among the neat signposts was one bearing the name 'Fifth Avenue' which the *Derby Evening Telegraph* reminded envious readers was 'a strictly "utility" one compared with America's most elegant residential thoroughfare'.

The new residents were told they could have the first week rent-free and those with children were promised that they would be provided with a permanent corporation council house 'within twelve months'. Some residents were delighted. Among them was Mrs N. Groves, wife of ex-Staff Sergeant Henry Groves, of the Royal Artillery and REME, who had never had her own home. She said: 'I think the Corporation has made a fine job of the conversion and I know we are going to be very happy here.'

However, by February 1947, there were reports of tenants' dissatisfaction. Many of the residents were threatening to withhold their rent unless the Derby Corporation housing committee agreed to meet with them to discuss the many grievances they had. Chief among their complaints was the belief that the corporation had bypassed camp tenants in the first allocation of new council houses.

There were also concerns about poor sanitation and inadequate street lighting, while during the worst winter in living memory, snow and ice had not been cleared from the main roads, deterring tradesmen, and causing housewives to have to fetch barrows of coal from the entrance of the park. There were also arguments about the enforced installation of electricity meters, and a complaint from one father that general dampness had caused mildew to form on his child's pillow. This type of complaint continued for another two years with one housewife claiming that condensation had caused mildew to form under the oilcloth in her bedroom and to warp the wood of her bedroom suite.

In September 1947 the *Derby Evening Telegraph* reported on the 'rust, decay and dilapidation that now meet the eye in the once spotless kitchens of Markeaton Camp'. By December Councillor Alec Ling had taken up the tenants' cause. He told a council meeting, 'I have medical evidence that some [properties] are not in a state to house adult people, let alone children.' It transpired that, by agreeing to sign a lease of eighteen months minimum, each tenant might well have to wait longer for their permanent house. The town's housing manager, Mr E.H. Gregory, noted that before signing, each tenant 'is advised that if he is comparatively comfortable where he is – in rooms perhaps – it would be advisable to remain and get an earlier chance of a house'.

Hull's housing shortage, meanwhile, was being addressed as early as 1944, with the introduction of the 'Tarran house'. In April that year the *Hull Daily Mail* reported that a two-storey house, containing kitchen, dining room, utility room, three bedrooms and a bathroom, could be built and fitted within four days, according to the 'energetic and pushful personality' of Robert Tarran of local company Tarran Industries. The following month Mr Tarran would begin a demonstration. Twelve people, three of whom would be women, would erect a house in one day, and three days later it would be ready for a tenant to move in. Made of wood and concrete, the factory-produced house weighing 26 tons would be 'pleasant, comfortable and durable'. Experts in civil engineering, architecture and science would watch this new development in modern house building, and the BBC and cinema units would also be there.

On 5 May Alfred Bossom, Conservative MP for Maidstone, a distinguished architect, and a member of the Burt Committee set up by the government to look at the nation's housing shortage, performed the opening ceremony of the first Tarran house, declaring, 'It is the leadership, vision and enterprise of such men as Robert G. Tarran that has made the speedy erection of such houses possible'. Bossom felt that 'the houses envisaged would, of course, take advantage of all the latest developments in electricity, gas, hot water, proper ventilation and heating, sanitation, and so on'.

The Burt Committee had decided by 1942 that the most cost-effective way to provide new homes – not only for people who had lost their houses in the Blitz but also for those who were still living in unsanitary conditions because the slum-clearance programme was unfinished – was Emergency Factory Made Homes (EFMs). In 1944 the Ministry of Works built the first demonstration prefabricated houses in Northolt and on Millbank in London and that year's Housing (Temporary Accommodation) Act aimed to deliver 300,000 prefabricated units within ten years, working to a maximum budget of £150 million. A total of 19,014 of the original Tarran homes were erected under the Temporary Housing Act with one- and two-storey variants built afterwards. There were many other types of prefabricated dwellings, and between 1945 and 1951, of the 1.25 million new houses built in Britain, 156,623 were prefabs. They were a small but important contribution to the national housing shortage.

In August 1944 Manchester Corporation announced that Tarran houses would be built on a council housing estate and let to tenants. The estate would also include Portal (a steel panelled experimental temporary bungalow named after a Minister of Works, Lord Portal) and possibly other houses 'so that the public may make their own judgements … because the true test of these houses is going to come from the people who live in them'.

The Tarran house received an enthusiastic reception when the first 100 were opened at Hull in July 1945, by the new Minister of Works, Duncan

Sandys. Mrs Florence Rooms, the very first occupant, said, 'I like the house very much. I wish everyone who needs a home could have one' Her 35-year-old husband, Lance Bombardier Walter Rooms, had been killed in Italy in September 1944, and her home had been bombed earlier in the war. She told the *Hull Daily Mail*:

> At first I wondered how I could cope on my own, but the Hull authorities have been most helpful, and after the first shock of my husband's death, I realised that it was up to me to make the best life I could for my children. Somehow, I felt that he has been helping me these last few weeks. I only wish that he were here to see how comfortable we are now.

One of Mrs Rooms' new neighbours, Isabel Innes, had lived in a caravan with her husband, a transport foreman at the docks, and their teenage son, ever since their home was bombed in May 1941. Then, one afternoon, they returned from the cinema to find that their caravan had been destroyed by fire. Looking around her new Tarran house she said, 'I think all working families should be able to have these sorts of homes.'

There were a few minor grumbles that day. One woman thought that her pantry door should have double, not single, hinges. Another felt that a wireless aerial lead aperture could have been bored through the wall to avoid having to keep a window open. Another housewife pointed out a design fault in her kitchen where the vegetable rack was next to the oven and got too warm. But, overall, everyone seemed happy.

'Prefabs' were intended to have a lifespan of fifteen to twenty years, but seven decades after the first were erected, there are those still providing accommodation for people who loved them, and who fought any plans to demolish them. However, the longer-term solution to the immediate post-war housing shortage was the 1946 New Towns Act.

In 1938 Prime Minister Neville Chamberlain had set up a Royal Commission, chaired by barrister Sir Anderson Barlow, that examined urban concentration of population and industry. It concluded that 'planned decentralisation' was the best way forward, but the Royal Commission on the Distribution of the Industrial Population – the Barlow Report – published in 1940 was shelved because of more pressing matters. The report eventually became the basis of a 'new towns' policy, and led to the creation of, in 1942, the Ministry of Works and Planning which decided that the relocation of population and industry would be a post-war objective. Thus, under the new Labour government, huge sections of the populations of bomb-damaged and overcrowded cities were to be rehoused in new communities in the provinces.

The New Towns Committee, chaired by Baron Reith, an engineer, briefly a wartime Minister of Information, and, most famously, founder of the BBC, sat from late 1945 until the middle of 1946. The committee included several leading figures in the Town and Country Planning Association, originally the Garden Cities Association that was founded in 1899. During the inter-war years, the success of 'garden city' and 'garden suburb' projects had seen many new council estates being built on similar lines. Now the New Towns Act gave the government power to designate areas of land for new town development. A series of 'development corporations' would be set up, each responsible for one of the projected towns. Most were intended to accommodate the overspill of population from London. The government saw it as essential to restrict the growth of large cities, a policy that would lead to the 1947 Town and Country Planning Act aimed to control urban sprawl into the countryside. The Act set a target of 300,000 new houses a year, and at the same time defined green belt land that had to be kept rural.

There would be two basic types of new town: those where there had previously been 'only a scattered and rural population'; those that formed 'extensions of existing small towns'. Stevenage, in Hertfordshire, fell between those two broad categories, and was designated as Britain's first new town. Stevenage dated back to Roman times. In the early eighteenth century it owed much of its prosperity to its position on the Great North Road. Twenty-one stagecoaches passed through Stevenage every day until, in 1850, the Great Northern Railway was opened, and the era of the stagecoach was over. In his 1861 short story *Tom Tiddler's Ground* Charles Dickens wrote of Stevenage, 'The village street was like most other village streets: wide for its height, silent for its size, and drowsy in the dullest degree. The quietest little dwellings with the largest of window-shutters to shut up nothing as if it were the Mint or the Bank of England.'

Eighty-five years later, locals were awakened to the prospect of their 'drowsy' town becoming overwhelmed by 10,000 new homes in six neighbourhoods, each with its own shops, pub, and community centre.

The plan also called for Stevenage to become the first town in the country to have a completely pedestrianised centre. Unlike other proposed new towns, such as Bracknell, Hemel Hempstead and Crawley, where the old centre became the basis for the new, Stevenage's new town would be developed next to the historic settlement that Dickens had found so dull. Around 6,100 acres were served a draft Designation Order as the site of Britain's first new town, and in October, after a public inquiry had been held, Lewis Silkin, the Minister of Town and Country Planning, decided to proceed with the plan. The final designation order for Stevenage was made on 11 November 1946. The intended population would be 60,000 people, many of whom were to be employed in the manufacturing industry.

While the plan had its supporters, including the local trades council which saw numerous advantages, it was a decision not universally welcomed by Stevenage's inhabitants. On 15 November the *Sussex Agricultural Express* reported, 'The Government department concerned has announced its intention of proceeding with the Stevenage project in spite of the strength and extent of the local opposition ... .' On the night of 19/20 December 1946, the boards at Stevenage railway station were changed to read 'Silkingrad' to highlight that locals were powerless against the will of the Government. Earlier that month, Lewis Silkin, had established the Stevenage Development Corporation that would play a vital role in the planning, building and management of the new town. Ironically, in 1973, the station was relocated to be nearer the new town centre.

In February 1947 a High Court judge found in favour of the Stevenage Residents' Protection Association, and quashed the Stevenage New Town Order, but the decision was overturned by the Court of Appeal and by the House of Lords (the Protection Association had raised £3,000 to finance this final appeal) and, in July 1947, the Designation Order for Stevenage was approved, although economic controls imposed that summer meant that it would be 1949 before the Stevenage Development Corporation began its compulsory purchase of land. The final scheme was not approved until December 1954 and it was 20 April 1959 before Queen Elizabeth II opened Stevenage's new shopping precinct, an early experiment in town centre pedestrianisation.

Seven further new towns were planned for around London: Crawley in West Sussex (designated in January 1947); Hemel Hempstead in

Hertfordshire (February 1947); Harlow in Essex (March 1947) where in 1951 the first residential tower block in Britain was built; Welwyn Garden City and Hatfield in Hertfordshire (both May 1948); Basildon in Essex (January 1949); and Bracknell in Berkshire (June 1949). Also in 1949, two new towns were designated in County Durham: Newton Aycliffe (April 1947) and Peterlee (March 1948). Corby in Northamptonshire followed in April 1950 and two new towns were designated in Scotland: East Kilbride (May 1947) and Glenrothes (June 1948), and one in Wales, at Cwmbran (November 1949). These were the first generation of new towns after the Second World War, second and third generations – such as Telford in Shropshire, Redditch in Worcestershire and Milton Keynes in Buckinghamshire – coming in the 1960s. Altogether, twenty-eight new towns were built in Britain in the half-century following the 1946 New Towns Act. The post-war programme was Britain's most ambitious large-scale town-building programme. Today, those new towns are home to almost 3 million people.

Chapter Five

The Petticoat Pilgrims

Mrs Forbes has introduced her husband to the tea-drinking habit – practically unknown in America

Michael Amnine, *Daily Herald*

On the morning of 26 January 1946, a special train pulled up alongside the American troopship SS *Argentina* docked at Southampton. Out of it poured more than 300 women accompanied by their children. They had arrived from Tidworth transit camp on Salisbury Plain and they were beginning a journey into the unknown. They were some of the so-called GI brides. Another train delivered more women and offspring to the quayside. They joined the others on board the *Argentina*, which had been refitted with kitchens where mothers could prepare food, and a nursery with playpens and every kind of toy. Mothers with babies averaged four to a cabin, each of which had been fitted with drop-side cots with pink and blue blankets. Dance music was being played on board. 'I think this is ideal,' said one mother as she was shown to her cabin. Another said, 'It's such a relief to see how well the ship is fitted up. We were all very anxious, as the camps were far from perfect, although the authorities did what they could.'

The Americans had organised two large camps near Southampton, where the mothers and babies were assembled a few days before they were due to sail. There they were given lectures on the American way of life, about the differences of language and they were told about the cultural changes that they would face. Writing from America to the *Cheltenham Chronicle and Gloucestershire Graphic* in February 1946, Mrs Gwen Drennan, who had just joined her husband in Louisiana, said that, when her party arrived at Andover, they were met by army trucks and taken to a reception camp just outside the small Wiltshire town of Ludgershall where German prisoners of war helped them with their luggage. She had shared a large hut with three other women although there was room for twenty-three. 'With all those rows of iron bedsteads, it was rather like being in the ATS,' she told the newspaper. An American Red Cross Club had provided tea and biscuits and there were facilities for cabling the United States. Meals were taken in the PX – the American equivalent of the NAAFI – where German PoWs served dishes the likes of which most Britons had not seen since before the war. Her elder sister expected to leave Cheltenham soon, to join her own husband in America.

In the late afternoon of 26 January, Colonel Floyd Lyle, known as Pete to his friends, had welcomed the women to the *Argentina*: 'We are cousins, not in blood and language alone, but in heritage of freedom and democracy.' His was a late appointment; the officer who should have taken charge had turned up drunk. Then the *Argentina* had slipped anchor and set out across the Atlantic for New York. Aboard her there were now 451 GI brides and 175 children and babies, all bound for a new life in a new land. Twelve newspapermen and photographers were also on board. As dawn began to break on 4 February, the passengers caught sight of the floodlit Statue of Liberty. They were probably much more relieved than they were excited. This had been the roughest Atlantic crossing the *Argentina* had ever made. Over 200 women had been seasick, one of them crying out, 'Let the bloody boat go down! It's not worth it!' Colonel Lyle, who during the war had taken charge of transporting GIs to Britain, and, later, prisoners of war sent to the United States from North Africa, and who had thus made more trips across the Atlantic than any other American officer, confirmed that it was the worst sea trip that he had experienced.

As the passengers disembarked, twenty hours later than scheduled, there was no army band to welcome them, although one had been planned. They didn't want to wake up the babies, explained an official. When the *Daily Herald* correspondent Michael Amnine attempted to snatch a few quotes, he was pleased when Daphne Dyer, a GI bride from Sanderstead in Surrey, asked him to include her in his story. 'Just say, "Mother and child doing well"' was all she wanted to relay back to home.

Six days later, the *Queen Mary* made her way through icy waters around Pier 90, bringing another 1,700 GI brides and 650 children to New York to begin new lives in America. The *Queen Mary*, which would eventually transport almost 13,000 GI brides and children to the United States, as well as 10,000 to Canada, had been converted in Southampton, with the installation of a nursery and a playroom as well as additional laundries. All cabins had cots and the first-class swimming pool had been used as a drying room for hundreds of nappies, or diapers as the Americans called them. Gwen Drennan had reported, 'Everything was repainted, and the lights on board were lovely.' The shops on the ship offered all sorts of goods which 'were much enjoyed, as were, too, the beauty salon and library'. There was also a newsletter, *Wives Aweigh*, produced by the ship's staff and by the women themselves. It contained public service announcements, recipes, international news, and, in a bid to prepare them for their new life, articles about the places to where the GI brides were ultimately bound.

On 10 February the 378th Army Service Forces Band greeted the brides with 'Brahm's Lullaby', 'Rock-A-Bye-Baby' and 'Here Comes the Bride'. Welcome to the United States. American Red Cross nurses and Army welfare officers had looked after the women on their voyage towards a new world. A message of welcome from the mayor of New York was broadcast over the ship's loudspeakers as husbands waiting on the dockside listened for the names of their wives to be called out.

Vera Cracknell was 18 and working as a junior hostess at an American Red Cross club behind Harrod's store in London when she met Sergeant Charles Long, who was working in military intelligence. Although she did not turn up to what should have been their first date, at Marble Arch, when the war ended, they married and in 1946 she found herself crossing the Atlantic, one of the 'Petticoat Pilgrims' as British newspapers had dubbed the war brides. Her memories of the *Queen Mary* differed from those of Gwen Drennan. In 1996 Vera recalled, 'It was no luxury ship. The quarters were cramped and uncomfortable. We weren't used to eating rich food and chocolates because of rationing, so we all got carried away.'

For those in Britain still wondering whether to make this life-changing trip, the *Daily Herald*'s Michael Amnine told the good news story of Mrs Ian Forbes, a 'pretty, young, brunette' from North Kensington, London, who had settled in well to her new life in Arlington, Virginia: 'Her courtship in the buzz-bombing of London seems far away as she goes about her daily tasks in a six-roomed wooden bungalow. She enjoys her modern American kitchen and tending her four-months-old daughter, Ann Kathleen, born soon after her arrival.' Mrs Forbes lived with her in-laws, but she and her husband 'dream of a house they will build some day, which will include all the gadgets including a "service-window" between dining-room and kitchen, a feature she has admired in American homes'. Mrs Forbes had also 'introduced her husband to the tea-drinking habit – practically unknown in America – and she has lost her British accent'.

She was one of more than 70,000 British women who, during the war and in the immediate post-war years, had married American servicemen. British men might have complained that the Americans were 'overpaid, oversexed and over here' but few British women were complaining. The arrival of American troops – the first contingent of GIs to arrive in the United Kingdom had stepped ashore in Belfast and Londonderry on 26 January 1942, only seven weeks after the Japanese attack on Pearl Harbor had brought the United States into the war – gave local girls a taste, perceived at least, of 'Hollywood' glamour. The Americans offered nylons, perfume, romance and, ultimately, the possibility of a new life in a country that the women thought they knew, albeit those impressions had been formed only through visits to their local cinemas.

Before crossing the Atlantic, American soldiers had been given a 32-page booklet entitled *Instructions for American Servicemen in Britain*. It contained advice on what to expect and how to behave. It reminded them:

> The British will welcome you as friends and allies but remember that crossing an ocean does not automatically make you a hero. There are housewives in aprons and youngsters in knee pants in Britain who have lived through more high-explosives in air-raids than many soldiers saw in first-class barrages in the last war.

The Americans were warned, 'Don't be a show off.' The US Army had tried its best to discourage marriages between GIs and local girls but, by the dawn of D Day, there were almost two million, mostly young and unattached, American men in the UK.

Officials were totally unprepared for the vast numbers of war brides who wanted to start a new life in their husbands' homeland at the end of the war. On 11 October 1945 British brides gathered outside the US Embassy in Grosvenor Square, protesting against the lack of transport to get them across the Atlantic to their demobbed American husbands. Earlier there had been a protest meeting at the Caxton Hall, where women, some of them carrying babies in their arms, had been queueing from one o'clock in the morning. One woman had with her four children – two sets of twins. Only two hundred tickets had been issued and hundreds more women waited outside. Some newspaper reports put the number at several thousand. Most of those who gained admittance had to sit on the floor, the few chairs there were being reserved for a committee led by Mrs Francis Rhodes, who, as Francis Henson, a newspaper reporter in Manchester, had married an American lieutenant.

The women's concerns were not simply that they had been parted from their lovers, they also had financial problems, and because of the housing shortage in British cities ravaged by the Blitz, many were living with relatives in wholly unsuitable arrangements. One GI bride was convinced that 'the American government does not want us over there, and it is doing its best to break up our marriages'. Lieutenant Commander Herbert Agar of the American embassy assured the girls that they were not 'lost people', although, some days later, he agreed with the argument of five GIs who had signed a letter to the *Daily Express*, pointing out that they had been separated from their own American families far longer than the war brides had been separated from their husbands. When it came to transport, the GIs wanted priority, and asked, 'Now girls, do you think you can bring yourselves to do without your husbands for a few months?'

At the Caxton Hall meeting, a resolution was passed, urging immediate steps to provide transport for GI brides, and the setting up of a special department to do so. Then some women, who were mostly from Manchester, Southport, Liverpool, Wigan and Yorkshire, marched through the West End to the US Embassy, chanting, 'We want boats!' When the march reached the American Red Cross club, Rainbow Corner, at Piccadilly Circus, it was joined by GIs who set up their own cry of 'We want boats too,' echoing the sentiments of their colleagues who had written to the *Daily Express*.

Two women were admitted to the embassy. When they eventually emerged, one of them, Mrs Emily France of Newport Road, Middlesbrough, said that the girls could not be seen by officials. They threatened to picket the embassy until 'something was done', but instead they dispersed peacefully. On 28 December that year the US government passed the War Brides Act, offering women married to American servicemen non-quota immigrant status and free passage to the United States. 'Operation War Bride' – or 'Operation Diaper Run' as US newspapers preferred to call it – was soon well under way. It is estimated that, in the years after the passing of the act, over 300,000 foreign war brides moved to the United States, including not only those 70,000 British women, but also some 51,000 Filipinos and 50,000 Japanese and between 12,000 and 15,000 Australians.

Not all found happiness. After all, the peacetime lives of their new husbands were a mystery. On the day that the *Argentina* had left for New York, British newspapers were also reporting the return of twenty GI brides, some of whom had paid up to £250 to cross the Atlantic from Britain by air in 1945 but who had now landed in Liverpool after sailing back home on board the *Mauritania*. One passenger said:

> They were simply fed up. The stories their husbands had told them about their life and their home were just not true. The girls found life in the United States not at all the carefree existence they had expected. One said that her husband told her that he owned a smart restaurant, employed thirty waiters, and had a fifteen-piece orchestra playing for him. When she got there, she found it was a snack bar in Brooklyn and she was expected to act as chief cook and bottle washer.

Others were trying for priority to get back to Britain. One found her husband was a knife-grinder in New York, although he had told her he was a theatre magnate. Another discovered that she was married to a criminal. He had jumped his bail to join the army and was re-arrested on his return to the United States.

In March 1946 a court in South Windsor, Connecticut, ordered William Karvells, an-ex-serviceman, to pay his English bride, Peggy, the daughter of Major and Mrs John Burgess of Shrewsbury, the equivalent of £5 per week, or go to prison for thirty days. According to the prosecution, Karvells had decided that his marriage was a mistake and that he was now interested in another woman. He had refused to meet his wife when her ship docked in New York and it was left to his parents and his sister to welcome Peggy to America. In November 1946 the *Essex Newsman-Herald* reported:

> A boat-train of beautifully dressed girls arrived at Waterloo this week. No, they were not another batch of Goldwyn Girls – they were all born and brought up among our own green fields and grey

cities. They were GI brides, returning, some for a visit, some for good. Those who came back for good could tell mostly unhappy stories, either of domestic or financial trouble in America.

Some marriages ended in tragedy. In September 1946 Bridget McCluskey, a nurse, originally from the small market town of Cootehill in County Cavan in Ulster, shot dead her husband, Frank Waters, in Las Vegas. She had married him in 1944 when he was a civilian worker with the Lockheed company in London, but after she became pregnant and he was posted to France after D Day, he told her that he wanted a divorce. Urged on by women's advocacy organisations keen to establish a legal precedent to protect deserted war brides, Bridget flew to Las Vegas, to where Frank had gone to take advantage of Nevada's short residency requirements when it came to seeking a divorce. In April 1946 she told the *Stars and Stripes* newspaper, 'After I wrote him that I had a baby, he replied saying the marriage was a mistake. He added he would send me $50 a month. I've got those letters and others. He can't get away with this.' He did not. She shot him dead with a revolver that she had found in a draw. She told a packed Nevada courtroom that 'the gun went off in my hand ... I didn't mean to kill him'. In his closing remarks, the deputy district attorney warned that, if Bridget was found not guilty, 'She may get a Hollywood contract or do a personal appearance tour. Perhaps the gun manufacturer will even seek her endorsement of his product.' A conviction for murder could have carried the death penalty but the jury, perhaps influenced by a groundswell of support for Bridget, both in the United States and Britain, found her guilty of involuntary manslaughter and sentenced her to one to five years in prison. She was released after ten months for good behaviour. She returned home to work as a nurse in Britain before emigrating to Canada to continue nursing. She died in 2005, well regarded for the care she had given to members of Canada's First Nation.

For most GI brides, however, the future was a happy one. Sixty-two years after arriving at New York aboard the Italian liner *Saturnia*, Eileen Marian Guaricci told the *New York Times* about the day she was re-united with her husband, Donato Guaricci, an army sergeant. When they had first met, at the Lord Nelson pub in Chelsea's Kings Road, Eileen was a 16-year-old girl from Battersea, the daughter of a sailor and one of ten children who had spent seven months sleeping in an air-raid shelter during the London Blitz. They married at the end of the war before Donato was returned to the United States. It was six months before she saw him again. He drove up to greet her in a black Buick with a bouquet for her on the dashboard. It was 17 March 1946, St Patrick's Day. The local newspaper in Richmond Hill, Queens, had the previous week published an article under the headline, 'Tea Time, Six More English Brides Head for Queens'. Eileen was one of them. Her first married home was a two-room apartment next to a window-washing business in Queens. Donato, or 'Danny' as she called him, worked as a car mechanic.

In New York, the war brides provided emotional support for each other, helping to find work, and sorting out child care. In 1994 Danny died, of heart disease, aged 76, In 2008 Eileen was one of the last surviving members of Astoria Crumpets, a Queens social club started by several war brides in 1947. Then aged 80, at her house on Long Island, she displayed a Union Flag in her study where there was also a sign that read, 'I'm British and Proud'. She told the *New York Times* writer Sarah Kershaw, 'I love this country. I love England, too, of course. It's my roots. But I always say if anything happened between America and England, put me in the middle of Atlantic Ocean in a boat, and I don't know which way I would go.'

Chapter Six

Mutiny in the RAF

'We have done the job we joined up to do ... We will go home in anything – a tramp steamer or a windjammer, if you like.'

RAF strikers

At the end of the Second World War there were around five million serving personnel in Britain's armed forces. Many of the men serving abroad when the war finally ended, in August 1945 with the surrender of Japan, had not seen their families for years. The men's demobilisation – not to mention their return to civilian life – would prove a huge headache for the government. They felt frustration at the slow business of taking them home, and in every branch of the services this resulted in a number of disciplinary incidents, none more so than in the RAF where it would eventually affect 50,000 men in sixty stations in the Far East, the sub-Continent, the Middle East, and even in Gibraltar. It was in India and South-East Asia, however, where it became a real crisis for the government.

There had been mutinies before, most notably at Salerno in September 1943 when, during the early phase of the Allied invasion of Italy, some two hundred British soldiers had refused re-assignments to other British units that were serving in the US Fifth Army. They were veterans of the Eighth Army's North African campaign and they wanted to rejoin their old units. The upshot was that 191 of them were shipped to Algeria, held in a prison near Constantine, and charged with mutiny. It was then the largest number of British servicemen ever to face prosecution at one time. Their trial lasted for five days, and not one of them was allowed to take the witness stand. All were found guilty and three sergeants were sentenced to death. Two weeks later, their sentences were commuted to twelve years' hard labour, and eventually, after the intervention of the Adjutant General, Sir Ronald Adam, they were suspended. All the men were released and sent to the units that they had refused to join in September. For the remainder of their time in the military, many faced constant harassment, and eighty absconded. One of them, a fiery little Scotsman, Private John McFarlane of the Durham Light Infantry, was stripped of the Military Medal that his bravery had earned in the Western Desert.

In 1946, even though it was peacetime again, and despite the sympathy that Sir Ronald Adam, the second most senior man in the British Army, had shown towards the disaffected servicemen of Salerno in the heat of battle, it still took courage to stand up to the authorities. There was, though, a resentment that had festered since October 1945 when, in a minute to his Ministry colleagues, Wing Commander John Strachey, the Parliamentary Under Secretary of State for Air, confirmed rumours that RAF personnel would be at the back of the queue when it came to demobilisation:

> My line in defence has been the obvious one that: first, a relatively large RAF and small army is by far the most economical way of meeting our world commitments; and second, that we face a huge transportation and trooping task, largely for the sake of the other two forces ... .

Transportation difficulties? The RAF men were now hearing stories of large liners such as the *Queen Mary* taking GI brides to start new lives in the United States. On 21 January 1946 a group of RAF 'repats' – serving men due to be sent home on completion of their tour of overseas duty – at Worli camp near Bombay, sent a cable to Strachey, alleging unfairness in their return to Britain. The repats said:

> As demobilised personnel have priority in both shipping and airlifts, approximately 1,000 tour-expired airmen have been awaiting repatriation for the past four weeks. The next two boat lists include only 50 and 200 repats respectively. We respectfully appeal to your sense of fairness, on behalf of the men and their families, to make an immediate substantial increase in the allotment of shipping space for tour-expired airmen.

The cable had resulted from growing discontent at the Worli camp where slogans such as 'No Boats', 'No Fatigues', 'No Guards' and 'We don't want speeches, we want action' had been pasted across official noticeboards. The men told the Reuters news agency:

> We are wondering whether we will ever get home. The injustice is that some demobilised men are sometimes getting home after only two or three months out here, while some of us have been overseas for nearly four years. We will go home in anything – a tramp steamer or a windjammer, if you like.

One week later it was reported that 850 RAF men stationed at Lahore, in the Punjab, had gone on strike as a protest at the rate and progress of demobilisation. The decision to strike had been taken at a meeting of men below the rank of sergeant, with no dissenting voice. The men alleged that favouritism had been shown to units stationed in Britain, or near home, in demobilisation. Another grievance was that when they finally got their ticket, they would each be permitted to take only 50lbs (22.67 kilos) of personal kit, while officers were allowed up to 4cwt (50.80 kilos), almost nine times as much. From Mauripur, near Karachi, 2,000 RAF strikers had sent Clement Attlee a petition for quicker demobilisation, while Indian airmen demanded better conditions for those who want to remain in the service, and the same pay, promotion and conditions as British other ranks.

On 27 January *The Times* reported:

> Twelve hundred men at Dum Dum, Calcutta, have been on strike since midnight on Friday. The men have no complaints against the authorities at the camp, with whom they are on the best of terms. The commanding officer, Air Commodore Slee, had a friendly discussion with them and a delegation of the strikers also talked with Major Wyatt of the Parliamentary delegation visiting India. With the strike now spread over a wide area, Air Vice-Marshal Sir Roderick Carr, AOC, BAFSEA, signalled the Air Ministry: 'I deplore the action of the airmen, but owing to the widespread nature of the incidents I cannot suggest any alternative to a general Government statement.'

The report of the new strike at Lahore came after a warning given the previous night by Air Vice-Marshal Sir Keith Park, Air C-in-C, South-East Asia, who, from his Singapore headquarters, said, 'The Government has made it clear that it will not tolerate disorders and intimidation, and disciplinary action will be taken against ringleaders.'

Sir Keith's announcement followed the return to duty of the 4,000 RAF sit-down strikers at Seletar airbase in Singapore. Official assurances had been given that grievances of a local nature, including lack of accommodation and canteens, would be rectified and that complaints against the slowness of release and repatriation had been referred to London. Sir Keith's statement was made 'to prevent actions by aircrew who fought the enemy, and the vast majority of loyal, hard-working airmen, from being confused with the actions of a few strike promoters'.

It went on:

> These men have clearly shown that they are determined to stage sit-down strikes as a means of bringing pressure on the home Government. On 26 January, the commanding officer at Seletar reported that some airmen threatened to stage a sit-down strike. The C-in-C instructed the base commander to parade the airmen to ascertain at first-hand their complaints. At this parade some were not satisfied and requested to speak to the C-in-C personally. The C-in-C attended a full parade a few hours later, to hear grievances and answer questions. A number of airmen drawn from units that arrived in the weeks after VJ Day refused to accept the fact and figures about relief schemes that have been supplied by the Air Ministry and the Government. A proportion of the airmen returned to duty, and some of these were subjected to violence after 'lights out' by a few rowdies who went as far as to beat up some of the loyal airmen in the barracks, thus using methods of extreme intimidation.

The first strike had begun at RAF Drigh Road – birthplace of the Royal Indian Air Force –in Karachi in mid-January 1946, when, wholly unexpectedly, came the order to parade in best blue uniform and that a kit inspection would be carried out. For months of excessive heat, men had worn open-necked shirts, lightweight shorts or trousers and sandals. Suddenly they were expected to don heavy woollen uniforms. Much of the kit they were now expected to lay out for inspection – after being cleaned and polished, of course – had been lost or stolen. It was resolved that more than a thousand men serving at the large maintenance unit would refuse to parade in their 'best blue' and would not prepare kit for inspection. Leading the protest was a small group of Communists, whose avowed intent had been to defeat fascism – job done there – and to help build a prosperous, socialist post-war Britain. Their immediate aim, of protesting at the conditions at Drigh Road, found massive support among even the most apolitical, for the problems were not confined to the fact that there was no word on when the men would be sent back to Britain and demobbed. For some, life at the camp was appalling. Most men were living in barrack blocks, but some were housed in bell tents – six men to a tent, all fighting off the attentions of mosquitoes and flies. The food was poor, often consisting only of emergency rations that the US Army did not now want to feed to its own soldiers, and the working day was a long one. What passed for the gents' toilet was a huge wooden box with holes cut into the top. There was no privacy. Illness and boredom also ate into the men's morale. The men sent a petition to Clement Attlee: 'We have done the job we joined up to do and now we want to get back home, both for personal reasons and because we think that it is by work at home that we can best help Britain.'

The Drigh Road protest went ahead and, overall, offenders were dealt with lightly, but scapegoats were needed. After pressure from above, Leading Aircraftman Arthur Attwood, a lifelong trade unionist, was court martialled. Found not guilty of incitement to mutiny, he was re-arrested when the RAF top brass objected to the verdict. Attwood was one of a number of left-wing sympathisers serving in the RAF in South-East Asia, and in the House of Commons, the Conservative MP Wing Commander Norman Hulbert declared that 'these Communist agitators who have brought disgrace' to the RAF had to be 'severely dealt with'. In Britain there was a public outcry – the Independent Labour Party MP John McGovern said that he had received more letters about Attwood's questionable court martial than on any other subject during the war. In June 1946, 33-year-old Attwood was released, the proceedings of his trial having been annulled and no re-trial planned.

Meanwhile, on 13 March 1946, the *Straits Times* reported that an RAF court martial had found 25-year-old Leading Aircraftsman Norris Cymbalist, a radar operator at RAF Kallang in Singapore, guilty of using insubordinate language to superiors and incitement to mutiny. Cymbalist, the son of an Inverness tailor, was sentenced to ten years' penal servitude and 'discharge with ignominy'. Again, there was outrage in Britain, and the custodial sentence was halved. Eventually, in November 1947, Cymbalist was released from Wakefield prison after serving twenty-one months.

In addition to Seletar, airmen at Dum Dum in Calcutta, and at Drigh Road and Mauripur returned to work, although strike leaders at Dum Dum warned that unless they received a satisfactory reply to their demands within ten days, their protest would be renewed. While 1,000 Indian airmen went on strike at Cawnpore, the 5,000 RAF airmen already on strike there said that they were prepared to return to work if they were given an absolute assurance that the RAF in India was informed that theirs was only a token strike, and that the people of Britain were told by SEAC radio, the BBC and the press of a 16-point demand by the men.

By the end of January 1946, after being given assurances that their demobilisation would be hastened, all the striking airmen began to return to normal duties. The strikes had lasted between three and eleven days, and they were peaceful. In February 1946 a court of inquiry found that, despite the allegations of a few rowdies beating up loyal airmen at Seletar, there was no evidence of intimidation or violence against regular or loyal airmen. It found that the airmen's complaints had not been directed against their own officers or RAF authorities. The strikes had followed a similar pattern and had common demands. The court noted that the overwhelming majority of men were merely civilians in uniform.

When, in February 1946, there were similar strikes by members of the Royal Indian Air Force, and, later, mutinies on seventy-eight of the Royal Indian Navy's eighty-eight ships, Lord Wavell, Viceroy of India, said, 'I am afraid that [the] example of the Royal Air Force, who got away with what was really a mutiny, has some responsibility for the present situation.'

There was more trouble ahead for Britain, however, this time from the Army when 255 men of the 13th (Lancashire) Parachute Battalion at Muar Camp in Malaya refused to obey the commanding officer's orders and were charged with mutiny. On 8 October the Secretary of State for War, Frederick Bellinger, told the House of Commons:

> On the evening of 13 May there was a certain amount of discontent in the canteen and the word 'strike' was mentioned. Later the lights were put out and someone asked those present if they were prepared to

stick to what had been arranged. At about 7am on 14 May, about 260 men congregated on the sea wall in a sullen mood, and when ordered to disperse by the orderly officer made no move. They later moved to the canteen and here they were addressed by the commanding officer who told them that they should air their grievances in the proper way, that he could not entertain collective grievances, and that if they refused to return to duty, they would be guilty of mutiny. He gave them a direct order to return to their companies. As the men did not respond to this order, the commanding officer reported the matter to his superior commander. During the afternoon the divisional commander arrived and addressed the men, who had again assembled on the sea wall. The commanding officer then put out company markers and ordered the men to fall in. They did not do so, and the divisional commander ordered another battalion to take them into custody. None of the officers or NCOs took part in the mutiny, nor had they any previous knowledge that it was going to occur.

Two Courts of Inquiry were assembled, on 17 and 22 May; one to inquire into the causes of the mutiny and the other to inquire into the conditions in Muar Camp. As a result, it was decided that all the 258 men concerned must be brought to trial for mutiny. The trial commenced on 12 August and was completed on 19 September. Of the 258 men charged three were acquitted and all the remainder were convicted. Of these, eight were sentenced to five years' penal servitude and to be discharged with ignominy. The rest to three years' penal servitude and to be discharged with ignominy. The General Officer Commanding-in-Chief as Confirming Officer did not confirm the proceedings in the case of twelve accused who were accordingly released, and in the remaining 243 cases commuted all the sentences to two years' imprisonment with hard labour and to be discharged with ignominy.

There can be no shadow of doubt that these men were rightly charged with mutiny. The law regards mutiny as a most serious military offence and provides death as the maximum penalty. Mutiny may be described as the act of two or more soldiers who join together, whether actively or passively, in resistance to, or disobedience of, lawful authority. The obedience of lawful orders is vital in any fighting Service, and it is obvious that in the Armed Forces any form of resistance to lawful authority, whether active or passive, cannot and will not be tolerated. I am waiting the advice of the Judge Advocate-General on the legality of the proceedings and I will make a further statement when I have received it. The proceedings of the trial arrived in this country only a week ago and it has not yet been possible, owing to their great length, to complete a full review.

There was much public sympathy. J.W. Smith of Hessle, wrote to the *Hull Daily Mail*:

I have read with very deep concern the sentences passed on the men of the 6th Airborne Division of Muar Camp, Kuala Lumpur. Is this the way to honour the men who were the first to jump into every battle this country has had in the war, men who have been given every honour for bravery and devotion to duty? How can we expect volunteers for the services when such sentences are imposed upon men for using the only way they could to get their grievances righted?

On 26 October *The Sphere* reported:

When the news reached Britain from Muar that the 243 paratroops who were accused of mutiny had been sentenced to terms of imprisonment averaging over two years per man, immediate action was taken in this country, and over one hundred MPs, besieged by their constituents, in turn tackled Mr Bellinger, the new War Minister with regard to the legality of the trial. Mr Bellinger made a spirited reply, declaring that mutiny would not be tolerated in the British Army, but within twenty-four hours, the Judge Advocate-General, after considering the matter of the trial and particularly the manner in which some of the evidence had been heard, reported that there had been 'legal irregularities of a substantial nature'. As a result, the sentences were quashed and the men at once set free.

Chapter Seven

Public Ownership is the Answer

At this somewhat critical stage in the youth of British Railways my complain may seem unreasonable but ... I can only say that the apathy of railway officials is matched but by those of us forced to trust ourselves to their mercies.

Charles G. Kennedy, writing to *The Scotsman*

In August 1948 W.L.B. Beales of Friern Barnet wrote to the *Thanet Advertiser and Echo* about a train journey that they had endured from a station on the Kent coast back to London. Ten adults and six children had been crammed into one compartment of a 'no-corridor' coach in which no toilet was available. It was, said the writer, 'a deplorable state of affairs for old people and young children to endure, especially as the train was 30 minutes late arriving at Victoria'.

He said that when the train did reach its final destination, 'I saw women and children rush for the ladies' toilet where the queue already stretched on to the platform'. During this journey:

> our compartment was without ceiling illumination ... at least two passengers showed a flame from lighters to keep young children quiet in tunnels ... an electric light shade in the roof of the carriage, and part of the fitting, was jolted loose in the Penge tunnel. It just missed my head and struck me on the hand. Had a bulb been there, that also would have fallen ... . It was clear from comments I heard on this journey that unless something is done to remove discomfort of travel to the Kent coast, some people will not return next year.

The newspaper's editor felt that their correspondent had been unlucky: 'Railway facilities this year are the best since the war, but shortage of coaches is the main stumbling block to more comfortable travel.' Beales's complaints were, however, typical of those that regularly appeared in newspaper letter pages following the nationalisation of the railways after the Second World War.

'Victory in war must be followed by a prosperous peace.' So declared the Labour Party's 1945 election manifesto. If only it had been that simple. Britain may have been on the winning side of war, but the country was groaning under a huge debt, its housing and its industry had been badly damaged by German air raids, and there was still the huge cost of maintaining an army of occupation in beaten and battered Germany, not to mention the men and resources still employed in an empire upon which the sun was finally about to set.

The Labour Party had promised to take control of the economy and to nationalise everything from the Bank of England to transport. Public ownership of road haulage (bitterly opposed by its owners), rail, canal, docks and air 'cannot be achieved without unification', said the manifesto.

Britain already had a state-owned airline, British Overseas Airways Corporation (BOAC), created in 1939 by the merger of Imperial Airways and British Airways. The 1946 Civil Aviation Act added two more: British-South American Airways (which, in 1949, would be absorbed by BOAC) and British European Airways (BEA). On New Year's Day 1946 the Lancastrian airliner *Starlight* took off from Heath Row airfield, which the *Coventry Evening Telegraph* helpfully explained, was 'on the verge of London'. It was the first proving flight preparatory to the introduction of a regular passenger and freight service between Britain and South America. The newspaper reported that in the post-war years, Heath Row would be Britain's major air junction estimated to cost about £20 million.

Air Vice-Marshal Donald Bennett took off, accompanied by a crew of six and five passengers, the latter all officials of British-South American Airways. Their stops included Lisbon, Rio de Janeiro and Montevideo. Twenty-four-year-old Miss Mary Sylvia Guthrie, of Basil Street, London, who had served as a pilot in the British Air Transport Auxiliary during the war 'went as the first air-hostess but will be known as the Star-girl'. Heath Row already had 'the finest runway in the world', and the *Coventry Evening Telegraph* declared that Air Vice-Marshal Bennett and those who accompanied him were 'truly ambassadors representing the spirit and determination of Britain to play the same leading part in the air as it always has at sea'.

Just as transport could not be achieved without unification, according to Labour, nor could public ownership of the water, fuel and power industries: 'For a quarter of a century the coal industry, producing Britain's most precious national raw material, has been floundering under the ownership of many hundreds of independent companies.' Amalgamation under public ownership 'will bring great economies in operation ... .' It was the same for iron and steel:

Only if public ownership replaces private monopoly can the industry become efficient.' A Labour Government would also 'keep the new food services, such as the factory canteens and the British Restaurants, free and cheap milk for mothers and children, fruit juices and food supplement, and will improve and extend these services.

So, one by one, Britain's key industries, and the welfare of her people, fell into state ownership. The public sector would run almost everything that was important to the public. The takeover was hugely popular in the coal-mining industry. The moment for which many had fought for so long was at hand. On New Year's Day 1947 Britain's coal mines were nationalised. It was the day on which 1 million men, many of them working in highly unpleasant and very often dangerous conditions, broke free from the grip of the 850 colliery owners (at a cost to taxpayers of £164 million in compensation). Many recalled 1926, when cuts in miners' pay resulted in the General Strike. That could not happen again. Now the miners, along with everyone else, owned the mines after the Labour Government, elected with a landslide victory only eighteen months earlier, fulfilled its promise.

Clement Attlee sent the miners a message:

> Today, January 1st, 1947, will be remembered as one of the great days in the industrial history of our country. The coalmines now belong to the nation. This act offers great possibilities of social advance for the workers, and indeed the whole nation. If all alike – workers, National Coal Board and Government – shoulder their duties resolutely and use their rights wisely, these great advances will be assured. I send my wishes to all engaged in this vital work.

Yet a post-war labour shortage in the pits meant that, in some areas of the country, the loss of manpower saw some mines being closed. In November 1950 it was proposed to bring over 6,000 Italians to work in Britain's coal mines. The move was opposed by the National Union of Mineworkers but a spokesman for the West Midlands Division of the National Coal Board pointed out that there were many foreign workers already in the pits and, were it not for Poles, Yugoslavians, Lithuanians and others, it would have been necessary to shut down even more mines.

One in ten British people would be employed in nationalised industries, which had cost £2,700 million in compensation to acquire. But while it had helped to put Labour in power, some aspects of nationalisation would soon become regarded with cynicism, no more so than British Railways which had replaced the regional private companies. The Railways Act of 1921 had seen the country's 130 or so individual railway companies re-organised into four regional groups (Southern, Great Western, London and North Eastern, and London, Midland and Scottish). In 1939 the government took control of railways as a matter of wartime necessity. The four railway groups continued but were placed under a Railways Executive Committee comprised of the representative general managers.

Under the Transport Act of 1947, Britain's railways passed into public ownership, overseen by the British Transport Commission that also looked after canals and road transport. On 1 January 1948 they were organised into six regions: London Midland, Southern, Eastern, Western, North Eastern and Scottish.

There was much work to do. Supporting the war effort, suffering damage from Luftwaffe bombing and an inevitable chronic lack of investment during that time, had worn the railway system to the bone, and following nationalisation there were complaints about late trains, dirty carriages, stations that were cold and falling apart – and even the catering. The British Railways refreshment-room sandwich became the standard comedy joke for everything that was wrong with 'BR'. If ever there was a bad time to take over, this was it.

The balance between principle and practice was hard to achieve. Most of the new state industries were gaining a reputation for being inefficient, overstaffed and stifled by bureaucracy. But especially so the railways. In November 1950 one Hamish Morison of Earlston in Berwickshire wrote a long letter to *The Scotsman* newspaper outlining some of his 'several experiences of British Railways which are not a good advertisement for nationalisation'. One instance would certainly have raised the hackles of animal lovers:

> During the very cold weather in the early part of the year I despatched some day-old chicks (a very perishable commodity and treated as such

prior to nationalisation) to Colinton. These duly arrived at Waverley at 12.40pm and one naturally expected them to be delivered in the early afternoon, but apparently the lorry conveying them from Waverley to Princes Street had broken down, and, in consequence, the chickens lay in Waverley till the following afternoon with dire results. It had not occurred to anybody in authority to get another lorry. Another lot were sent to the North and arrived with several dead and the box flattened. This had been run over by one of the porters wheeling a barrow in Inverness station. About the same time a weekly consignment was left lying in Aberdeen station overnight with a loss of several chickens ... no compensation has been paid ... as I have been unable to prove wilful damage on the part of the railway.

Mr Morison had also run into a tangle of bureaucracy when he attempted to purchase forty railway sleepers. When he had dealt with the private railway companies of pre-nationalisation days this had always proved a simple matter. But now long delays caused by red tape had eventually led him to 'giving up the contest as unequal'.

Then there was the Sunday when he visited the coal sidings of a goods station, where 'a very large body of men' were employed in lifting and relaying the line.

> On the word of command, sixteen men fell in beside the rail; on the word 'lift' every man straightened; and on the word 'throw' the rail soared about three feet through the air to land with a resounding crash ... it was a relief to see that, after lifting four rails, a considerable period for relaxation was allowed. It occurred to me to wonder whether it was absolutely necessary to do this work on a Sunday at double-time, and to speculate on how many men would have been employed under private enterprise. One thing was quite clear, and that was why British Railways show a deficit on their working.

When it came to overspending 'Onlooker' wrote to complain to the *Dundee Courier*:

> In the old days [railway] officials travelled on inspection work by railway transport at no great expense. Now it seems that three or four in a bunch tour the country in expensive motor cars, plus a

liveried chauffeur. How many of these gangs are employed up and down the country is difficult to estimate. It certainly looks like 'jobs for the boys'.

'Onlooker' also had the nationalised power industry in his sights:

> A few days ago it was reported ... that three representatives from the Electricity Board had called on a Cupar manufacturer with the idea of selling him new electric power. Apart from the fact that the Electricity Board are quite unable to give efficient service just now, the necessity of no less than three representatives calling seems a waste of manpower and uncalled for expense. How long would the firm called upon remain in business if they employed three travellers to contact one prospective customer?

There were plenty of critics lining up with an answer.

While it took power from private owners, nationalisation did not mean the end of industrial action. Just before Christmas 1949 an unofficial strike at Barking power station spread to other areas when military personnel were drafted in to maintain supplies. Traffic lights in South London failed during rush hour, and at South London Hospital for Women paraffin lamps and candles were lit, while the admission of casualties was stopped at the South-Eastern Hospital for Children at Sydenham. Trolley buses in the East End and Northern Line underground trains stopped, and London telephone exchanges were also affected. There was load shedding in the Midlands, the North-East and the South-West. It was a cold winter and a spokesman for the British Electricity Authority said that the low temperatures had been aggravated by the loss of power from the London power stations. The strike lasted for a week before the workers' trade union brokered a new pay deal.

Chapter Eight

From the Cradle to the Grave

The National Health Service has got off to an encouraging start ... an example of how the nation can co-operate in a great enterprise.
                                                            Daily Mirror

In January 1946 a flood of resolutions from units of the Student Nurses' Association, which represented 15,000 young nurses, was received by the Royal College of Nursing, imploring the college to take up their plea for extra and better shoes. A hospital nurse, it had been calculated, covered between twelve and fifteen miles a day while at work. The college promised that it would make further approaches to the Board of Trade. Ten months later the National Health Service Act was passed. It took two years to come into effect, after which student nurses would apparently have no further concerns over their working footwear. More than that, healthcare was no longer exclusive to those who could afford to pay for it.

The day that the National Health Service (NHS) was born in the post-war United Kingdom was a historic moment in the nation's history. For the first time anywhere in the world, healthcare was freely available to anyone based on citizenship only, not on their ability to pay fees or insurance. Previously, free treatment had been available only at charitable hospitals or at hospitals run by local authorities, where local ratepayers could be treated under a system that owed much to the Poor Laws that stretched back to late medieval times. Much depended on where one lived. If postcodes had been invented, then healthcare would have been a postcode lottery. Now, at a single stroke, hospitals, doctors, nurses and dentists, as well as opticians and pharmacists, came together under one service. And they were available to everyone in the country, whatever their age and whatever their circumstances.

The NHS came out of the Beveridge Report – officially entitled *Social Insurance and Allied Services* – that had been published in November 1942 as a blueprint for social policy in post-war Britain. Beveridge, a social economist who was 63 at the time his report appeared, had been working for the Toynbee Hall charitable organisation in East London where he saw the need to right social inequality. He realised that philanthropy was not enough and that a coherent government plan was the only way forward. As early as 1912 Beveridge had created the State Medical Service Association, but it was to be another thirty years before his ideas were accepted by government. By the outbreak of war Beveridge was working in Whitehall where he was commissioned to lead an inquiry into social services. His vision was to battle against what he called the five giants: idleness, ignorance, disease, squalor and want. His 'cradle to the grave' approach called for, among other things, a free national health service.

His vision was met with opposition from many quarters. Many of the doctors who opposed the setting up of the NHS feared they would lose income. Nor did they wish to become employees of the state. Local authorities and voluntary bodies objected because they did not want to lose control over their hospitals. The Conservatives, who voted against the National Health Service Act twenty-one times, thought that the cost of the NHS would be too great a burden to bear. Churchill just felt that it was the first step 'to turn Britain into a National Socialist economy'. Comparing it to Nazi Germany was a step too far for many. But then, during the 1945 election campaign, Britain's wartime leader had declared that Labour 'would have to fall back on some form of a Gestapo' in order to impose socialism on peacetime Britain. The public, however, soon warmed to the idea of a 'free' health service, and Atlee's support for it helped Labour to win the election.

The Act received royal assent in November 1946. The *Daily Herald* re-assured its readers:

> Don't expect an immediate change to something new and frightening. Above all, don't think that your friend the family doctor will be swept away in favour of some impersonal clinic. You will still have the same freedom to choose your doctor as you have now. Ten to one your present doctor will join the service, so you won't have to change at all.
>
> But there will no longer be the haunting fear of the expense of an illness or accident, and the knowledge that you cannot afford the best

treatment for your wife and family if they fall sick. The service will cover hospital and specialist treatment, midwifery, home nursing, domestic help when needed on health grounds, immunisation against infections, spectacles, false teeth, drugs, ambulances, laboratory aid in diagnosis, X-ray examinations, and all the thousand and one necessities of modern medicine.

It will also introduce a system of health centres, which is new to most parts of the country, but will enable your family doctor to treat you more efficiently because he will have other doctors at hand to consult, the apparatus that he needs, and more regular hours of work.

Who would pay for all this? The newspaper said:

The cost will be shared between the Exchequer, the local rates, and your own contributions to the National Insurance Fund. The weekly contribution to the Health Service will be 10d [4p] for men, 8d [3p] for women and 6d [2.5p] for children. And there will be no extras: when your contribution has been paid, you won't be asked for more a penny more.

The British Medical Association (BMA), which represented doctors, polled its 50,000 members. In December 1946 the *Daily Mirror* reported that only a small number were against negotiations continuing and that, among younger doctors and specialists, there was a substantial majority for negotiating. The newspaper said that 'the general pictures is that the old men are against it, and the young men are in favour of the Government scheme'.

In fact, of the 42,082 replies received, 18,972 were in favour of their negotiating committee entering into discussions with the Minister of Health; 23,110 voted 'no'. Dr Guy Dain, chairman of the BMA council, said that it was important to remember that the National Health Service Act was not a conscription act, and that a decision not to join was not disloyalty to the country. 'Whatever the ultimate outcome, the doctors will be loyal to their patients, to whom, as always, they owe their first duty.' That was all very well, but to the question, 'Can the Act be operated without your co-operation', Dr Dain replied, 'No.'

The Minister of Health, Aneurin Bevan, remained undaunted.

Within three hours of the result of the vote being announced, he declared, 'I can no longer postpone the consultations which are necessary preliminary to setting up the administrative machinery. I am therefore proceeding to consult with all the many other interests which will be concerned in the National Health Service.'

In January 1947 Bevan told the three Royal colleges of the medical profession that he could now negotiate with the doctors within the terms of the Act. There was, apparently, 'a lightening of tension between the Government and the profession'. Inevitably, the government had been forced to make compromises. Local doctors would not become state employees. Instead, GP surgeries could remain private business that could be bought and sold, and they would be contracted by the government to provide healthcare. Meanwhile, senior hospital doctors – consultants – would be allowed to continue providing treatment privately to those who could afford to pay. Similar compromises were agreed with dentists.

Thus, despite all the initial opposition, on Monday, 5 July 1948, the National Health Service came into being. Some 94 per cent of the public were now enrolled with the NHS, and the newly-created health boards controlled 2,751 of Britain's 3,000 hospitals that had previously been administered by local authorities or charities. In England and Wales alone, the NHS had taken over the running of 1,545 municipal hospitals with about 390,000 beds (190,000 of them in mental illness hospitals), and 1,143 voluntary hospitals with around 90,000 beds. In one fell swoop everyone now had access to the best medical care available. *The Times* felt that the masses had, overnight, joined the middle classes.

Two days earlier, the *British Medical Journal* had published a message from Bevan:

> On 5th July we start together, the new National Health Service. It has not had an altogether trouble-free gestation! There have been understandable anxieties, inevitable in so great and novel an undertaking. Nor will there be overnight any miraculous removal of our more serious shortages of nurses and others and of modern replanned buildings and equipment. But the sooner we start, the sooner we can try together to see to these things and to secure the improvements we all want. On July 5, there is no reason why the whole of the doctor-patient relationship should not be freed from

what most of us feel should be irrelevant to it, the money factor, the collection of fees or thinking how to pay fees, an aspect of practice already distasteful to many practitioners. Yet it has been vital, if this is to be the new situation, to see that it did not carry with it either any discouragement of professional and scientific freedom or any unfair worsening of a doctor's material livelihood. I sincerely hope and believe we have secured these things. If we have not, we can easily put that right … . My job is to give you all the facilities, resources and help I can, and then to leave you alone as professional men and women to use your skill and judgement without hindrance. Let us try to develop that partnership from now on.

An editorial in the same edition of the *British Medical Journal* warned that 'the doctor will need to exercise much patience and tact in the coming months if his patients demand – as some of them will – the impossible,' adding 'but with goodwill many of these difficulties will be overcome'.

On that first day, the chairman of the London County Council held a reception for the capital's old and new health services. Guests included the departing members of the hospital and social welfare committees and representatives of the new Metropolitan regional hospital boards. The Leader of the House of Commons, Herbert Morrison, made a speech, there was a display of new ambulances and dental units, there was music and dancing and around County Hall were posters illustrating 'The passing of Bumbledom'. 'Mr Bumble', of course, was the fussy, self-important beadle of the workhouse where Charles Dickens's Oliver Twist was raised.

Up in Manchester, meanwhile, Aneurin Bevan was visiting Park Hospital in Davyhulme. Today it is Trafford Hospital and is known as the first NHS hospital and thus 'the birthplace of the NHS'. Opened in 1929, by Barton upon Irwell Board of Guardians, during the Second World War, Park Hospital was occupied by the 10th US Station Hospital and Glenn Miller was said to have entertained troops in its grounds. The Americans left in July 1945, and Park Hospital was de-requisitioned two months later.

There Bevan met the NHS's first patient, 13-year-old Sylvia Beckingham, who was suffering from a life-threatening liver condition, which had affected her kidneys causing acute nephritis. She later recalled,

'Mr Bevan asked me if I understood the significance of the occasion, and he told me that it was a milestone in history, the most civilised step that any country had ever taken.' Sylvia Beckingham, who became a teacher, married and became Sylvia Diggory, always felt indebted to the NHS and enrolled her son in medical school. She died in 2006. In 2017 her grandson, George Diggory, married Kate Dorman, the great-granddaughter of Clement Attlee. When the couple met while working in a laboratory at Newcastle University, they had no idea of the connection.

History was being made everywhere. Two days after Bevan met the NHS's first patient, the *Gloucestershire Echo* reported that the first baby to be born at the Sunnyside Maternity Home in Cheltenham since the commencement of the NHS was a baby girl, with the appropriate surname of Bevan. No relation.

The *Coventry Evening Telegraph* called the NHS 'the greatest social experiment ever undertaken by any country', pointing out that how it would work remained to be seen because it was an experiment that began without the resources that might ensure success. 'We have provided ourselves with a measure appropriate to a wealthy nation, and social security is unattainable without the economic prosperity we still have to win.'

The NHS has always had its financial problems and, in 1951, Aneurin Bevan, now the Minister of Labour, resigned from the Cabinet when it voted to introduce fees for dental care (£1 flat fee), spectacles, and prescriptions charges of one shilling (5p). In his resignation letter to Attlee, Bevan said, 'It is the beginning of the destruction of those social services in which Labour has taken a special pride and which were giving Britain the moral leadership of the world.'

Chapter Nine

Lessons Learned

The same thing happened in the last war. Following upon it, a great Education Act was passed, but we had to wait for another major conflict before the attention and interest of the country was again aroused.

Rochdale Observer

In January 1946 the president of the National Union of Women Teachers described the current shortage of teachers as 'calamitous'. Miss O.M. Young told the union's annual conference in Folkestone of the 'enormous difficulties' standing in the way of the full implementation of the Education Act of 1944. To provide an adequate secondary education in accordance with 'age, ability, and aptitude,' as interpreted by the new Ministry of Education, three separate schools were necessary: grammar which would be modelled on elite public schools; the technical school; and the less intellectually rigorous secondary modern school. Children would be directed to the appropriate school at the age of 11 by means of selection tests, known as the '11-plus'. Miss Young said that 70,000 teachers were now needed. The raising of the school leaving age alone, from 14 to 15, meant that by April 1947 an additional 13,000 teachers would be required. She blamed 'the short-sighted policy of the last Government for this deplorable situation'.

The post-war Welfare State had arrived with a raft of legislation. The 1945 Family Allowance Act provided that parents were given five shillings (25p) per week for each child from the second-born. The 1946 National Insurance Act paid unemployment pay for six months, and sick pay for as long as the recipient was ill. There was now a maternity grant, and a death grant to help bereaved families pay for funerals. The 1946 National Insurance Act meant that, from 1948, a state pension, on a contributory basis, was available to everyone. Men were eligible from the age of 65; women from 60. The 1946 Industrial Injuries Act provided additional benefits for those injured at work. The 1948 Children's Act required local councils to provide good homes and care for every child 'deprived of a normal home life'. The 1946 New Towns Act, and the 1947 Town and Country Planning Act, were meant to take care of the post-war housing shortage. The 1946 National Health Service Act, which came into force in 1948, meant that hospitals, GPs, dentists, opticians, midwives and health visitors were available to everybody, free of all charges.

Education was also to undergo a huge change. In a broadcast in March 1944, Winston Churchill said, 'I do not think we can maintain our position in the post-war world unless we are an exceptionally well-educated people, and unless we can handle easily, and with comprehension, the problems and inventions of the new scientific age.'

Before the outbreak of war in 1939, British society had been divided strictly by class and education was a clear defining factor in that. The 1944 Education Act, set up under a coalition government but driven by a Conservative politician, Robert Austin Butler (better known as simply 'Rab'), sought to offer a decent free secondary education to children of all backgrounds up to the age of 15. Conceived during the dark days of the Blitz, the Bill to make that universally free secondary education a reality received its Royal Assent on 3 August 1944 as the Allies were busy liberating Europe from the Nazis.

Previously 90 per cent of British children attended elementary schools until they started work at 14. As Miss O.M. Young pointed out, the new system saw grammar schools intended for the more academically able pupils and technical schools and secondary modern schools for those more likely to benefit from learning practical skills. The Act renamed the Board of Education the Ministry of Education and gave it a bigger budget and greater powers. It made it the duty of the 146 local education authorities in England and Wales (previously there had been 315) to provide lunches and free school milk, and to waive the charge for meals in cases of hardship. The essential features of the 1944 Act that covered England and Wales were reproduced in Acts in Scotland (1945) and in Northern Ireland (1947).

Yet if school life in the early post-war years now provided the same opportunities for well-off and poor alike, other aspects did not change overnight. Anton Rippon recalls his own days at primary school during the post-war years:

Becket School in Gerard Street was one of Derby's earliest 'board schools', built in Victorian times. I doubt the building itself had changed since it was opened in 1879. Big draughty classrooms, perilously steep steps leading down to a concrete playground that looked like a barrack square, and outside toilets that froze in winter – they all added up to something out of a Dickens novel.

Lessons were basic but solid, the 'three Rs' taught in an old-fashioned way: arithmetic, including learning by rote the times tables until we possessed what amounted to a mental pocket calculator; reading and writing; history and geography. What more did we need? PT lessons were usually conducted outside, no matter what the weather, and the poorer kids had to make use of the plimsolls provided by the education authority; these were kept in the 'pump cage' and there were stories of all manner of diseases and terrible foot conditions caused by wearing communal footwear.

Discipline could be harsh. The headmaster, Bob Stanley, was one of the old brigade. He wasn't too bad – although he could still dish out the cane – but some of his teachers were to be feared. The worst of all was a chap called Widdowsen who, unfortunately, was my class teacher for two years. Widdowsen was bald and his whole head reminded me of a grinning skull. Only he didn't do all that much grinning. He had several party pieces, including strolling up to a desk and then bringing down a ruler on the knuckles of an unsuspecting child whose only offence might have been to let his gaze wander when they should have been trying to absorb the joys of long division. Worst of all, before our classes were streamed according to ability I saw many instances where pupils who really should have been in a remedial group were beaten for just not grasping what they were being told.

Widdowsen's eyes really lit up when he could administer properly considered corporal punishment. Unlike his pre-emptory strikes with the ruler, canings gave him a moment to relish. There were two sorts of cane at Becket School, a whippy effort made of thin bamboo, and a thick stick. Both hurt like hell but the thicker version, which Widdowsen favoured, left the longer-lasting pain, like trapping your hand in a door. You could get yanked out for anything – talking, daydreaming and even scratching your nose. Widdowsen's face would twist until it looked as though he was wearing some sort of maniacal mask, and then he would bring the cane down from a great height and with a follow-through that would have done justice to Len Hutton smiting Ray Lindwall through the covers. It was always on the hands, sometimes two strokes on each, and the trick was to drop your palm ever so slightly a split-second before impact. If Widdowsen spotted you doing this, then the punishment was doubled, but it was worth the risk because the manoeuvre could cushion some of the pain. It still hurt a lot, however, and anyone with any pride would fight back the tears and resume their seat while trying to look as if it hadn't really hurt at all. Otherwise, Widdowsen had won. On one occasion a particularly nervous pupil removed his hand altogether which resulted in Widdowsen cracking the cane against his own knee. You can imagine what happened next.

I enjoyed playing football, wherever we had to go to find a suitable pitch in the concrete jungle that was inner-city post-war Derby, but one activity with which I was less than enamoured was the Friday morning hymn practice that took up about two hours. A good solid Christian education was the basis for any British school in the 1940s and 1950s, and I have always been grateful for the fact that, at grammar school, we had a proper religious service each morning. But two hours of hymn practice? Eventually I worked my ticket on that one. The whole of Thursday afternoons was given over to painting, and two volunteers were needed to clean up the following morning. Up shot a forest of hands and me and a boy called Roy Reed were selected, perhaps on the premise that neither of us could sing. Thereafter, Roy and I spent Friday mornings happily washing brushes and palettes to the muffled accompaniment of *Onward Christian Soldiers*.

While the 1944 Education Act aimed to remove the inequalities which remained in the system, its flaw was that this was decided by a life-defining 11-plus examination, which children sat in their final year at primary school. Grammar schools had infinitely better resources and facilities – although teachers needed no teaching qualifications, only a degree in a specific subject – and only their pupils would stand a chance of going on to university. Yet there were plenty of children who wasted their chance of a grammar school education, while many of those who went to secondary modern school eventually did rather better. One such boy was Stanley Guy, a fair-haired lad from Derby, who 'failed' his 11-plus in 1950, but went on to work for MI5, in banking and became a best-selling author of crime fiction set in Japan where he spends most of his time. Our classmate, Julian Grant, also did not pass the 11-plus examination but still went on to greater things. He joined the Merchant Navy as a radio officer and later became chairman of the Hydrographic Society. They were just two of countless thousands who defied the logic that a child's future can be mapped out for them before their teens.

There was also immense financial pressure on children from less well-off families if they passed the 11-plus. Grammar schools required all pupils to wear uniforms and to be kitted out with kit for winter and summer sports, whether or not they had the slightest aptitude for football, rugby, cricket, or athletics. Anton Rippon again: 'After I passed the 11-plus, my mother wheeled me off to a local clothier to be kitted out in the maroon and white uniform of my new grammar school. It was years later before I realised what an outlay that had involved.'

Chapter Ten

A Betrayal of British Values?

The German SS prisoners at Wollaton Park are better fed than the ordinary working men and women in Nottingham.

Major S.F. Malcolm

On 26 March 1946 Labour MP Richard Rapier Stokes asked the Secretary of State for War, Jack Lawson, how many Italian and German prisoners of war were still in Britain. He also wanted to know how many were engaged in useful work, how many were receiving direct payment for their labour, and what were their rates of pay. Lawson replied that the answer was so long that a written reply would be circulated. Stokes responded:

> You cannot get out of it that way. Is it not a fact that while those prisoners are paid only a nominal rate for their labour, the Government charges the full rate for the job? If that is so, when do you propose to discontinue this practice which amounts to nothing more or less in slave labour?

Lawson said he had been asked about the number of prisoners of war and that 'it would take the rest of the day to answer, if I got the figures out'. Stokes said that he asked about the rates of pay. That, he said, required no figures at all, a remark that prompted laughter in the Commons chamber. Stokes was not amused, 'If it happened to be the case that they were paid next to nothing, why can the minister not tell the House? Is it because he is ashamed of them?'

The matter that Stokes raised was one that was engaging many people in Britain. Writing in *The Spectator* in May 1946, the politician and author Harold Nicolson argued that the repatriation of German PoWs should begin immediately.

> It is wrong that we should treat human beings in this manner while proclaiming aloud our belief in the sanctity of human values; but it

is more than wrong, it is blind and stupid. There are three things which should be done immediately. A statement should be made in Parliament as to the probable length of their captivity. Men in the White and Grey categories should be given preferential treatment similar to that accorded to the White Italians. [German PoWs were graded as follows: Grade A (White) were considered anti-Nazi; Grade B (Grey) had less clear feelings and were considered not as reliable as the Whites; Grade C (Black) had probable Nazi leanings; Grade C+ (also Black) were deemed ardent Nazis.] And all proved anti-Nazis, irrespective of their technical qualifications, should be repatriated at once ... . We do not today possess the physical power to impose our will upon the peoples of Europe; but we do possess enormous moral power which, if rightly used, will give us the willing co-operation of many millions.

People in ordinary walks of life were also concerned. A correspondent who signed themselves 'Pax' wrote to the *Staffordshire Sentinel*, 'Let me register a strong protest against the suggestions to employ German and Italian prisoners of war on English farms, in coalmines, and in the brick and tile industry. According to the Hague Convention these men should be repatriated.'

Not everyone was sympathetic. A writer in the *Gloucestershire Echo* commented:

At present there is some agitation for German prisoners of war to be sent home, and sympathy is not only being expressed for them, but for the German nation as a whole. Unfortunately, this agitation generally comes from persons who did not serve during the Great War or World War and did not suffer from either.

For the time being, however, PoWs were proving a useful source of labour. The Rehabilitation Committee of Chelmsford Rural District Council heard that, while building had not yet started on an estate near the Springfield by-pass, German prisoners working there had nearly completed the roadways. It was also reported that German prisoners-of-war might be used on refuse disposal work. Public health chiefs in London and in out-of-London boroughs were having to employ men who were not dustmen, and, in several areas, efforts to get locals to do the work had failed. Watford Rural Council had asked the Ministry of Health to find them four German prisoners to help empty the bins. Meanwhile, as a result of the employment of German prisoners, civilian workers at the REME workshops at Buntingford in Hertfordshire had been given notice. The Secretary of State for War said that he was enquiring into the matter.

The *People*, though, had no qualms:

> As for employing foreigners, it is already clear that some thousands of extra miners, whether they be Poles, German prisoners or others, would be worth more than their keep to us, and if we could not get enough coal to keep our factories running, we should be glad enough to employ them.

Foreign labour was indeed essential and would have to continue. By December 1946, a full nineteen months after the war in Europe had ended, despite a repatriation scheme that had started at the end of that summer, there were still more than 355,000 German prisoners of war housed in more than 600 camps all over the UK. Thanks to the arrival of 130,000 'British-owned' prisoners released by US forces, in September the number had peaked at 402,200. The prisoners that the Americans had passed on thought that they would be returned to Germany but instead found themselves docking in Liverpool. Hitherto unaware that they were technically prisoners of the British, they, too, would remain in captivity, not knowing their expected date of release. Tom Driberg, the Labour MP for Maldon, said:

> It may be that the American officers who got them on to the boats on that pretext had no authority to give that undertaking. It may be that they only said that in order to get them to go quietly, but nonetheless it was an undertaking that was given, and while that is in their minds, we cannot possibly preach to them that democracy is a particularly fair or desirable system of government.

It was, said Richard Stokes, 'an affront to their human rights' and therefore a betrayal of British values.

The problem was that, while under an international convention of 1929, prisoners of war had to be repatriated after a peace treaty was signed, Germany had surrendered unconditionally. There was no peace treaty.

Germany was an occupied country suffering atrocious living conditions. Arranging transport for tens of thousands of men would also pose a huge logistical problem. And there was the vexed issue of repatriating ardent Nazis who were known to be among the ranks of PoWs. Prisoners had been categorised as either anti-Nazis who had always been opposed to the ideology (they had to provide proof of this, which was not easy), those who were disinterested by politics and were fighting Hitler's war not from choice but rather from expediency, and those who were either ardent Nazis or young Germans who, from the age of seven, had not known anything other than the Nazi way of life. The conversations of thousands of prisoners, including those of high-ranking generals, Luftwaffe pilots and naval personnel, had been overheard using bugging devices at two camps in Buckinghamshire – Latimer House near Amersham and Wilton Park near Beaconsfield – and at another at Trent Park near Cockfosters in north London. Eavesdropping were German refugees who had fled the Nazis and who now tuned in at the 'M [microphoned] Room'.

So, when the war ended, what to do with tens of thousands of enemy aliens? Many were set to work repairing roads, making bricks and, when one of the harshest winters in living memory arrived, shifting snow and helping to re-open essential road and rail links. By September 1946 up to 20 per cent of all farm work in Britain was being undertaken by 158,00 PoWs, many now billeted on the farms where they were employed under minimal supervision. Previously, they had worked in groups of thirty, escorted by armed guards. Another 50,000 were engaged on labour work for the War Office; 36,000 comprised camp staff under the War Office; 35,000 were clearing housing sites for the Ministry of Works; and 19,500 were employed in various ways by the Air Ministry. And then there were preparations for the 1948 Olympic Games. It had been planned for prisoners of war to collect rubbish during the Games – they had been used for just that purpose after the VE Day and VJ Day celebrations – but Philip Noel-Baker, the Labour MP for Derby who, as well as his regular role as Secretary of State for Commonwealth Relations was now the country's 'Olympics Minister', felt that using former enemies for such demeaning tasks would reflect badly on Britain. Instead, Noel-Baker, who won a silver medal in the 1,500 metres at the 1920 Olympics in Antwerp, decided that they would be used on construction. Forty-four Germans were employed to help construct Wembley Way, although, despite their help, Germany would not be invited to compete in the first post-war Olympics.

It had taken only a few days after war was declared in 1939 for the first prisoners to arrive in Britain. On 14 September, 30-year-old *Kapitänleutnant* Gerhard Glattes, commander of *U-39*, had attempted to torpedo the aircraft carrier HMS *Ark Royal* off the Rockall Bank, north-west of Scotland, but instead his submarine was damaged by depth charges, and he had to surface. Glattes and his crew of forty-three were rescued, and Glattes began seven and a half years as a prisoner of war, being released on 8 April 1947. The German authorities would have been aware of his fate, and that of all other prisoners. At the Foreign Office on 4 October 1939, a meeting called to discuss setting up a Prisoner of War Information Bureau was told that information about German prisoners was available for communication to the German government via the International Red Cross or through the intermediary of the Special Division of the Swiss legation in London.

Initially, two prisoner-of-war camps had been established, at Grizedale Hall near the village of Satterthwaite in the Lake District, where a forty-room mansion was reserved for officers and became known as 'U-boat Hotel', and in a former cotton mill in Oldham, where 2,000 prisoners with ranks of sergeant and below were held. Eventually, the numbers of prisoners swelled after victory in North Africa, and then again following the D Day landings. The Allies' success in the Western Desert had also seen a large number of Italians imprisoned in Britain. Following Italy's surrender in September 1943, 100,000 Italians volunteered to work as 'co-operators', and, in return, were given considerable freedom and mixed with local people. Only diehard supporters of Mussolini were gathered together and isolated in 'non-co-operator' camps. The number of co-operators was substantial. In March 1945, 154,082 Italians were being employed in various sectors of the British economy. In fact, even though the war in Europe was still going on, some 66,500 German prisoners were also working in Britain, usually on farms. But while most Italians were quickly accepted by the British public, there were instances where German PoWs most certainly were not, sometimes with good reason. In June 1946 A.E. Chubb of East Knoyle in Wiltshire wrote to the *Western Gazette*:

Walking along the road a few days ago in company with a warrant officer just returned from Burma, it was surprising that groups of lorry-borne German prisoners of war should make various insulting signs to my comrade and myself, and, as an ex-soldier, I felt very hurt. Cannot the camp officials do something about this as this brave man of my county regiment faced the Japs for three years as well as the privations of the jungle?

The same month, during the debate that raged over the introduction of bread rationing, Major S.F. Malcolm, the Conservative candidate for South Nottingham, told a meeting at Sneiton Hermitage that 'the German SS prisoners at Wollaton Park are better fed than the ordinary working men and women in Nottingham'. In contrast, on the annual Children's Festival Day procession at Grangemouth, a group of German prisoners of war joined with RAF personnel from a nearby aerodrome to watch from the top of two RAF lorries parked outside the town hall.

But the matter engaging people like Harold Nicolson and Richard Stokes, not to mention the *Staffordshire Sentinel*'s correspondent 'Pax', had still not been resolved. On 21 August 1946, 'gravely concerned about the position of German prisoners of war in Britain', 875 representative men and women in all walks of life, including three archbishops, 118 MPs, and university heads, sent to the Prime Minister a petition sponsored by the Save Europe Now organisation calling for prisoners to be released at the earliest possible date. The petition declared that 'there comes a point at which men cannot live without hope'. It asked the government to draw up a definite scheme for the release of the men, if necessary, by various categories.

On 29 August a London-based news agency reported that Clement Attlee had called for a review, by all departments concerned, on the whole question of German prisoners of war in the UK. The subsequent report embodying their views would be considered by the Cabinet before the next meeting of the House of Commons, and a policy statement made 'at the earliest possible moment'. There were many problems which had to be considered:

> First, a careful review of the prisoners themselves was necessary because there were a number whose repatriations to Germany would be politically dangerous.

Second, there was the economic position of the Germany itself. Until the Government received decisions on the orientation of the British and American zones, and on the level at which German industry was to be allowed to develop, very large repatriations at that time would have meant that considerable numbers of Germans would return home to find there was no employment and they would then become a liability on the British administration.

Third, Britain's own economic position had to be taken into account. The Government felt that due regard had to be paid to the fact that Britain was faced with a definite shortage in manpower for reconstruction and harvesting. The shortage was due, in part, to the necessity of maintaining substantial numbers of troops abroad, many of them in Germany. According to the news agency report 'that raises the problem of whether we ought not to consider whether, both economically and on grounds of justice, we ought not supplement, to some extent, British labour which is having to be used overseas, and replace it in Britain by using prisoners-of-war, for the time being, on essential work which we should otherwise be unable to carry out'.

Pressure from the public had the desired effect, though. On 13 September 1946 the Government announced that it had decided to repatriate German prisoners of war at the rate of 15,000 a month. The scheme covered all prisoners with the exception of senior officers and ardent Nazis. The first contingent, men definitely democratically minded and non-Nazi, would get to Germany about the beginning of October and would number about 8,000. The rate of departures would be speeded up, otherwise it would take more than two years to repatriate everyone. About 3,000 prisoners had already been repatriated to Germany each month, mainly on compassionate grounds.

A statement from 10 Downing Street said that priority would be given to prisoners who had shown a positive attitude and who therefore would be likely to play a positive role in the rehabilitation of Germany. In the meantime, 'the Government intend to announce very shortly certain improvements in conditions for prisoners-of-war engaged on work of national importance and awaiting repatriation'. A full explanation of the scheme would be made to all prisoners of war.

By December 1946, the rules against fraternisation were relaxed but there were still many who harboured deep resentment against men whose country had, not so long before, rained bombs upon them. Love ignores borders, of course, but for British women who fell for German prisoners, there was a painful price to pay. In 2007 June Fellbrich told the *Daily Mail* how, at the age of 18, she fell in love with a 25-year-old PoW called Heinz. They were celebrating their 60th wedding anniversary when she told the newspaper that, when she was June Tull, she became pregnant by Heinz. 'Aren't our boys good enough for you?' yelled one woman. Another punched her. Others spat in her face. How could she, they asked, fraternise with the enemy when their own fathers, husbands and sons had been killed by the Germans? The fact that, wherever they went, PoWs had to wear brown uniforms with orange felt patches, served only to further inflame the situation. Many girls were shunned by their families, although June said, 'My father, Frank, was all right about it, but my mother was against the relationship. She worried about what people would think.' Heinz said, 'Since falling in love with June, I have never once felt homesick for Germany. This is my home. I like the people, the country and being here. We have been very lucky.'

In September 1946 'Another Disgusted Girl' wrote to the *Lancashire Evening Post*:

> Sir, 'British and Proud of It' (*Post*, September 18) says, 'Remember Belsen and the rest of the horror camps.' I've been wondering why the boys in Germany don't remember when they are fraternising with the frauleins. They can even marry them now and bring them home to England. So, if our men can do all that, our girls should be allowed to go about openly with German prisoners of war.

The last German PoWs were repatriated in 1949, but after being released from prisoner-of-war status, some 25,000 chose to remain in Britain, either because, like Heinz Fellbrich, they had met a British girl or because their hometowns were now in Soviet-occupied territory, which meant the likelihood of further imprisonment, this time in Russian hands.

Efforts to 're-educate' former soldiers of the Third Reich, to show them the evils of Nazi ideology, and that democracy was the only way to live, seem to have been successful. In 1957 the German federal government set up the *Kommission fur deutsche Kriegsgefangenengeschichte* (the *Scientific Commission for the History of German Prisoners of War*, chaired by Erich

Maschke and often known simply as the Maschke Commission). It concluded:

> Although, as a whole, many critics saw the re-education efforts made by the victorious powers as problematic and questionable, it is a fact that none of the powers made such a decisive effort as Great Britain — particularly in respect of the PoWs — to assist Germany's return to a free and democratic European group of nations ... in this respect the prisoners held in Great Britain ... were way ahead of their compatriots in Germany.

One of the German prisoners who spurned the chance of repatriation was Bernhard Carl Trautmann, who decided to make a new start in a new land. After jobs on a farm and with a bomb-disposal unit – a controversial use of prisoners and work forbidden by the Geneva Convention which Britain maintained was not valid in the immediate post-war period – he showed sufficient prowess as a goalkeeper to be signed by Manchester City. As Bert Trautmann he would become a household name in his adopted country. Years later, he recalled:

> I was brought up under Hitler, and I volunteered, like many others, at 17. When I became a PoW, I was a boy of 22. Not yet a man. I think my education began in Britain, because people understood the predicament that we were in. I think the English showed something of forgiveness. You know, 'The war is over, you are PoWs, and we understand how you feel.'

Chapter Eleven

Good, Thrifty, Hard-working People

A little Europe in the heart of Yorkshire, a people compelled to drive down new roots into strange soil, to acquire another language, to found new homes.

Yorkshire Post

In 1946 Britain was now home to tens of thousands of Polish troops who had chosen to remain in the UK after the end of hostilities in Europe. They would eventually be joined by their families from wherever the fortunes of war had landed them – many in displaced persons' camps run by the British in West Africa and India – and by people from other parts of Eastern Europe, who would arrive in Britain under the European Voluntary Workers (EVW) scheme set up in 1946 to help people who had become homeless and destitute during the war, and also aimed at helping to solve Britain's post-war labour shortage.

Following their defeat by the unholy alliance of Hitler's Germany and Stalin's USSR in September 1939, Polish forces had been ordered to make their way as best they could to France, where a Polish Government in Exile under the premiership of military and political leader Władysław Sikorski had been set up. Sikorski would be killed in an air crash in 1943. The Polish army that reformed in France was part of the 338,000 Allied soldiers who were evacuated from Dunkirk in 1940, and, after the USA and Britain, the Poles became the third largest Allied fighting force in the West. They included those who had escaped from Siberia in 1942. Their airman fought in the Battle of Britain, and their battle honours included Narvik, Tobruk, Monte Cassino, Normandy and Arnhem.

After the war ended, and following the deal between the Allies – Churchill warned Roosevelt not to trust Stalin but the American president ignored the advice – to incorporate Eastern Poland into the USSR and the rest of the country to become a puppet state with a Communist government, most Poles who had fought so valiantly against fascism elected to remain in the West where they could maintain their language and culture, and continue their fight for an independent homeland to which they might one day return.

The war over, and Britain struggling to help her own people rendered homeless by German bombing, the only way to take in such numbers of Poles was to accommodate them in camps vacated by departed American and Canadian troops. The War Office assured everyone that the Poles were to be looked after in old wartime camps 'which, generally speaking, have been disposed of through normal channels'. They would not be housed in properties requisitioned for locals.

By October 1946 around 120,000 Polish troops were quartered in 265 camps throughout the UK. These camps consisted mostly of Nissen huts, lit by electricity, and heated by slow combustion wood-burning stoves. In due course, wives and other dependents arrived, bringing the estimated total to a figure of 250,000 and, in 1947, the Committee for the Education of Poles, funded by taxpayers, was set up. Its aim was to prepare the Poles for 'absorption into British schools and British careers whilst still maintaining provision for their natural desire for the maintenance of Polish culture and the knowledge of Polish history and literature'. During the seven and a half years that it operated, the committee spent £9 million on its various programmes.

In 1946 a Polish Resettlement Corps (PRC) was raised as part of the British Army. It was designed to hold members of the Polish armed forces who had served with the Allies and who did not wish to return to now Communist Poland. The aim was to ease the troops back into civilian life – British civilian life, of course. Despite the bravery of the Poles during the war, it was not a universally popular decision and leading trades unions initially tried their best to turn public opinion against the newcomers. It was eventually agreed with the trade unions that prospective Polish employees could be recruited only from the PRC, and placed only in jobs approved by the Ministry of Labour, but that did not appease every critic.

In June 1946, two speakers at the British Legion's silver jubilee conference in London were warmly applauded when they 'denounced Mr Bevan for giving employment preference to the Polish Resettlement Corps when British ex-servicemen could not have preference'. The *Birmingham Daily Gazette* reported that one of the speakers, Mr F.C.W. Glitz, claimed that half of the Poles – who now enjoyed preference over

British ex-servicemen who themselves had to line up at the employment exchange – had in fact fought in the German forces.

Using the rather unimaginative nom-de-plume 'A Reader', a letter writer from Torquay pointed out to the *Daily Herald* that the Minister of War, Jack Lawson, in a written reply, had estimated 'that the estimated cost of the Polish Resettlement Corps during the present financial year was £33 million'. Lawson had further stated that there were 83,000 Polish armed forces in Britain in August 1946, and, according to 'A. Reader', 'it would appear therefore, that each Polish soldier is costing the British taxpayer just over £7 a week'.

On 30 September 1949 the PRC was wound up as a military force, and 150,000 former soldiers, sailors and airmen, together with their dependents, now formed a significant Polish community in several British towns and cities. In October that year, Emanuel Shinwell, Secretary of State for War – a demotion that meant he was no longer a member of the Cabinet – told the House of Commons that former members of the corps were now living either in private accommodation or in hostels. Those in hostels who were unemployed and had no resources were provided with free board and lodgings, and pocket money. Those in private accommodation might also, if in need, apply to the National Assistance Board for benefit payments. Some 2,000 men whose engagement had expired when the corps was disbanded were receiving ex-gratia payments from the board, based on what they would be receiving if the corps had not been wound up. That would continue until their original term of engagement had expired unless, in the meantime, they found employment or been repatriated.

Herschel Austin, the Labour MP for Stretford and one of the new intake in the 1945 General Election, asked, 'Will the Minister bring to bear the scrutiny of the Treasury on this with a view to economies?' Manny Shinwell replied, 'We cannot allow any prejudice against these people to influence us in showing them what sympathy we can. We accepted the obligation, and we must see that it is properly carried through.'

The 1947 Polish Resettlement Act – the first mass immigration legislation ever passed by a UK government – provided for any Polish immigrant to be entitled to apply for employment, and to receive unemployment pay. There was, of course, also an element of self-interest for the British government. The country needed workers, and many of the Poles and others from Eastern Europe, all white and Christian, were skilled in work where labour was most needed – in building, coal mining, engineering and textile manufacture, as well as in nursing, hotels and catering. The Government established resettlement schemes in areas where such workers were most needed.

In March 1948 the Home Secretary, James Chuter Ede, announced that Poles would be granted the right to become British citizens, and applications would be accepted from Polish ex-servicemen. In September 1951 the *Yorkshire Post* reported that there were 'many good citizens among Yorkshire European Volunteer Workers'. The newspaper said that the 'Lithuanians, Latvians, Poles, Czechs, Estonians and Ukrainians ... are a little Europe in the heart of Yorkshire, a people compelled to drive down new roots into strange soil, to acquire another language, to found new homes'.

Their impact on Yorkshire, said the paper, was bound to be felt and may be disturbing:

> Now and again, some crime of violence by a foreigner brings angry protests to the *Yorkshire Post* against allowing aliens to come in so freely. But, generally speaking, reports from all parts of the area show that complaints about their behaviour are diminishing and they are gaining increasing acceptance as good, thrifty, and hard-working people.

In January 1949 the Dublin-based *Catholic Standard* newspaper reported that the British Joint Committee for Polish Affairs had revealed that 72.4 per cent of the Poles living in Britain were earning wages, compared to 40 per cent of the British population. Of course, this was explained by the fact that the Polish community comprised mostly of men, especially former soldiers, and it had relatively few women and children. 'Still, said, the newspaper, 'these figures are the best answer to the accusations that the Polish community is a heavy burden on Britain.'

The Polish weekly *Orzel Bialy* (White Eagle), said that a study showed that, in December 1948, there were 164,000 Poles in Britain, of whom 24,000 arrived as European Voluntary Workers. Out of the 96,000 former Polish soldiers gainfully employed, 91 per cent were manual workers, 20 per cent of whom had formerly been 'intellectual' workers.

About 1,800 young Poles were studying for university and schools were receiving help from the Committee for the Education of Poles.

Given the Russian takeover of Poland, there were bound to be some concerns regarding Britain's national security. In August 1949, at the annual general meeting of the Scottish-Polish Society in Edinburgh, 'Communist agents planted in this country under the shelter of diplomatic immunity' were attacked by the society's chairman John J. Campbell. He denounced what he called 'the persistent campaign of the Moscow-controlled Polish Government of its policy of interference with Poles resident in this country.' 'There was,' he said, a 'Communist-inspired agitation in British trades unions to deny Polish ex-servicemen the right to work.' The Polish consul in Glasgow, Stanislaw Teliga, had also paid a visit to a Polish boys' school in the city and threatened to deport the boys to Poland 'where the Government would deal with them'.

In July that year, answering a question from Richard Rapier Stokes, the Labour MP for Ipswich, in the House of Commons on 'the espionage organised by Major Julian Kajdy', an assistant military attaché at the Polish Embassy in London, and 'activities by Polish Communists in order to create bad feeling between Polish and British workers', Minister of State at the Foreign Office, Hector McNeill, said that Major Kajdy had left London a month earlier and would not return. McNeill said that Foreign Secretary Ernest Bevin 'has no doubt that we may count upon the good sense and loyalty of the Polish community in this country, and he has been happy to note the excellent relations which now exist between Polish and British workers here.'

In January 1948 Poles employed in agriculture, brickyard and other industries in Bedfordshire had been enrolled in the Transport and General Workers' Union. Mr J.W. Grove, a district organiser for the union, told the *Bedfordshire Times and Independent*, 'We are trying to help them all we can, and we shall see that they get exactly the same conditions as British workers – no better and no worse.' He said that it was important to realise that the Poles did not get better food than other workers, although the impression was about that they did. 'We feel that only by enrolling these men can we control them. We want them to toe the line and do a good day's work, the same as our other members.' On the same day, the Bedfordshire committee of the Agricultural Workers' Union renewed

Clement Attlee, Britain's first post-war Prime Minister. (*Eon Images: www.eonimages.com*)

Four weeks after bread rationing was introduced in the summer of 1946, these London housewives find that the system where surplus points for other items could be exchanged for bread has been suspended. (*Alamy*)

Left to right: Winifred Shotter, McDonald Hobley and Jasmine Bligh during a rehearsal at Alexandra Palace for the return of the BBC's television service in 1946. (*Alamy*)

British GI war brides and their children during lifeboat drill on the *Queen Mary* bound for a new life in the United States. (*Alamy*)

Crowds at the Old Bailey hoping to see prominent witnesses at the murder trial of Neville George Clevely Heath. (*Alamy*)

King George VI meets Derby County's players before the start of the first post-war FA Cup Final in 1946. Derby beat Charlton Athletic 4-1 after extra-time. (*Authors' Collection*)

Two-year-old Pat Buckler pictured on the beach at Scarborough in 1946, as Britain's seaside resorts reopened for business. (*Authors' Collection*)

Health Minister Aneurin Bevan meets 13-year-old Sylvia Beckingham, the NHS's first patient, at Park Hospital in Davyhulme in July 1948. (*Alamy*)

Five thousand pigeons are released at the opening ceremony of the 1948 Olympic Games. (*Alamy*)

Front cover of the Festival of Britain official guide. (*Authors' Collection*)

Men of the 1st Battalion Royal Northumberland Fusiliers aboard the troopship RMS *Empire Halladale* at Southampton, about to sail for Korea where, in April 1951, they were involved in the Battle of the Imjin River during the Chinese Spring Offensive. (*Alamy*)

Queen Elizabeth, Queen Mary and Prince Henry, Duke of Gloucester, visit the Festival of Britain on the South Bank. (*Alamy*)

Post-war style: a modern kitchen, part of the Britain Can Make It exhibition. (*Alamy*)

A familiar wartime image, Winston Churchill was returned to power in the 1951 General Election. (*Illustrated London News*)

A 'non-austerity' fashion show in progress at London's Dorchester Hotel. (*Alamy*)

Crowds watch the coffin of King George VI as it passes Marble Arch and turns into Edgware Road on its way to Paddington Station in February 1952. (*Alamy*)

The Coronation Coach carrying Queen Elizabeth II passes through Trafalgar Square in June 1953. (*Alamy*)

their protest against the employment of Poles and displaced persons in their industry.

There were troubles, of course, and throughout the post-war period there were plenty of Polish names appearing on court schedules, some for relatively minor infringements. In January 1948 Anselm Gruzinski, a Pole who was working in the building trade and now living at Woolwich, appeared before Horsham Petty Sessions where he admitted having failed, until six weeks later, to report his change of address. For the police, Superintendent Wright said, 'I do not press this case, but the authorities are getting rather alarmed about the number of Poles who fail to carry out the directions which are posted in their own language on all notice boards in their own camps. They just do not bother.' The summons was dismissed on payment of 14s (70p) costs, and the court heard that since the first summons for this offence, sixty Poles had called at the police station to report changes of address.

There were more serious charges. In November 1950 the *Birmingham Daily Gazette* reported that bail for a Pole and a Ukrainian had been refused by Coventry magistrates after a detective inspector had warned that their release would lead to 'serious racial trouble' among the city's 3,000 foreigners. Their faces bearing signs of injury and their clothes bloodstained, the men stood in the dock charged with the malicious wounding of two Lithuanians and a Latvian. All the men, victims and accused, lived at the Brooklands hostel in Coventry. The magistrates adjourned the case for a week and refused bail.

Language might have been a barrier for some Poles but there was laughter at Cirencester magistrates' court in October 1950 when Bronislaw Koziol, then resident at a hostel in the Cotswolds village of Daglingworth, faced charges concerned with the insurance of a motor vehicle and the use of a provisional driving licence. Asked if he understood English, the defendant gave a confident 'No'. Asked if he knew whether an interpreter was available, he gave another prompt and confident 'No'. Then asked how, if he could not understand English, he could understand the question, this time there was a smile but no reply. He was told that his case would be adjourned for a week while an interpreter was available. 'Do you understand?' asked the chairman of the court. 'Yes,' replied Mr Koziol. There were roars of laughter, and, according to the *Gloucestershire Echo*, the defendant left the court with 'a smile on his face'.

In Halifax, one of the leaders of the Polish community described the housing problem for his people there as a serious one. While single people were well housed in hostels run by their employers, married people had to find their own accommodation. In the Pontefract, Featherstone and Ackworth districts, where there were about 300 EVWs, most of them Poles and most of them miners, the local feeling was that they had settled into normal community life, and that their interests had broadened.

The *Yorkshire Post* said:

> A darker picture is painted of the conduct of the EVWs in Bradford, where hardly a week passes without the names of some of them appearing on court charge sheets. Most of these people in Bradford live in large houses converted into flats, and it is more than a possibility that these conditions encourage brawling.

But then the paper said, 'The large majority of Bradford's EVWs, however, satisfy the requirements of their employers, and those with families are anxious to give their children a good start in life'.

In June 1949 the *Glamorgan Advertiser* said that there were around fifty Polish men employed at collieries in Maesteg and district. Most of them could give first-hand accounts of life in German concentration camps. Recently, the Polish community in the Maesteg area had been visited by Revd Father Lucien Luszcki, who had been a slave labourer in the gold mines of Northern Siberia for three years. After liberation, he had served as a chaplain with the Polish forces and he was surprised to find that some of the men he met in in the Lower Rhondda Valley had been in his unit at Monte Cassino during the Italian Campaign. During a special service that he held, 'members of the Polish congregation sang delightfully plaintive hymns in their own language'.

Slowly, the new Polish communities settled in. They set up clubs, churches and Saturday schools and, in July 1952, the *Melton Mowbray Times* commented, 'Their assets and pastimes may differ, but that very difference is an asset to the joint community of the town.'

Chapter Twelve

No Dogs, No Blacks, No Irish

Even landladies at boarding houses will not have us as residents. Why, I do not know.

Horace Halliburton

On the cloudy Tuesday morning of 22 June 1948, 802 migrants from the Caribbean, many of them veterans who had fought for the Allies during the Second World War, disembarked from the HMT *Empire Windrush* that had docked at Tilbury the previous day. Their arrival heralded the beginning of largescale immigration from the West Indies. They were the first of what would become known as 'the Windrush Generation', and they arrived in a Britain where there was a shortage of workers – estimated at 1.346 million at the end of 1946 – to help rebuild a country still bearing the deep scars of the war, a country where there was a huge backlog of repair work and essential maintenance, and where workers were also needed in factories, transport and in the new National Health Service.

That labour shortage had been worsened by the introduction of peacetime military National Service. Britain still had commitments abroad – in Germany, India, Palestine, and later in Korea, Malaya, Cyprus and Kenya – and from January 1949 until 1960, a total of 2.3 million young men were taken out of the workforce initially for eighteen months each, and then for two years. It was the prospect of filling the gap in the labour market that brought most of those who sailed on the *Empire Windrush*. After their initial reception, however, the newcomers, and those who followed them, found no warm welcome in Britain, only prejudice.

The ship on which they undertook their voyage of hope to a land that many regarded as the 'mother country', but which most had never seen, was originally named the MV *Monte Rosa*, a German cruise ship that had been turned into a troopship by the Nazis. Claimed by the British as a prize of war, she had been renamed and used as a troopship until March 1954, when she caught fire in the Mediterranean and sank. Her immortality was by then assured.

In 1948 the *Empire Windrush* sailed from Australia en route to London and called at Mexico where sixty-six Poles were picked up – they had travelled there from Siberia via India and the Pacific and were aiming to settle in the United Kingdom under the terms of the 1947 Polish Resettlement Act – and then at Kingston in Jamaica to pick up British servicemen coming home on leave.

The ship had plenty of capacity and, in April 1948, an advertisement was placed in the Jamaican newspaper *The Daily Gleaner*, offering cabin-class accommodation to London for £48, and troop-deck travel for £28. The 1948 British Nationality Act conferred the status of British citizen on all Commonwealth subjects and recognised their right to work and settle in the UK and to bring their families with them. The Act was still going through Parliament but hundreds of Jamaicans decided to take a chance, either because they hoped to rejoin the RAF or the army, or, mostly, because they looked for better civilian employment.

Also aboard the *Empire Windrush* were three 'once fed-up with England' housewives who saw the Thames again and together said, 'Thank God. We won't leave England ever again.' The *Daily Mirror* reported:

> With their ex-RAF, West Indian husbands they had gone to Jamaica full of hope ... disillusioned, they arrived back at Tilbury yesterday ... Ex-Waaf Doreen Zayne, from Blackpool, with husband Herbert and two children, told how, in sixteen months in Jamaica, Herbert, a painter, got two months' work – at £3 12 a week ... and you had to pay 4s 6d for 1lb of bacon.

'All I want to see now is Blackpool,' said Doreen.

Initially, the Jamaicans were promised a warm welcome. The *Daily Herald* reported that 'they will find that no effort has been spared to look after their welfare'. An official welcome party would greet the ship when it anchored in midstream, and Customs and Immigration officials would carry our checks on board 'so that the men will walk straight ashore'.

Workers at the Colonial Servicemen's Club in London's Wimpole Street would welcome the eighty immigrants who had volunteered for the armed services, and the remainder would be housed in the Clapham South deep air-raid shelter where they would be looked after until they found work and accommodation. The Ministry of Labour promised that 'everything will be done to fix them with jobs best suited to them'. Their first meal at the Clapham shelter was 'roast beef, potatoes, vegetables, Yorkshire pudding, suet pudding with currents and custard, and tea'. According to the *Daily Herald*, 'one of the greatest disappointments of the men was when Colonial Office officials killed the rumour that each would be given £4 on arrival'. According to the *Birmingham Gazette*, ten stowaways served brief prison sentences before being allowed to remain, while the *Daily Herald* reported that in Kingston, a further 2,000 Jamaicans were awaiting ships to bring them to Britain. The arrival of those on the *Empire Windrush* had not been anticipated by the British Government, however, and George Isaacs, the Minister of Labour, assured Parliament that there would be no encouragement for others to follow in the wake of the *Empire Windrush*. Three days before the ship docked, however, Arthur Creech Jones, Colonial Secretary, wrote a Cabinet memorandum noting that the Jamaican government could not legally prevent people from departing, and the British government could not legally prevent them from landing. However, he said that the British government was opposed to this immigration, and all possible steps would be taken by the Colonial Office and the Jamaican government to discourage it. In fact, from 1948 until 1952, between 1,000 and 2,000 people from the Caribbean entered Britain each year, followed by a steady and rapid rise that would eventually see over half a million Commonwealth citizens settle in Britain between 1948 and the 1971 Immigration Act.

Few of them would escape the prejudices that faced incomers for years to come. In 2018, 80-year-old Winston Howells told the *BirminghamLive* website how, in 1957, as an adventurous 19-year-old, he left Jamaica and sailed for England with high hopes for a bright future.

> The Second World War had not long ended and there was a big labour shortage in England. Obviously, the climate was a huge shock to the system to start with. But then there were the houses, which were cramped and with an outside toilet. We had an inside toilet in Jamaica and the houses had lovely verandas.
>
> I got a job in a factory. There was racism in the workplace, but I certainly didn't expect the level of racism I encountered. Seeing the

signs on pubs and guest houses saying, 'No dogs, blacks or Irish' was a shock to me. I would often be racially abused and told to 'go home'.

Although the dominant narrative of racial tension in Britain begins with the beginning of largescale immigration from 1948, and the anti-black riots of the 1950s in places like Notting Hill and Nottingham, trouble had flared long before the *Empire Windrush* set sail.

In December 1946 the West Bromwich hostel of the National Service Hostels Corporation which had been set up in 1941 as an independent non-profit making organisation to cater for the needs of workers arising out of their employment during the Second World War, reported that it was continuing 'to have a certain amount of trouble ... owing to our having 70 West Indians in this hostel'. The trouble had arisen 'largely owing to the fact the West Indians dance a good deal with the female members of staff and this leads to strong feelings on the part, principally, of the Irish residents'.

The situation continued at overcrowded hostels throughout the country. In August 1949 there was serious violence among the 700 men at the Causeway Green hostel near Oldbury in the West Midlands, where Jamaican immigrants were housed alongside European Volunteer Workers from Poland, as well as men from the British Isles. Again, the trouble appears to have started when some of the West Indians began dancing with white women. First the West Indians and the Poles began fighting 'with bottles in the main reception hall' and it carried on all week. One police officer required stitches after being hit on the head by a stone. The *Birmingham Gazette* reported that 'Poles armed with sticks, stones, razors and bottles surrounded the Jamaican quarters'.

The newspaper continued:

> The police managed to restore order .... Some Jamaicans, however, decided to leave. They packed their bags and demanded police escort. As they walked through main gates of the camp, they were followed by catcalls and jeering from other residents. Girl residents, who number 120, ran from their rooms when fighting began and sought refuge outside the camp. Local residents, behind barred doors, watched Jamaicans pursued by Poles armed with sticks and bottles hiding in a nearby cornfield.

A resident of Brook Road, at the rear of the hostel, told the newspaper, 'This sort of thing happens frequently, and we are thoroughly fed up with it.'

It was decided that the best course of action would be to evict the West Indians before the white residents returned from work the following evening but, as the *Birmingham Gazette* reported, the West Indians decided to 'stay put'.

Three days after an uneasy peace was finally restored, a quota of twelve black people per National Service Hostels Corporation hostel was suggested. Apart from the obvious accusation of colour prejudice, it was also pointed out that the overall number of residents could vary from 1,000 to less than 100. Eventually, a figure of accepting black men up to 10 per cent of total capacity subject to a maximum of thirty was set, although that could be reduced in potential trouble spots.

Writing in the *Birmingham Daily Gazette* on 11 August 1949, 24-year-old Horace Halliburton, who had worked in the engineering section of the Jamaican Public Works Department – and 'who has knowledge of Latin and can speak Spanish fluently,' the newspaper added – said that he had lived in the Causeway Green hostel since arriving in Birmingham in search of job, eight months earlier.

> The problem of Causeway Green is by no means unique in this country. It is an example of Great Britain's colour bar ... my sixty fellow West Indians in the hostel know only too well that the ill-feeling and fighting of the past week cannot be blamed on individual differences of opinion and local domestic arguments – the story of the Causeway Green riots really started at the beginning of the year when the management suddenly decided to segregate the coloured inhabitants from the Polish and the British. This created considerable resentment among the West Indians. They felt that they had been singled out and herded together because other people had found them unsuitable to live with ... many Birmingham people have placed the cause of the trouble on the question of women friends ... I would like to point out this is a very minor cause of dissension.

Mr Halliburton said that the West Indians were jeered at and were 'the subject of constant baiting'. 'Even landladies at boarding houses will not have us as residents. Why, I do not know.' Sadly, perhaps, he felt that the only answer was a separate hostel altogether for black people. And 'to firms whose policy is not to employ coloured men, I would say, have one or two on trial for a time.'

It would take many more years – and only after legislation – for the post-war immigrants to Britain to stand an overall fair chance when it came to finding employment. Not only West Indians, but workers from the Indian sub-continent who arrived in Britain after Partition in 1947, found this to be the case.

In May 1959 the *Derby Evening Telegraph* published a feature by one of its regular columnists 'Albert Street' asking: 'Has Derby a Colour Bar?' As new immigrants had begun arriving from the Commonwealth, there had been much talk of non-white school leavers finding it difficult to obtain suitable work in the town because employers were selecting white workers ahead of them, regardless of qualification or ability. As the columnist pointed out, it would be hard to prove this was the case since 'No firm will admit publicly … that the colour of an apprentice's skin could affect his chances of securing an apprenticeship.'

He also suggested that fear of an unfavourable reaction from existing workers might put employers off taking on immigrant workers. The previous year, factory workers at Milford had gone on strike when a Punjabi was given work there. The strikers had claimed that the management had agreed not to take on 'coloured' workers when white workers were available. 'Albert Street' was horrified to relate that, although the two sides had eventually reached an agreement, this had occurred only after the Punjabi had been dismissed.

Post-war prejudice against non-white people continued, though, and it is remarkable to think that even in 1966, the year that London was 'swinging' and England won the World Cup, a West Indian man, Asquith Xavier, a 44-year-old train guard from Dominica, was refused a promotional transfer from Marylebone Station to Euston, not because he was unqualified for the job, but because of the colour of his skin. The new job would have meant a pay increase of around £10 a week for Mr Xavier who had started work for British Railways as a porter ten years earlier. He was informed about his rejection, and the reason for it, in a letter from Euston's local staff committee whose members belonged to the National Union of Railwaymen. The letter was unequivocal: 'I have to inform you that staff representatives for Sectional Council No. 3 at

Euston are not prepared to accept on promotion the transfer of coloured staff to Euston.'

The Race Relations Act had been passed the previous year but contained only measures to combat racial discrimination in public places such as hotels and pubs. Employers were still at liberty to refuse someone a job on grounds of their colour alone. In July the ban at Euston – which had apparently been in existence for twelve years and which was reported to be in force at other London stations including Camden and Broad Street – was overturned. Mr Xavier, who was unwell at the time, took up the job in August 1966, but not before asking for police protection after receiving hate mail and death threats.

Chapter Thirteen

Murders Most Foul

She noticed three gentlemen were prepared to defend that inhuman monster ... she placed me and, I suppose, my learned friends, in the category of Hitler.

Joshua Caswell KC

On 16 October 1946, 64-year-old Mrs Violet Van der Elst was fined £2 at Clerkenwell magistrates' court for obstructing free passage of the highway. Behind that brief news report lay a remarkable story. Mrs Van der Elst was a most formidable woman. A former scullery maid, born Violet Dodge, in Feltham in Middlesex, she was the daughter of a garden labourer and a washerwoman. When she was seventeen, she married Henry Nathan, a civil engineer thirteen years her senior. After developing the world's first brushless shaving cream, Shavex, she began to amass a fortune. After Henry Nathan died in November 1927, she re-married. Her new husband was Jean Julien Romain Van der Elst, a Belgian who had been working for the couple. A talented artist – he was descended from the seventeen-century Flemish painter, Pieter Van der Elst – who had served as a captain in the First World War, Jean Julien had been living with the Nathans at 30 Belsize Park in north-west London.

After Jean Julien died suddenly, in August 1934, in Ostend, Mrs Van der Elst, a student of witchcraft, blamed the mummified hand that a Bedouin had sold her in the Upper Nile three years earlier. She told a journalist:

> Don't mention it to me. It is a curse. An archaeologist told me that it was 7,000 years old, and the hand of a princess. My husband never wanted it, but it was my unbridled desire to have it. Ever since I have had it, I have been ill. My husband, too, was ill. Now he is dead.

During the next few years, Mrs Van der Elst attempted to contact her dead husband, holding séances at the stately pile, Harlaxton Manor in Lincolnshire, that she purchased in 1937. She paid £90,000 for the derelict 1830s building, restored it, and renamed it Grantham Castle. She wrote a collection of short stories, *The Torture Chamber and Other Stories*, and, most tellingly, a book entitled *On the Gallows*, for Violet Van der Elst was a vehement opponent of the death penalty. She set up her own newspaper called *Humanity*, in which she published evidence that she believed proved the innocence of condemned people. She had stood, unsuccessfully, for parliament three times, most recently as an independent in the 1945 general election when she had come fourth in the Hornchurch constituency poll.

On that October day in 1946 she was arrested outside Pentonville Prison after handing out leaflets calling for the reprieve of Neville George Clevely Heath, a 29-year-old former airman who was due to be hanged that day for the brutal murder of Mrs Margery Aimee Gardner, a 32-year-old occasional film extra, at a Notting Hill hotel on 20 June. The magistrates' court heard that Mrs Van der Elst arrived in a chauffeur-driven Rolls Royce at 8.55am that day and began to address a crowd of about 200 people who were assembled on the footpath adjoining the prison. She threw a number of handbills into the crowd. Traffic ground to a halt as press photographers, some twenty in number, stood in the roadway trying to get the money shot. Mrs Van der Elst told the court, 'I had no sooner got out of the car then I was arrested. There was nothing in that pamphlet against anybody. There was fresh evidence in it, which should have been read.' She said that as she walked to the prison gates, a police inspector crossed over to her and said, 'You come with me.' She said, 'I was astonished as I am generally allowed to walk a little distance. I did not give utterance to anything. I never had the chance.' Earlier, at the same court, a man was fined £1 for fixing posters, protesting at the execution, to a bridge near the prison without the consent of the owners. Similar charges against a soldier and a Land Girl were dismissed.

There was never any doubt that Neville Heath was guilty of murdering Marjorie Gardner. The case was the most sensational of recent times. His execution pushed even the suicide of Herman Göring, one of the primary architects of the Nazi police state in Germany, into second place on the nation's front pages. The previous night, the former head of the Luftwaffe had crunched a glass phial of cyanide in his mouth in a Nuremberg prison cell, thus avoiding his own date with the hangman.

Heath was a charmer. On Sunday 16 June 1946 he took a room at the Pembridge Court Hotel in Notting Hill, booking-in using his real surname but promoting himself to the rank of lieutenant colonel. His companion was a woman called Yvonne Symonds, whom he introduced to the hotel receptionist as his wife. In fact, they had met for the first time only a few days earlier, at a dance in London. He persuaded her to spend the night with him at the Pembridge Court, under the promise that, in due course, he would marry her. The following day, Yvonne Symonds, who lived with her parents in Worthing, returned home.

Three days later Heath spent the evening at the Panama Club in Old Brompton Road, dancing with Margery Gardner, who had a young daughter but who was living alone in Earl's Court after separating from her alcoholic husband. They arrived at the Pembridge Court Hotel at around midnight, Heath's arm around Margery's waist. At about 4.00pm the following day, Alice Wyatt, who assisted her father in law in managing the Pembridge Court, found room no. 4 in semi-darkness. When she pulled back the curtains, she saw someone lying in the bed nearest the door. The bedclothes were drawn up around the shoulders in the usual way but, when Mrs Wyatt pulled them back, she saw Margery Gardner's naked body. Police found that it had been subjected to the most appalling sexual assault, including lash marks caused by a whip. Home Office pathologist Keith Simpson told the investigating officers, 'Find the whip and you've found your man.' The cause of death was suffocation but only after all the other injuries had been inflicted.

There was no sign of the man with whom Margery Gardner had arrived at the hotel. On Friday 21 June Heath telephoned Yvonne Symonds, told her that he was in Worthing, and that he would like to have lunch with her that day. He booked a room at the Ocean Hotel and the following day they met again. News of Margery Gardner's murder was now in the Sunday papers and Heath told Yvonne that he was closely connected with the case and would tell her all about it later. Then he said his goodbyes and left Worthing for Bournemouth where he booked a room at the Tollard Royal Hotel under the name of Group Captain Rupert Brooke. There he wrote a letter to Detective Superintendent Tom Barratt, one of the officers investigating Margery Gardner's murder, claiming that he had let her use his hotel bedroom so that she could sleep with another man, and that when he returned at 3.00am, he found her in the condition of which you are aware ... I realised I was in an invidious position and rather than notify the police I packed my belongings and left. Since then, I have been in several minds whether to come forward or not, but, in view of the circumstances, I have been afraid to.

Staying at the Norfolk Hotel in Bournemouth was Doreen Margaret Marshall, a 22-year-old former Wren who was convalescing from a bout of measles. On 3 July, as she was walking along the promenade, she met 'Group Captain Rupert Brooke'. Handsome, well-spoken and polite, he seemed an agreeable companion and she accepted his invitation to take afternoon tea with him at the Tollard Royal. She accepted a dinner invitation that evening too, but after dinner, in the hotel lounge, she appeared to be uncomfortable in his presence and she asked a fellow guest to call her a taxi. Heath cancelled it and said that he would walk her back to the Norfolk Hotel. As they left the Tollard Royal, he told a porter that he would be back in half an hour. Doreen Marshall interrupted, 'He will be only a quarter of an hour.' It was the last time that she was seen alive. On Friday 5 July the manager of the Norfolk Hotel reported her missing. Heath rang the Tollard Royal to ask about her and its manager told him that his dinner companion had disappeared.

Heath visited Bournemouth police station and, from a photograph, identified Doreen as the young woman with whom he had dined. The detective investigating her disappearance, 31-year-old George Suter, soon suspected that Group Captain Rupert Brooke was in fact Heath, the man wanted in connection with Margery Gardner's murder. He pointed out to 'Brooke' his remarkable similarity to a photograph of Heath that the Met had circulated to all forces. 'Brooke' agreed but denied that he was the wanted man. His claim that he had an aircraft at Hurn airfield was soon disproved and, by the time officers from Scotland Yard arrived, 'Brooke' admitted that he was indeed Heath. A whip and other trophies were found among his possessions and he was taken back to London where he was charged with Margery Gardner's murder. The following day a waitress, Kathleen Evans, out walking her dog, came across the body of Doreen Marshall in Branksome Dean Chine. Doreen had also been brutally murdered, her body bearing many injuries similar to those inflicted upon Margery Gardner.

On 24 September 1946 there was a long queue for the public gallery when the trial of Neville George Clevely Heath for the murder of Margery Gardner – the charge of murdering Doreen Marshall was not proceeded with – opened at the Old Bailey. After first telling his counsel, Joshua Caswell KC, to plead guilty, when Caswell – who had, in 1913, represented families of victims of the sinking of the *Titanic* – queried this, Heath, who was described on the charge sheet as a 'civil airline pilot' and living in Wimbledon, is alleged to have said, 'All right, put me down as not guilty, old boy.'

Smartly dressed in a grey pin-striped flannel suit, Heath listened intently as Detective Inspector Reg Spooner of Scotland Yard detailed the accused's career to the jury. Spooner said that Heath, who was born at Ilford in June 1917, had been dismissed from the Royal Air Force, the British Army and the South African Air Force. Heath had joined the Artists' Rifles as a Territorial when he was seventeen. He joined the RAF in February 1936 but the following year was dismissed from the service for being absent without official leave. In November 1937 a Nottingham court placed him on probation for two years for obtaining credit by fraud and attempting to obtain a car worth £175 by false pretences. On two occasions he had posed as Lord Dudley. In October 1939 he enlisted as a private in the Royal Army Service Corps, and, after being commissioned as a second lieutenant, was posted to the Middle East. In July 1941 he was court-martialled and cashiered for obtaining a second pay book by false statement and making a false statement to his commanding officer to enable him to be absent from his unit. Sent back to England on a troopship, he disembarked illegally at Durban and began issuing false cheques, passing himself off as Captain Salley MC of the Argyll and Sutherland Highlanders. He then changed his name to Armstrong and joined the South African Air Force. In May 1944 he was seconded to the RAF with the rank of captain and sent to 180 (Bomber) Squadron of the 2nd Tactical Air Force. Inspector Spooner said that Heath had been shot down in October 1944. There is an account that, during a bombing raid over Holland that month, Heath's plane was hit by flak, and he ordered his men to bale out, but stayed behind to free the navigator, who had become trapped; the pair then jumped together.

In 1945 he returned to South Africa, whereupon his wife, Elizabeth, whom he had married there in February 1942, divorced him on grounds of desertion. The couple had one child, a boy. In December 1945 he was convicted on three charges of prejudicial conduct and three of wearing decorations to which he was not entitled and dismissed from the service. He returned to London and, on 5 April 1946, was fined at Wimbledon for unlawfully wearing decorations and uniform. Eleven weeks later he met Margery Gardner.

Caswell decided not to call Heath to give evidence but instead to rely on a defence of insanity. He told the jury:

> I am not going to call Heath before you. You would probably not believe a word he says. If he were called, moreover, you're not mental experts and nobody, I suppose, even from hearing a man give evidence in court, unless he has a been a psychiatrist or psychologist, can estimate that man's mental quality. You will be told more about the Bournemouth case, so that all the facts maybe before you, on which Dr Hubert has based his opinion.

William Henry Duval Hubert, a psychotherapist at Wormwood Scrubs prison from 1934 until the outbreak of the war, said that while Heath knew what he was doing, he did not know that it was wrong. He was, said, Hubert, 'morally insane'. The prosecution destroyed that argument. Hubert, a drug addict who, within six months of Heath's trial, would be dead from the effects of self-administered barbituric acid and chloral hydrate, on his forty-third birthday, was arguing that anyone, if they thought that their acts were right or necessary, had an indiscriminate licence to commit crime.

Two prison medical officers testified that while Heath was a psychopath and a sexual sadist he was not insane. It took the jury of ten men and two women just one minute under an hour to find Heath guilty of murder. He was sentenced to death by hanging. As he heard his fate, Heath, standing between two prison warders, appeared unperturbed, gazing directly ahead as sentence was passed. Only when he turned to descend from the dock did he seem to struggle to maintain his composure, but he had regained self-control before he disappeared from public view. A few minutes before his execution at the hands of Albert Pierrepoint, as was the custom, he was offered a glass of whiskey by the governor. It has been claimed that Heath replied, 'While you're about it, sir, you might as well make that a double.'

This sensational murder trial that gripped the nation in 1946 had inflamed passions throughout the country. Caswell said that he had received a letter from an anonymous woman: 'She said she had noticed three gentlemen were prepared to defend that inhuman monster, Heath. She placed me and, I suppose, my learned friends, in the category of Hitler, and she hoped our consciences would haunt us for the rest of our lives.'

There had been some fascinating twists. During the trial a young woman called Peggy Waring had told a Fleet Street news agency reporter that she had met Heath, or 'Bob Brooke' as she knew him, at Bournemouth on 25 June. He had joined her party at a tea dance and later they had sat on the beach before dinner at the Tollard Royal. She said:

> Bob appeared to be in need of someone to talk to. He gave the impression that he had something on his mind. He always seemed to have a distant look in his eye. They are light blue and occasionally the most troubled expression came over his face. He drank very heavily most of the time. After dinner that same night, four of us went for a walk along the seafront, where he said 'good evening' to a number of people. Suddenly, as we were walking along, he said he was in great need of being looked after, and asked me to marry him. All along the promenade he kept taking hold of my arm and kept pushing his attentions on to me, pleading for sympathy … . I would not have tolerated it had I not felt he was labouring under some unhappiness, for he kept asking me to marry him all the way back to the hotel. He also told me he had an income of £2,500 a year as a test pilot. In the hotel that evening he was in a heavy, morbid frame of mind. He asked me if, as I would not accept marriage, whether I would agree to other suggestions. I told him not to be ridiculous but that I was prepared to give him my friendship and sympathy if he was ready to behave himself. When he was sober, elderly ladies in the hotel thought he was charming … . He tried very hard to persuade me to stay on in Bournemouth for another week but, of course, I refused … . Before I left the hotel, he came to me and said, 'You have won a magnificent victory. I only hope you can congratulate yourself on Monday.' … Later, a police officer told me I was the luckiest person to be alive.

Meanwhile, it had emerged that, in February 1946, a young woman called Pauline Brees had been found naked and bound in a bedroom at the Strand Palace Hotel in London. Over her, ready to thrash her, was Neville Heath. Hotel staff had been alerted by her screams but, because she wished to avoid publicity, she refused to press charges against the man she knew as James Robert Cadogan Armstrong. After Margery Gardner's body was found, staff at the Strand Palace Hotel wrongly identified her as the woman they had rescued. This found its way into the newspapers, suggesting that Margery Gardner had been fully aware of Heath's sexual tastes and so probably had her own masochistic tendencies, but it was soon established that they had only just met. But had Pauline Brees chosen to go ahead with charges against Heath, then he would probably have been imprisoned and Margery Gardner and Doreen Marshall would have lived.

And Violet Van der Elst? Her campaigning against the death penalty, her unsuccessful political career and her general behaviour combined to lose her a fortune. In fact, she told a *Picture Post* reporter: 'I have made three fortunes and lost five.' In reduced circumstances she lived in a flat in Knightsbridge and she died at Ticehurst House Hospital, a mental health facility, on 30 April 1966, having lived to see the abolition of the death penalty the previous year.

Chapter Fourteen

A Perfect Orgy of Crime

The end of the Second World War has switched public attention to many other evils, lesser in extent and enormity, but almost equally difficult to combat.

Northern Daily Mail

'It is quite clear that there has been organised smuggling going on at Halton.' That was the allegation made by Mr B.R.C. Noble, a solicitor representing HM Customs and Excise at Aylesbury magistrates' court in February 1946, when seven serving and former airmen were charged with offences against Customs laws.

The men were Flying Officer William John Crimmin, Warrant Officer John Roy Luly and Leading Aircraftman Dennis George Brice, all of the RAF's Bomber Command Communications Flight; Flight Lieutenant Albert Leather of the BOAC Training Unit; Flying Officer Roy Viggo Gordon Frandsen of the Empire Air Armament School; Edward Alfred George, a former leading aircraftman; and George William Grieve, a former RAF corporal. They were variously charged with offences that included evading duty on bottles of champagne, whiskey, brandy, cherry brandy, Benedictine, cigarettes, gramophone records, a standard lamp and cards of fancy buttons.

Mr Noble told the court that, at the time the offences were committed, the defendants were stationed at RAF Halton where a courier service to the continent came into operation. The actual flying people concerned with that service worked and lived together and formed a small community. 'Between September and November 1944,' alleged Mr Noble, 'there was a considerable amount of smuggling going on at this airport and the smuggling in some cases continued until June 1945, when investigations started.'

A charge against George Grieve, of being knowingly concerned in the fraudulent evasion of duty on twelve bottles of brandy, was dismissed, but the other six were found guilty on all counts. Five were fined between £10 and £40 on each offence, with an alternative of two months' hard labour on each charge. Edward George was not given a choice; he had previous convictions for receiving stolen petrol and stolen tyres and was sentenced to two months' hard labour. Crimmin alleged that George had given him four pounds of tea, which he in turn gave to his mother, in exchange for a bottle of champagne and a bottle of brandy, 'both of which were fairly cheap in France'. The chairman of the magistrates, Lieutenant Colonel H. Bruce Dresser DSO, a former wine grower in Argentina, said that while Crimmin seemed to have been doing the smuggling on a systematic scale, George had been 'more than systematic in this matter'. George's solicitor, Reginald Johnson, told the court, 'I was a little hurt to hear an officer, and presumably a gentleman, say that a leading aircraftman was the brains behind this organisation.'

With no Customs officials stationed at Halton to check incoming flights, the defendants were 'making hay while the sun shone,' said the Customs and Excise solicitor, and, of course, opportunity is everything, and the Second World War had presented plenty of opportunities to those in positions of authority. At the height of the Blitz, the ranks of the police force, Air Raid Precautions and Home Guard had all been well represented in the dock at magistrates' courts. In November 1940, when three Coventry firemen were each sentenced to six months' hard labour for stealing from a shop that had received a direct hit, the judge told them, 'I cannot think of conduct more detestable than that, during the most dreadful air raid which has ever taken place, you should be found looting.'

Smuggling alcohol, cigarettes and fancy buttons in no way compares with looting from bombed-out shops and houses, but the case of the Halton airmen is but one example of the crime wave that continued after VE Day and well into the post-war years. In January 1946 the *New Statesman and Nation* commented that 'crimes of violence are usually common in the aftermath of a great war in which habituation in killing has dulled all the sensibilities and loosed the normal restraints of civilised men'.

That month the Home Secretary, James Chuter Ede, published figures showing the percentage increase in crime in London since 1938. They were quite startling: 'Shopbreaking up 92 per cent, larcenies from dwelling houses 155 per cent, car thefts 25 per cent [even though there were fewer cars to steal], robberies and assaults 106 per cent, petty larcenies 61 per cent.' Writing in the *New Statesman and Nation*, a former City of London police inspector, Cecil Rolph Hewitt, (writing under the name of C.H. Rolph), drew attention to an interview with the Home Secretary, who said:

> No one would have thought of stealing second-hand shirts in 1938, but to large numbers of people today the sight of a shirt on a clothes line has become a temptation. Everything is worth stealing and everything is much easier to steal. Any amateur can get into a bombed house which has still got its windows boarded up with cardboard.

Although the number of criminal acts had more than doubled, convictions of people under the age of 21 had gone up by only 10 per cent. It was the 10,000 deserters from the armed forces who posed a particular problem. Here were men with no identity cards, no ration books and no clothing coupons – passports essential for civilian life – who could not report to their local Labour Exchange for work. They ended up taking casual, low-paid and often unpleasant jobs, and that often led them to drift into an underworld of petty criminals, and from there to their recruitment into organised crime gangs. Quite often these men had not run away from danger in the forces but had simply overstayed their leave, and had then, in fear of being imprisoned in the 'glasshouse', gone on the run and dropped out of organised society. But they still needed to eat and to find somewhere to lay their heads at night.

In July 1946 the *Belfast Telegraph* published a story about one such case:

> This man had heard stories about his wife. He found they were quite unfounded. Ashamed to admit what he had done, he said he was on leave and ostensibly returned to his unit. Actually, he went to London. Down to his last few shillings, he was considering giving himself up when he met a stranger over a drink. One drink led to another, and at last he was telling his story, saying he was going to give himself up. The stranger told him not to be a fool and that he would get three years [imprisonment]. Why not demob himself? He offered to find identity card, ration book, clothing. He named the price. The soldier could not afford it. But the stranger said he was

looking for someone to drive his car and the soldier could work it off in that way. Before he appreciated properly what he was doing, the soldier was driving the car on various nefarious errands ... why do men desert? In the first instance, desertion is not generally intended to be permanent. A few men do desert to take to crime or because anything seems preferable to life in the army. But many cases start either with compassionate leave being refused, or even by a man failing to ask for it and simply going home because he's worried about something. It does not become real desertion until he decides not to go back, generally because he is afraid of the consequences.

It was reported that 80 per cent of recorded crime had been carried out by deserters and a general amnesty for them was suggested as one way of bringing down the crime figures. The *Belfast Telegraph* addressed that:

> Obviously to let all deserters simply go scot-free would be impossible. Desertion must always be a serious offence, and, quite apart from discipline in a conscripted army, it simply means that other men have to serve. But it cannot be good for the country to have such large numbers of deserters, with a strong incentive to civilian crime, at large. An offer for a limited period to treat leniently any deserters who surrendered and had not been guilty of civilian crimes might have the effect on greatly reducing the numbers. It would allow the authorities to concentrate on the really 'bad' cases, where the deserter is not only a threat to discipline but also to civilian society. It might also be the means of preventing men taking to crime and adding other offences to their desertion because of the difficulties of getting employment in a highly regulated society.

In the Lanarkshire newspaper the *Bellshill Speaker*, one letter writer, signing themselves 'Cavalcade', made a more impassioned plea:

> if you will all enter your pulpit some Sunday and demand that this Socialist Government of ours grant an amnesty to all those poor hunted souls who, through desertion or otherwise from the services, are roaming like haunted criminals throughout our land and also for those who, for conscience sake, still linger in our prisons.

In fact, it would be February 1954, when Winston Churchill was once again leading a Tory Government, that wartime deserters from the services were granted an amnesty. It affected 10,393 soldiers, 1,784 airmen, and 863 naval personnel, and ended what Lieutenant Colonel Marcus Lipton, the Labour MP for Brixton, called 'this eight-year-old manhunt'.

But it was not only deserters who were turning to crime in 1946. On 22 March Mr Justice Humphreys told Sussex Assizes, 'There is at present in this country a perfect orgy of breaking into shops and warehouses and stealing goods, and I regret to say that a very high proportion of the people who do that are either in or just out of the services.' He told an 18-year-old Royal Marine, who had been convicted of theft, that the current crime wave had caused the whole Borstal system to break down. Justice Humphreys said that youths would have to wait their turn to get into Borstal, as they would a fish shop or any other place, because of overcrowding. Travers Humphrey was well qualified to comment: his sixty-year legal career involved him in many high-profile cases including the trials of Oscar Wilde and of murderers Hawley Harvey Crippen and John George Haigh, 'the Acid Bath Murderer', as well being a member of the Court of Criminal Appeal panel that rejected the appeal of William Joyce, 'Lord Haw Haw', against his conviction for treason.

However, not everyone sent to gaol was a deserter, a young serviceman or a hardened professional criminal. In March a 65-year-old widow, Jannet Maud Capper, was sentenced to six months' imprisonment after pleading guilty at Gloucester City Quarter Sessions for 'collaborating in the crime wave that is sweeping this country' by receiving a watch, knowing it to be stolen.

In January 1946 the *Sidney Morning Herald* reported a different view on the main causes of increased crime in Britain:

> Five murders, eight pistol-point robberies, and a large number of less spectacular crimes within a week recently drew public attention to the extent of the wave of gangsterism .... Scotland Yard chiefs admit that armed gangsterism is behind the black market activities linking London with provincial industrial centres producing consumer goods still scarce or severely rationed ... those few American gangsters who came to Britain on bogus passports before the war and tried to break in on the London underworld were usually marked by London criminals, not only for professional jealousy or

infringement of 'territorial rights' but because the presence of armed alien hoodlums brought the police down on the criminal fraternity in general. Today, however, there are in England a host of foreign servicemen who, lacking emotional control, reach for a gun where, in similar circumstances, a Britisher would use his fists.

That was perhaps an over-simplistic view, but it was a fact that Britain was flooded with illegal weapons. The *Sidney Morning Herald* reported:

> Demobilisation and leave from Europe bring home daily thousands of men with weapons to sell and the ability to use them. Port military police say it is estimated that one in every ten soldiers smuggles in a weapon as a souvenir or for sale. Homecoming troops are warned by unit commanders, and on ships, that arms smuggling is a court-martial offence as well as a civil crime, but thorough searches of all returning soldiers' kits for arms would cause too much delay at the disembarkation port, so only spot-checks on individuals and appeals to common sense are made. From one port of arrival (for leave and demobilisation troops from Central Mediterranean Forces) on one day last month, 10 machine guns, 12 handguns, 18 automatic rifles and 60 revolvers and pistols were collected. Police consider that should unemployment become prevalent, or the black market continue to pay such huge dividends, crime will increase and enlist young men who could plan a bank robbery with the same skill and ruthlessness as they planned commando raids.

On 14 February it was announced in the House of Commons that no proceedings would be taken in Scotland against anyone surrendering firearms by 31 March. Two weeks later, Motherwell police reported a mixed bag of weaponry handed in: two rifles, five pistols, six automatic weapons and 480 rounds of ammunition; most, however, were of 1914-18 vintage.

The *Motherwell Times* advised people to continue to heed the temporary amnesty: 'If you have a gun that could still make a bang at all, you should tote it along, just to be on the safe side. After all, you yourself might never think of using it, but you can't guarantee that nobody else will – and these are troubled times.'

Many police officers said that they knew the identities of the major black marketeers but lacked sufficient evidence to convict them because the buyers on the market would not give evidence. One solution suggested was the application of such measures as indefinite detention, under the wartime provisions of the Defence of the Realm Act, of known but unconvicted blackmarketeers and gangsters, with a general clean-up of underworld figures 'who infest the pin-table saloons, racecourses, dog tracks and other sources of "easy money"'. In a recent speech the Home Secretary had declared that, should the circumstances arise, he would not hesitate to use the military to break armed gangsterism.

While news of the crime wave in Britain had reached even Australia, closer to home there was also plenty of reaction. A comment column in the *Northern Daily Mail* ran:

> The end of the Second World War has switched public attention to many other evils, lesser in extent and enormity, but almost equally difficult to combat. Some, like the shortage of houses, for example, are inevitable, but others, like the increase in crime, are merely fashionable and, it is to be hoped, of temporary duration .... How is it to be quelled? Some interesting suggestions have been made this week by police chiefs and judicial bodies. Judges and magistrates in various parts of the country have stated bluntly that they intend to do more than merely make the sentences fit the crimes because leniency may be mistaken for licence by people other than those in the dock. The task of the criminal will be much more difficult, and that of the police correspondingly far easier, if, as the chief constable of Durham advocates, we could get active co-operation between civilians and police in the work preventing and detecting crime.

That would happen. In November 1946 it was announced that the Hull branch of the National Housewives' League had decided to co-operate with the police 'not by active service in an anti-burglary squad, but in various practical ways of crime prevention'. The chief constable of Leeds, Frank Swaby, said that he did not approve of citizen patrols or vigilantes because of complications that might follow their actions. He was reassured that the idea was simply that the housewives of Hull should, on the request of neighbours during absence from home, remove any signs, such as newspaper showing in a letterbox, that may tell thieves that the occupants are away. The *Yorkshire Post*, however, saw a greater role for the women:

> If the burglar is as wise as he is enterprising, he will give careful thought to the news from Hull that housewives there are to take a more active share in the defence of their homes against his intrusion. Until now the burglar has had to contend with comparatively mild opposition from the constabulary and the male householder, forces which, while being resolute in their support of law and order, can see that even the thief has certain civil rights and that the campaign against him must be conducted according to specific rules ... . It is not simply that women are impulsive and liable, upon confronting an intruder in sufficient numbers, to attack him without weighing either consequences or weapons that they use. What makes this promise of a new development so menacing to the lawbreaker is the fact that house burglary is a crime peculiarly hateful to women. The home is their treasure.

The shortage of police officers made matters worse. On New Year's Eve 1946 additional police had been drafted into the West End to keep order but, as another year dawned, the Metropolitan Police force was in danger of being overwhelmed. By midnight, 2,740 men – time-served, war reserves, or full-time specials – had walked out of London police stations for the last time, leaving the Met more than 4,000 officers below strength. The wartime emergency that had seen the enlistment of extra officers was over – and there was now a post-war crime wave

The chief constable of Middlesbrough wanted to enrol many more special constables to do monthly tours of duty near their homes as wartime auxiliaries had done during air raids. This was a growing problem: after the release of wartime reserve police officers, every force was reduced to pre-war numbers of personnel; but crime had more than doubled since before the war. In October 1946 it was reported that, of more than 500 applicants for the Manchester police force in the previous nine months, only 190 – 38 per cent – had passed both the physical and educational tests set by the force. Manchester still needed 200 more policemen, and several policewomen, to bring the force up to strength. It was maintained that only by placing a larger number of men on street duties, with freedom to mix at will with the general public, could the force perform its work effectively. Most police officials agreed that the right answer to the present crime wave in the country would be found only by employing more men on outside duties.

In November the lord mayor of Bristol, Gilbert James, drew the attention of the first meeting of the city's newly elected watch committee to 'the appalling crime wave which was sweeping the country, and the shortage of police recruits in Bristol'. 'We must have sympathy with the police and the extraordinarily difficult task they have got,' he said. The committee's chairman, Alderman Frank Sheppard, said:

> Our greatest difficulty is getting recruits for the police force. While it is true that there is a wave of crime going on throughout the country at the present time, we have to take into consideration the difficult circumstances in which we are living. After the last war there was the same kind of attitude in regard to possessing other people's property. I suppose this thing will right itself in time. We hope the development of a higher standard of culture and education will have some influence on the population of the country.

Irvine Fell, a magistrate and churchwarden in the Lancashire town of Nelson, felt that it was the duty of the church to help stamp out the current crime wave which, he said, was becoming a menace to the community. This, he suggested, 'should be attempted through the youth of the country keeping up their interest in church and Sunday School'. The *Lancashire Evening Post*, referring to the 'crime wave, following in the wake of world war, [that] continues to be profoundly disturbing,' saw the causes as

> the growth of unmoral forces let loose by armed conflict ... a short-sighted weakening of police strength ... and, finally, to the effects of lax control in the homes during the years fathers have been away fighting and mothers have been commandeered for munitions-making and other national work ... the age-old problem of what form of correction wayward tendencies in childhood should take is present with us in greater seriousness than ever. The stern repressiveness and punishment practised during Victorian and Edwardian days came to be frowned upon and gave place to what is called child self-expressionism, often a mere euphemism for unbridled wilfulness which laughs at discipline and control.

Although London had been the first area of the country to report a massive increase in crime, everyone now seemed worried. In March Sir

Noel B. Goldie, the Recorder at Manchester Quarter Sessions, said. 'At last, the wave of crime spreading in Britain has reached Manchester. One only has to look at this calendar of more than ninety prisoners to see that the majority are charged with either house or office-breaking.' Sir Noel sentenced to three years' penal servitude, a 25-year-old labourer, Ernest Vernon of Cheadle Heath, who pleaded guilty to three counts of stealing and asked for twenty-four offences involving a total of £720 to be taken into consideration. In November the chief constable of Gloucestershire, Colonel William Henn, speaking at a re-union dinner at Cinderford, said that it was more than possible that a good many of the criminals now operating in London would, when they found that the Metropolis was 'too hot for them' drift into the provinces. 'Although that we don't expect anything in the nature of a serious crime wave, we must be on our guard.' Everyone was taking additional measures. The *Rugby Advertiser* reported that:

> the 999-emergency telephone call system, which has already played a considerable part in combating the crime wave in London, will be introduced at Rugby ... special equipment has been installed at the Rugby exchange, so that when 999 is dialled, an emergency lamp and loud buzzer will indicate to the operator that the call is especially urgent.

Despite the *Northern Daily Mail*'s assertion that judges and magistrates had 'stated bluntly' that they intended to do more than merely make the sentences fit the crimes, not every judge was wholly unsympathetic to the plight of men who pleaded that they were 'victims of poverty'. Even here, though, leniency generally carried conditions. At Burnley Quarter Sessions in March, the Recorder, Neville Laski, told 35-year-old labourer Frank Gregory, who had been found guilty of stealing 25 shillings (£1.25):

> I am going to give you one more chance. I want to say with the greatest emphasis that if you come before me again for any offence there will be nothing that will stand between you and imprisonment. You are a worthless scamp. Don't go out of this court laughing at me, because I have the last word and if anything happens to jeopardise your liberty it will not be safe with me. It will be very unsafe.

Not everyone was convinced that lenient sentences would result in criminals seeing the error of their ways and setting out on the road to their reform. In April 1946 a letter writer to the *Liverpool Echo* asked, 'What are we coming to? In Liverpool a man pleads guilty to robbing an old woman of 75 of 12s 10d after getting into a house at midnight – and is bound over! How do we expect to stop the crime wave?'

In December 1946 William Johnson, previously the chief constable of the Birmingham city force, and now HM Inspector of Constabulary, wondered what all the fuss was about. Addressing a conference of detective officers at Tunbridge Wells, he said that while in the aftermath of war there was 'a certain type of unpleasant offence' the bulk of crime was 'not of a serious nature'. The same month, Frank Swaby, retiring as chief constable of the Leeds city force, said he thought that the present crime wave would pass, as did the one after the First World War. The training was different in the Second World War, he said, and that accounted, to some extent at least, for the present level of crime. A second reason was that 'lack of parental control'.

Whatever the causes, Britain's post-war crime wave would continue way beyond 1946, not least in that black market that had flourished during the war, when many producers, traders and, of course, career criminals had taken advantage of rationing to fulfil people's desire for a little extra and not really caring whether it came from under the counter or had fallen off the back of a lorry. As rationing became even more strict in peacetime, the black market inevitably continued to prosper. In the late 1940s in Derby a small woman could regularly be seen scurrying from house to house after dark, lugging a heavy sack over her shoulder. One January evening she knocked on the door of Anton Rippon's home and whispered, 'Ask your mother if she wants any tea.' His mother, who in any other situation was honest almost to the point of eccentricity, did want some tea, over and above the two ounces (56.69 grammes) a week allowed for each adult, and the transaction was completed, in cash, obviously, in a darkened doorway. Besides the tea, the little woman said that she could offer sugar, bacon, cigarettes and tobacco, all of which, as it happens, were refused. In the following day's *Derby Evening Telegraph* it was reported that, two days earlier, the glass in the front door of a local Co-Op store had been smashed during the small hours and 'thieves took quantities of tea, sugar, bacon and other foods, and cigarettes and tobacco, valued at approximately £20'. It was a perhaps a coincidence, but it made uncomfortable reading for someone who, when it came to putting that little extra on her family's table, generally could not give much thought to the source. Crime in the form of the post-war black marketeers prospered because people usually turned a blind eye.

Chapter Fifteen

If They Win the Cup, We Don't Mind Feeding Them

What a lovely time to play football. Families were being reunited, the blackout had ended, and there was a great feeling of comradeship.
                                        Dennis Herod, Stoke City

For over a million people there was only one place to be on Saturday 31 August 1946: at a Football League ground. Unusually for the first day of the football season, the weather was cloudy and overcast, the forecast for rain. The previous week had seen gale-force winds and torrential downpours, rivers swollen, roads blocked by fallen trees. In Germany the Nuremberg war crimes trials entered their last day and that afternoon Göring, Hess and von Ribbentrop were among major Nazi leaders making their final impassioned pleas. In Britain the days when football matches were interrupted by air raids, and teams made up their numbers by borrowing from their opponents, or even from the crowd, were over. Now there were no guest players, but there was promotion and relegation. Now there was a return to the old ways of football.

The fixtures were a replica of the 1939-40 season which meant that Sheffield United were making another attempt to establish themselves in the top division, seven years after they had been promoted. Twenty-eight thousand fans made their way to Bramall Lane, where Liverpool, fresh from a trip to North America, were Sheffield United's visitors. Liverpool effectively won the title on 31 May when they beat their closest rivals, Wolves, on a scorching day at Molineux, but they had to wait another two weeks to be sure; thanks to yet another dreadful winter, the 1946-47 season went on until 14 June.

The FA Cup, however, had resumed for the previous season and, on 9 March 1946, all roads leading to Burnden Park were packed. Bolton Wanderers were playing host to Stoke City in the second leg of their FA

Cup quarter-final tie, and the visitors had the great Stanley Matthews in their ranks. Burnden Park stood on the south side of Bolton, about half a mile from the town centre. Throughout the morning crowds built up in the streets around the ground as supporters arrived early. Home fans queued up, waiting for the turnstiles to open. They were joined by away fans who had arrived on early trains before making the ten-minute walk from the railway station. There was no segregation of rival supporters. Everyone had come to see a football match, not to cause trouble.

Bolton held a two-goal advantage from the first leg – up to and including the quarter-finals the first post-war FA Cup competition was played on a home-and-away basis. Would Bolton prevail? Could Matthews, who had spent most of the war guesting for Blackpool where he was stationed in the RAF, turn the tide Stoke's way? Over 85,000 people wanted to see the outcome at first hand. But the record attendance, and the capacity, for the ground was just under 70,000.

When the gates opened at 1.00pm, tens of thousands moved forward in orderly fashion into Burnden Park to take up their positions on the terraces. However, not everyone was prepared to stand around for hours. Many could not anyway. First they had factory jobs to do, arriving at Burnden breathless after grabbing a cup of tea and a sandwich before jumping aboard a Bolton Corporation bus. They, too, shuffled their way into the ground. Behind them still more fans flocked towards the stadium that, like almost all football grounds in Britain, had grown from small beginnings in Victorian times and had been extended with no real thought for crowd comfort. Health and safety was not even a work in progress. Thousands more supporters arrived, and the streets became choked as a seething mass of supporters, now growing increasingly anxious about getting in, made their way towards the turnstiles.

By 2.15pm – still forty-five minutes to kick-off – conditions were already becoming uncomfortable both inside and outside the ground. The pressure was so great around the turnstiles that many would-be spectators were being pushed against the walls of the stadium. On the terraces there was hardly any room to move. Keeping one's feet became a priority. Yet still the turnstiles clicked and clattered, feeding more people on to the terraces. Those at the front were being pressed further forward, but it was now impossible to move in any direction.

The streets surrounding the ground were as packed as the terraces inside. There were no police radios; it was impossible for officers in the ground to communicate with those controlling the tens of thousands still hoping to gain admission. A call from a PC Lowe to close the turnstiles reached the head checker too late to make a difference. Discomfort now turned to distress as people began to fall to the ground, and others could not avoid standing on them. With ten minutes to kick-off the crush outside the turnstiles was relieved almost at a stroke. A spectator, trying to escape the ground with his young son, had picked the padlock on a large exit gate designed to spill large numbers back into the streets at the final whistle.

But people were not leaving Burnden Park; thousands more were pouring in. The pressure on the terraces was now unbearable. At five minutes to three, a huge roar signalled the appearance of the teams. On the terraces tens of thousands of people craned their necks to catch a first glimpse of their favourites. This sea of humanity rolled forward. Most were held in place by a series of strategically placed crush barriers that prevented the swaying masses from pressing down to the front of the terracing.

But there was one area, near the bottom of some steps, where no crush barriers had been erected. Thousands of people were compressed into this gap, funnelling down uncontrollably. Then barriers elsewhere started to buckle under the strain, and down went the crowd, tumbling forward. Bodies began to pile up, two, three, four deep. Twelve minutes into the game, a police sergeant walked on to the pitch and spoke to the referee. George Dutton stopped play and took the teams off the field. The players sat in their dressing rooms for twenty-five minutes. Word spread that two or three spectators had been killed. Then referee Dutton re-appeared, telling the players that, on the advice of the chief constable of Bolton, he was resuming the game. When the teams took the field again, they saw that the pitch had grown smaller. Thousands of spectators were sitting over the original touchline and new markings had been made with sawdust.

At half-time the teams turned straight round with no break. The players were unaware that this was English football's worst tragedy: thirty-three people had been killed and over 500 more injured. Best to get the game over with as soon as possible, said the officials. It ended goalless. Bolton were through, Stoke were out. That night few people really cared.

A Home Office enquiry, chaired by Ronw Moelwyn Hughes KC, found that while the Bolton club and the police had taken proper steps, procedures were inadequate. The real trouble lay in the fact that there had been no scientific assessment of the ground's capacity – this was simply regarded as the greatest number of people to have been safely accommodated there on a previous occasion. There was also no means of knowing when that figure was about to be reached, nor were there facilities for the immediate closing of the turnstiles. An attempt had been made to open exit doors, but the keys could not be found.

Matters had been made worse by the fact that several turnstiles had been rendered unusable, which meant that over 28,000 destined for the Railway Embankment end had to enter from the Manchester Road end. Also, ticket holders for the Burnden Paddock had been admitted through turnstiles in this area and then escorted around the pitch to their places, adding to the huge build-up in the north-west corner of the ground. In addition to those fans who had poured in when the exit gate was opened by a panicking spectator, thousands more had simply climbed over turnstiles and walls. Some had walked along the railway line and down the embankment before breaking into the ground through a fence. One thousand people climbed over the entrance to the boys' enclosure. They had free rein: the police were reluctant to release any officers from the Burnden Stand where they were guarding food stockpiled by the Ministry of Supply.

A relief fund for the injured and their families and those of the dead realised £40,000, and a series of government recommendations were made so that, in future, football supporters could attend matches in safety. Yet, despite the huge amount of money pouring into the game through the turnstiles in the post-war years, when players were still on a maximum wage, little was spent on ground improvements.

Seven weeks after the Bolton disaster, the first post-war FA Cup final was staged at Wembley. It was contested between Charlton Athletic and Derby County. More than half the players were over 30. Charlton Athletic skipper John Oakes was 42, the oldest man ever to play in a Wembley final. The teams emerged from the Wembley tunnel into the brightness of a gloriously warm, sunny, late spring day before a crowd of

98,215. The atmosphere was charged with emotion, tears rolling down the cheeks of hardened men during the singing of the traditional FA Cup final anthem, *Abide With Me*. For all that had happened since VE Day and VJ Day, this was the first real indication that life was returning to normal after six years of war. Charlton waited to be introduced to King George VI, who, despite the warm day, was wearing a grey overcoat. Queen Elizabeth and the two princesses, Elizabeth and Margaret, watched from the stand. First it was Derby's turn, their boots repaired with sticky tape, some of the numbers on their less-than-white shirts fraying at the edges, a sign of the austere post-war days to come. A month earlier there had been a rather mournful appeal in the Charlton match programme, 'We are collecting coupons for kit. Can anybody help us?'

The game went down in football folklore – because the ball burst. Twenty-four hours earlier Cumberland referee Eddie Smith, when asked the question on radio, put the chances of that happening as 'millions to one'. Yet footballs were bursting all over the place. Two of Charlton's recent League South matches had to be resumed with a new ball. The League game between Charlton and Derby on the Wednesday after the final would see another burst ball. And when Charlton returned to Wembley to meet Burnley in the 1947 FA Cup final, the ball burst yet again. The Japanese invasion of Malaya in 1941 had meant that rubber was a rare commodity and better spent on things like aircraft production. Good footballs were simply in short supply at the end of the war. At the end of ninety minutes, the game was all square at 1-1, Charlton's Bert Turner having scored for both sides. After an extra half-hour's play, Derby won 4-1.

Now, however, there was the issue of a celebration banquet for the victors. Derby Town Council's special purposes committee had voted to give the team a civic welcome on their return, whatever the result at Wembley. The players would be met by the mayor of the borough, and parade on an open-topped beer dray through the town. On 6 May it was announced, the council would host a dinner for 250 people – players, directors, MPs and county and civic dignitaries. In those times of shortages and food rationing, the idea of a civic junket for the local football club, even if they had just won the FA Cup, did not go down well with many locals. Letters soon began to appear in the *Derby Evening*

Telegraph. J.R. Kendall thought that while meeting the players at the borough boundary was an excellent idea:

> when one reads that this is to be followed by a dinner for about 250 people when every day one reads of world food shortages, economy etc ... would it not be more in keeping with the principles of the Council ... that the occasion be symbolised by small gifts to the more needy townsfolk such as old-age pensioners?

'Two Volunteer Workers' said that they were 'amazed that in these times of austerity and famine, Derby Corporation should dream of spending the ratepayers' money on entertaining themselves and their friends'. They asked, 'Why not appropriate this money for the benefit of our wounded and disabled soldiers who fought and gave their limbs so that Derby County footballers should be able to play?'

When plans for the dinner were mentioned at a meeting of the Derby Food Control Committee, Mr A. Houseman, the deputy food executive officer, said that it would probably be done through British Restaurants, the communal kitchens created in 1940 to help people who had been bombed out of their homes, had run out of food ration coupons, or who otherwise needed help. A member of the committee said, 'If they win the Cup, we don't mind giving them a bit of a feed.'

On 17 April, however, the council bowed to public pressure. The mayor, Alderman Thomas Johnson, told the *Derby Evening Telegraph* that 'in view of the food situation it was felt that a reception ... along the lines of that given to American troops ... would be more acceptable than a dinner'. So, on the evening of 6 May, a reception, concert and dance would be held at a local grammar school. The same day as the announcement, the *Evening Telegraph* reported that Cornish new potatoes were now available in Derby, at ten shillings per pound, and English asparagus was for sale at £1 5s 0d per bunch. The average weekly wage in Britain was just over £7. No wonder many people had been angered by plans for a civic meal for some footballers.

As with Derby Town Council's dilemma over providing a banquet for the FA Cup winners, so in May 1946 the Majlis Asian Society, led by Amalendu Bose, an Indian student reading for his doctorate in English at Christ Church college, and in co-operation with another group of students at Oxford called the Hermits, decided to organise a dinner for the touring Indian cricket team. It would be held at the Angel restaurant in that city. Those private restaurants still in business were not subject to food rationing but they could charge no more than five shillings per head. The Indian cricketers and their hosts sat down to hors d'ouevre, soup, chicken and vegetables, trifle and coffee.

The first full season of first-class cricket to be played in England for seven years was about to get under way – Yorkshire would retain the County Championship they had won in 1939 – while a three-match Test series was hastily arranged against India, who were captained by a pre-war England player, the Nawab of Pataudi, and whose party contained Hindus, Muslims, a Parsi and a Christian. It would also be the last team to represent an undivided India. The players arrived in England in different groups, travelling by various means including an RAF Dakota, a BOAC Avro York, and a flying boat from Karachi to Poole.

After England won the first match, the last two were drawn, the third being ruined by persistent rain. But people were desperate for 'proper' sport, and in its review of the season, an era of Len Hutton, Denis Compton, Wally Hammond and Cyril Washbrook, *Wisden Cricketers' Almanack* commented, 'The weather in 1946 might have been dreadful, but it didn't stop the crowds flocking to games.' It was one of wettest of English summers but the *Cricketer's* annual issue for 1946 reported, 'It is satisfactory to know that, in spite of the bad weather, the tour produced a considerable profit, and this will be an asset in the development of Indian cricket.'

In 1946 the Northern Rugby League began its longest season on record, again thanks to the appalling winter, and in Rugby Union – then strictly an amateur game – the remarkable Dr Kevin O'Flanagan played rugby for Ireland against France (in an unofficial international) and then soccer for the Ireland national football team against Scotland seven days later. He then won an official rugby international cap, against Australia.

The University Boat Race returned to the Thames and was won by Oxford, by three lengths. No official races had been conducted between 1940 and 1945 which meant that none of the rowers had previously participated in a Boat Race.

In February 1946 the last of 16,000 troops left Aintree racecourse that had been used a vehicle depot during the war. The remarkable Mirabel Topham, owner of Aintree, then achieved something that few thought possible: by the first weekend in April she had the racecourse ready for the first true Grand National since 1940. Racing fans, starved of their sport, poured towards Aintree – some estimates give the crowd that Friday (the last time that the face would be run on a Friday) at 300,000. The race was won by the 25/1 shot Lovely Cottage, ridden by Captain Bobby Petre and coming home four lengths ahead of the second-placed runner, Jack Finlay, a 100/1 chance.

When, in June 1946, the Derby was run at Epsom for the first time since 1939 – the course had accommodated an anti-aircraft gunsite – an estimated half a million people, including the King and Queen, saw – in fact, most of them probably did not see very much at all – the grey colt Airborne, at 50/1 and ridden by Tommy Lowrey, catch Gulf Stream in the final furlong to win by a length. The race was filmed by Movietone, using a precarious looking 120-feet-high tower of scaffolding. Airborne's owner, a wealthy manufacturer of plastics, Old Etonian Mr J.E. Ferguson, had not fancied his horse, backing him only for £5 each way. However, the *Daily Herald* reported that many men of the 1st Airborne Division – the 'Red Devils of Arnhem' – had placed a bet on the winner, 'if only for sentimental reasons'.

Sport was helping to heal many different wounds. In 1946, the Devon village of Bradworthy raised a football team to play German PoWs from the local camp. The Germans, who included former professionals in their ranks, won 10-1. At Poppylot PoW camp in Feltwell, Norfolk, the prisoners were mostly infantrymen aged from 25 upwards. They had a very good football team and played against other camps. On one occasion, they, too, met the village team, on the prisoners' 'home' ground, a farmer's field opposite the camp. Footballing prisoners of war were not confined to village life. Brian Harris was an 11-year-old London schoolboy in 1946, 'I remember regularly playing football with the German PoWs who were housed in Richmond Park. The gates were left open so they could come and go. Better than going home I suppose.'

After six long, war-weary years, sport generally provided a huge release from the grind of the factory floor, rationing and everything else that helped to make life so grey. And so it continued. The post-war years were football's so-called 'golden age'. From the 1946-47 season to 1951-52, over 237 million people passed through the turnstiles of England's Football League clubs with a peak in 1948-49 of 41.2 million. Individual match attendances were staggering; on 17 January 1948 the First Division match between Manchester United and Arsenal at Maine Road (United's Old Trafford stadium was still unusable after German air raids) attracted a record gate of 83,260. Two months later there was a crowd of 143,570 to see Rangers play Hibernian in the semi-final of the Scottish FA Cup. Even friendly games saw huge attendances: the Newcastle United versus Liverpool friendly at St James's Park in February 1948 was played before 44,840 spectators.

The post-war game was so popular that, when vital matches were played, mass absenteesim from vital industry was a problem. As late as 1951 docks authorities in Manchester ordered workers not to attend a Manchester United FA Cup match because they were needed, ironically, to clear a backlog caused by a strike. The men went to the match anyway and plans to import dockers from Fleetwood foundered when men at that port preferred to watch Blackpool, who were also playing in the cup. In the days before floodlit football, replayed cup-ties on midweek afternoons conincided with a spate of dear, departed grandmothers in urgent need of burial and the government considered banning midweek football in important industrial areas. Instead, it opted for staggered working hours to accommodate the tens of thousands who wanted to watch football.

Throughout the post-war years, almost every professional sport enjoyed record attendances, from cricket, especially in the summer of 1948 when Don Bradman made his farewell tour with the Australians, to horse racing, greyhound racing, boxing, Rugby League and even ice hockey. And then there were the Olympic Games … .

Chapter Sixteen

Austerity Olympics – A Glorious Reality

The organisers of the London Olympic Games, which ended on Saturday, did an excellent job with comparatively few errors ...
Manchester Guardian

IN the summer of 1948 a young news reporter called Terry O'Connor, not long demobbed from the RAF after wartime aircrew service, thought that the forthcoming Olympic Games in London 'might prove interesting'. So, he decided to accept the offer to become a sportswriter. It would be only a temporary move, however. Once the Games were over, he would return to hard news. But O'Connor never made it back to the newsroom. Forty years later he was still covering the Olympics.

In 2012, as London prepared to host the Olympic Games for a third time, he said:

> Of course, the 1948 Games were light years away from what we see today. The war hadn't long been over and there was still food and clothes rationing. There was certainly no money to spend on facilities for the Olympics. For instance, the cycling events were held at Herne Hill velodrome that had been built in the previous century. A gun battery had been sited there during the war. Some improvements were carried out, but when the foreign competitors first saw it, they thought it was just the practice facility. The swimming was held in the Empire Pool at Wembley, the shooting at Bisley, the yachting at Tor Bay, and the rowing at Henley. There was no Olympic village. Athletes were put up mainly at military camps around London, including RAF Uxbridge. The whole thing was a gloriously amateur affair. It wasn't like it is today. People weren't queuing up to spend a fortune on staging the Olympics.

The Olympic flame had last burned in Berlin in 1936 when Nazi Germany had used the Games for propaganda as much as for sport. In those twelve years, the world had become a different place. Tokyo was scheduled to hold the 1940 Games and London the 1944 Games, and so in 1948 it was London which staged them, for the first time since 1908.

As Terry O'Connor said, the first post-war Olympiad was no lavish spectacle. There was no Olympic village nor any newly built venues. Male athletes from the record fifty-nine nations that took part – Germany and Japan were not invited; the Soviet Union declined – were housed in military camps at West Drayton, Uxbridge, and the former Army Convalescent Centre in Richmond Park, while, for the duration of the Games, female competitors lived in London colleges. Local athletes simply remained at home, travelling to their events on public transport. The Olympics then were steadfastly amateur (the only perk was free Horlicks), and British athletes, some of whom trained at Butlin's at Clacton-on-Sea, had to pay for their own uniforms. The 1948 Games were the first Olympics to be shown on home television, although relatively few people owned a set, and, for the first time, starting blocks were used for sprint races from 100m to 400m.

King George VI formerly opened the Games in blazing sunshine on Thursday 29 July 1948 before a crowd of 80,000 people who included the Queen and Princess Margaret, Lord and Lady Mountbatten, the Shah of Persia and the United Nations' first secretary-general, Trygve Lie. Trumpeters of the Household Cavalry sounded a fanfare, 7,000 pigeons were released to greet the Olympic flag, and a twenty-one-gun salute heralded the arrival of the Olympic flame. As the guns thundered, the Boy Scout holding the banner of Ceylon fainted. Another boy immediately took his place.

The great pageant of athletes marched past the Royal Box, turning their heads to the right, their standard bearers dipping their flags in salute. After the Greeks, traditionally leading the athletes' entrance, the remaining nations arrived in alphabetical order, first the Afghans wearing green blazers, white trousers and astrakhan caps. The British men wore blue blazers, white trousers and blue berets, the women blue blazers, white skirts and shoes and white berets.

Lord Burghley, chairman of the organising committee, told the huge crowd, 'The hour has struck. A visionary dream has today become a glorious reality.' The 580-page *Official Report of the Organising Committee for the XIV Olympiad* reported:

Austerity Olympics – A Glorious Reality 121

To end the formal ceremony, one verse of the *National Anthem* was played by the massed bands, and sung by a choir, joined by all those assembled in the stadium.

Once again, the bands broke into continuous march rhythm; in turn the teams, headed once more by Greece, wheeled to the right and gradually filed out of the arena; and the vast crowd, deeply impressed by the ceremony they had witnessed, dispersed with thoughts now turning to the competitions yet to come.

Thus were launched the Olympic Games of London, under the most happy auspices. The smooth-running ceremony, which profoundly moved not only all who saw it but also the millions who were listening-in on the radio throughout the world, and the glorious weather in which it took place, combined to give birth to a spirit which was to permeate the whole of the following two weeks of thrilling and intensive sport.

The *Daily Herald*'s Clifford Webb commented, 'There was colour, warmth, dignity, and ceremony. Yet with all a gay holiday atmosphere, good fellowship in the air, and all the promise of a fine sporting occasion.' It was, said Webb, 'a magnificent sun-drenched start'.

A standing ticket to watch the athletics at Wembley cost 3s 6d (17.5p) when the average weekly wage was £8.15s (£8.75). At the London Games of 2012 the same ticket cost £202; the average weekly wage was £500. Outside the Empire Stadium would-be spectators baulked at the touts' price of £4 for a one guinea (£1.05) ticket to see the opening ceremony. According to the official report, total receipts for the Games amounted to £762,000, of which £732,000 went in expenditure.

The star of the 1948 Olympics was Fanny Blankers-Koen, a Dutch housewife who won four gold medals on the track: 100m, 200m, 80m hurdles and 4x100m relay. During the war she had set six new world records, including the long-jump, in the German-occupied Netherlands. Terry O'Connor recalled:

> The so-called 'Flying Housewife' was a remarkable athlete, especially when you consider that she was 30 years old, had two children and had survived the Nazi occupation. Ironically, she'd competed in the 1936 Berlin Games. Her husband, Jan Blankers, had taken part in the 1928 Games in Amsterdam, but I knew him as a journalist. He

became sports editor of the daily *Der Telegraaf* based in Amsterdam. I used to see him at Olympics around the world.

When the 1948 Olympic Games ended, Britain finished with a total of twenty medals, three of which were gold, good enough for twelfth place. The United States topped the medals table with eighty-four, including thirty-four gold.

Said Terry O'Connor, 'Today there is a lot of emphasis on an "Olympic legacy", but there was certainly no legacy from the 1948 Games, not so far as facilities went anyway. They were starting to dig up the athletics track at Wembley Stadium almost before the Games were over.'

In 1948, 17-year-old Bob Mathias became the youngest winner of the Olympic decathlon. He won it again in 1952, in Helsinki, but his abiding memory was of the London Games, In his autobiography *A Twentieth Century Odyssey: The Bob Mathias Story*, the double Olympic decathlon gold medallist (as well as US Marine Corps officer, actor and US Congressman) wrote:

> The [Wembley] stadium had been designed originally for daytime greyhound racing and had only some dim lights about waist-high every 15 yards or so along the track. Well, what they did to brighten things up, those clever Brits, was to bring a bunch of cars into the stadium, aimed the headlights at the finish line, shot off a gun and said: 'Have at it, lads.'

On the same day that the 1948 London Olympics began, fourteen ex-servicemen and two ex-servicewomen competed in an archery event at the Stoke Mandeville Hospital in Buckinghamshire which ran sports programmes for the rehabilitation of patients with spinal injuries. The event, organised by the German-British neurologist Professor Sir Ludwig Guttmann, aimed to 'unite paralysed men and women from all parts of the world in an international sports movement'. The Paralympic Movement was born in 1948.

Chapter Seventeen

That's Entertainment

Good afternoon, everybody. How are you? Do you remember me?
                                                    Jasmine Bligh

On Sunday 29 July 1945 BBC radio's General Forces Programme was no more, at least so far as Britain's civilian population was concerned. Launched in February 1940 to provide popular music, comedy, drama and general variety shows for servicemen, the Forces Programme meant that civilians could also hear this rich mixture of entertainment, and it soon proved more popular than the Home Service. After France fell and the war came much closer to Britain, the BBC decided to continue broadcasting the Forces programme to the entire United Kingdom. It was now the light entertainment station of choice for the nation.

Initially the Forces Programme aired from 11.00am to 11.00pm daily, but from 16 June 1940 it began at 6.30am every day. Programmes that had been designed for specific services, such as *Garrison Theatre*, which starred Jack Warner, for the Army, and *Ack Ack Beer Beer*, which featured Wing Commander Kenneth Horne, for anti-aircraft units, barrage balloon stations and coast artillery, soon became essential listening for civilians too.

After D Day the Forces Programme that was broadcast on long wave became the BBC's Light Programme, while the service continued broadcasting on shortwave to troops still fighting in the Far East, and after VJ Day to occupying forces in vanquished countries until civilian rule was restored. The Forces Programme closed altogether on 31 December 1946.

Listeners at home, meanwhile, had already seen a major change in their entertainment on the wireless. In July 1945 radio critic Harold Watkins said:

Getting any information about the new regional alphabetical programmes from the BBC is rather like asking a censor not to be a censor. But I have discovered the reason why. The wavelength problem has been a major difficulty, and the BBC powers are truly anxious to use what new wavelengths can be spared from war and propaganda service to the best entertainment purpose.

There would soon be three, not two, BBC radio stations from which to choose. The *Gloucester Citizen* reported:

The third station will cater for highbrows only – those who like opera, chamber music, symphonies, and long plays. The Light Programme will be for people who prefer variety, thrillers, bands, and comedians. The Home station will steer a middle-of-the-road course ... the regions, seven of them, are also to come back.

There were already those who challenged the privileged status of the BBC. In his 1945 book *Time's Winged Chariot*, Ernest Thurtle, who was Parliamentary Secretary to the Ministry of Information in the wartime coalition government, felt that 'the BBC has not been, is not, and cannot be impartial on controversial issues ... . Suppose the BBC were biased in favour of the Government of the day, then the parliamentary safeguard might be illusory'. Thurtle thought that parliament would be wise to favour a number of rival broadcasting concerns as an alternative to the BBC's monopoly. That would be a long time coming.

First there was the launching of the new station. On Saturday 28 July 1946 the Allied Expeditionary Force programme, which had been on air since 7 June 1944 – D Day + 1 – had closed down with an outstanding tribute paid by General Eisenhower to all the British, Canadian and American personnel who had operated that service. The next day the Light Programme was launched to the sound of Big Ben and the words:

Good morning, everyone. This is the BBC Light Programme ... . It's the first time we have said those words, 'BBC Light Programme', which we hope are going to mean for you now and in the days to come all that is best in radio entertainment, from nine o clock in the morning until midnight.

Then came the first news bulletin of the day, followed by a wide selection of programmes including *Transatlantic Quiz, Britain versus America*; the drama *Alf's Dream* by W.W. Jacobs; *Sandy McPherson at the Theatre Organ; As The Commentator Saw It: Cricket and Tennis; Variety Bandbox* starring comedian Issy Bonn, ventriloquist Peter Brough and Edmundo Ros and his Rumba Band; a concert - *Tyneside Salutes the Merchant Navy*; the religious programme *Sunday Half Hour*. The day ended with *In a Sentimental Mood*, and *Songs of Three Decades*, before the late-evening news and Big Ben once more.

Over the next few post-war years The Light Programme would introduce many programmes, both those fondly remembered and those still going strong more than seventy years later. The names evoke a golden era of radio listening: *Housewives' Choice, Have A Go, Letter From America, Down Your Way, Mrs Dale's Diary, Take It From Here, Woman's Hour, Dick Barton – Special Agent, The Archers, Life With The Lyons, Educating Archie, Much Binding in the Marsh (*which started life as a recurring sketch in the wartime variety programme *Merry-Go-Round), Twenty Questions, Round Britain Quiz, How Does Your Garden Grow?, Sports Report, Any Questions?, The Billy Cotton Band Show, Ray's A Laugh, A Book at Bedtime, Up The Pole* (starring first cousins from Sheffield, Jimmy Jewel and Ben Warriss), *The Goon Show, Listen With Mother* and *Children's Hour*.

There was also the abrupt end of a national broadcasting institution when, in January 1949, Tommy Handley, the star of BBC radio's *It's That Man Again*, or *ITMA* as it was universally known, died after suffering a brain haemorrhage. After 300 episodes the show died with him. First broadcast in July 1939, throughout the war *ITMA* had sustained a generation of radio listeners. Handley, a variety artist and scriptwriter who during the First World War had served in a kite balloon section of the Royal Naval Air Service, was already a veteran of radio entertainment, having worked in the medium in its infancy. Through *ITMA* he was now a national treasure, undertaking several bizarre posts, fictional of course, such as Minister of Aggravation and Mysteries at the Office of Twerps; the major of a down-at-heel seaside resort called Foaming at the Mouth; and governor of a South Sea island, Tomtopia. Barely twenty-four hours after Handley died in a London nursing home, the show's scriptwriter, Ted Kavanagh, told reporters, 'I can't quite grasp the fact. The whole cast is stunned. The show will end. It can't go on without him. Without "That Man" there can never be another.' Handley was said to be the Royal Family's favourite comedian, and a letter writer to the *News Chronicle* demanded to know why he had never been knighted.

Handley had also appeared in two cinema films, *It's That Man Again* (1943) based on his radio series –the *Radio Times* called the film 'disappointing' – and *Times Flies* (1944), where he played a variety performer who, along with three others, accidentally travels back to Elizabethan times in a time machine. He had never, though, appeared on television.

The BBC's television service, which had been closed down on 1 September 1939 and remained in cold storage throughout the war, began broadcasting again at 3.00pm on 7 June 1946, when it was estimated that there were 20,000 TV sets in Britain, all within the London area. The *News Chronicle* reported, 'The first transmission this afternoon will show the television mast, accompanied by a drum-roll and fanfare, and then cars will be seen arriving for the ceremony.'

The first words heard were those of Jasmine Bligh, one of three BBC TV presenters of pre-war days – Leslie Mitchell and Elizabeth Cowell were the others – who said, 'Good afternoon, everybody. How are you? Do you remember me, Jasmine Bligh?' The final programme shown before the service shut down on the eve of war was the Mickey Mouse cartoon, *Mickey's Gala Premier*, and it was shown again on the day of the BBC television's resumption, along with ballet featuring Margot Fonteyn from Sadler's Wells, and a talk, with drawings, by cartoonist David Low. The following day, on tiny screens, viewers could watch black-and-white pictures of the nation's Victory Parade through London.

June 1946 also saw the return of the televising of Wimbledon; the All-England Tennis Championships had first been televised in 1937. In July children's television returned and in August, *Muffin the Mule* made his small-screen debut. In October part of the Athenian Football League match between Barnet and Wealdstone was televised. The *Harrow Observer* reported that with the 'added attraction' of television cameras, the ground was packed to capacity. But television viewers missed the best bit. The newspaper said, 'The last 20 minutes proved the most exciting of all and produced two further goals, neither of which were televised, the service having to close down on account of bad light and a steady downpour of rain'. The Boat Race and the Lord's Test Match against India were both televised in 1946 and, in 1948, the opening ceremony of the sixteenth modern Olympic Games was broadcast from the Empire Stadium at Wembley.

Only the relatively few viewers in London saw any of this. It would be 1949 before the first great network of transmitters was opened in December with the Sutton Coldfield transmitter bringing television to the Midlands for the first time. It radiated the same programmes as the London station at Alexandra Palace. In October 1951 the Holme Moss station near Manchester began serving a heavily populated area of the industrial North; again, its programmes were the same as those in London. In 1952 Scotland and Wales would finally join in the television revolution with Northern Ireland following suit in 1953.

On 1 June 1946 the first television licences were issued, at £2 each and combining sound and TV. At the same time the price of a sound licence alone was increased to £1. The cost of a television set in post-war austerity Britain could be ruinously expensive. In October 1948 Taylor's radio shop, opposite Rayner's Lane station in Harrow, was advertising the latest Pye television set for £48 17s 3d ('immediate and expert installation'). The same month, the Clerical and Administrative Workers' Union, pressing for a wage rise for its members, said that the total weekly wage for an adult male clerk at an engineering works was £5 9s 6d.

Thus, radio was still the cheapest mass entertainment medium with only cinema coming near to it. Picture houses were packed, people watching films through a haze of blue tobacco smoke during what was to become the 'golden era' of British film with Ealing Studios leading the way. Ealing had come to the fore during the war, with comedies starring George Formby, Tommy Trinder and Will Hay. The studios continued throughout the latter part of the 1940s and into the 1950s, with films such as *Hue and Cry* (1947), *Passport to Pimlico* (1949), *Kind Hearts and Coronets* (1949), *Whisky Galore* (1949), *The Lavender Hill Mob* (1951) and *The Titfield Thunderbolt* (1953). Although best known for those 'Ealing Comedies', the studio, led by Sir Malcolm Balcon, who was knighted in 1948, also produced dramas such as *It Always Rains On Sunday* (1947) which featured Googie Withers, and *Saraband for Dead Lovers* (1948) which starred Stewart Granger and Joan Greenwood.

In 1944 Ealing Studios had been taken over by the Rank Organisation which now controlled a large proportion of the British film industry. Founded by the industrialist J. Arthur Rank, the Rank Organisation was Britain's first vertically-integrated film business where production, distribution and exhibition came under one very large umbrella. Another of Rank's purchases, in 1941, was the Gaumont-British Corporation that owned Gainsborough Pictures which had been created by Michael Balcon in 1924. Famous in the 1930s for its comedies, in the late 1940s Gainsborough was making the *Huggett Family* series of films starring Jack Warner, Kathleen Harrison, Petula Clark and Diana Dors. Rank was also responsible for films that gave audiences a couple of hours' escape from the realities of post-war austerity. Films like *Spring In Park Lane* (1948), *London Belongs To Me* (1948) and *Maytime in Mayfair* (1949). And, of course, there was the 1949 film, Carol Reed's *The Third Man*, set in post-war Vienna and starring Orson Welles. Based on Graham Greene's novella of the same name, its theme tune, played on the zither by Anton Karas, was one of the most haunting melodies of the era. British Lion's *The Third Man* beautifully captured the mood of an uncertain post-war world, although the *Leicester Chronicle's* film critic Douglas Goodlad was 'worried about the assertive camera work ... there were far too many angle shots'.

Perhaps the most bizarre film of the early post-war years was *What A Life!* which was released in 1949. Commissioned by the Central Office of Information and produced by the Crown Film Unit, the eleven-minute-long film was effectively a propaganda effort aiming to persuade the public that life in austerity Britain was not so bad after all, a tongue-in-cheek look at the shortages that still dogged everyday life. Written and directed by Michael Law, and starring Richard Massingham who was principally known for appearing in public information films, and the Scottish actor Russell Walters, it showed two men 'Mr and Mr' sitting in a pub. They decide to end it all by drowning but their attempt fails because the water is so shallow that they can stand up. They burst out laughing and return to the pub where they see two men, images of their earlier selves, looking miserable at the bar. They begin laughing again.

The *Gloucestershire Echo* described the film as 'depicting the world of the inveterate grumbler ... ending with a blinding glimpse of its absurdity'. The British Film Institute later felt that the film failed to fulfil its brief: 'The uncontrolled laughter of the two men after their failed suicide attempt is prompted more by an absurd acceptance of misery than by proving that things are better than they seem.'

When it came to holidays, for those who wanted something more than the pre-war seaside boarding house experience there were holiday camps, although in and around them there were still plenty of reminders of the war itself. Butlin's at Skegness – officially opened in April 1936 by Amy Johnson, the first woman to fly solo from England to Australia – had been used as a naval training centre, HMS *Royal Arthur*. Another Butlin's camp, at Clacton-on-Sea, opened in 1938, was earmarked to be used as a prisoner-of-war camp during the war but became a training facility for the Pioneer Corps before re-opening to the public in 1946. When war broke out, Butlin was building another camp, at Filey, and until 1945 it was used as a military training base, RAF Hunmanby Moor. Butlin's Pwllheli camp, built at the request of the Admiralty, become the naval training base HMS *Glendower* until holidaymakers took over in 1946. In 1947 Ayr, also built for the Admiralty during the war, was opened to the public for the first time. In the drab years of post-war Britain, all the camps returned to providing workers and their families with a basic chalet – cold water and communal bathrooms in the early days – a week of colourful entertainment, plenty of activities, and robust menus. The post-war boom saw new Butlin's camps at Minehead, Bognor Regis, Barry Island, and Mosney in the Republic of Ireland.

Smaller and less expensive that those run by Billy Butlin were Pontin's holiday camps. In 1946 Fred Pontin, who during the war had been involved in establishing hostels for construction workers, opened his first holiday camp on the site of a former US Army base at Brean Sands, near Weston-super-Mare. To help raise the £25,280 cost to restore it, Pontin formed a syndicate in which he owned 50 per cent. Osmington Camp, near Weymouth, soon followed, and within a year Pontin had six camps, each run by him for a year to get them into shape before selling them to the syndicate, in which he still owned 50 per cent. The Pontins company was formed in July 1946, with 400,000 shares, all of them placed in one day. Over the years his empire grew to thirty sites.

Seaside resorts could fully re-open after the war – even in the summer of 1944, after the D Day landings, swimming was allowed on some small beaches – but only after clearance work had been carried out, particularly on the south coast which had been heavily defended against a German invasion. Removing barbed wire and barricades was easy enough, but when it came to clearing mines sown during the early years of the war, there were plenty of challenges.

As late as May 1955 five schoolboys were killed when a mine exploded on the beach where they were walking in Swanage, Dorset. A teacher from their local Forres Preparatory School said, 'The boys were walking in an area that had officially been declared to be clear. It has been used by members of the public, holidaymakers and others for some years since the war.' Seaman John Dawson, who was a mile away, said, 'I saw a huge stretch of sand at the foot of the cliffs exploding. It seemed to blow a ton or more of sand into the air.'

An inquest was told that one of the boys was using a shoehorn to remove the top from a rusty object that was apparently made of iron when the object exploded. A Royal Engineers' bomb disposal expert told the hearing that metal found was the type used when the area was mined in 1940. In 1950 a certificate had been issued saying that the area had been swept with a mine detector and those found had been disposed of by controlled explosion or removed and disposed of elsewhere. No guarantee could be given, but the area could be considered safe except for the possibility of mines being washed up. The Engineers officer said that he was convinced that the mine that killed the boys had been in the sea because there were traces of marine growth on the fragments. About warning notices, he said, 'People should obviously be told about these dangers, that they exist, but I don't know whether local authorities would accept such notices.'

The coroner recorded a verdict of death by misadventure on David North Lewis (13), Robin Ardagh (12), Jeremy Dennis (12), Richard Birch (12) and Jason Oliver (11). A full decade after VE Day, the *Portsmouth Evening News* warned, 'Hitler can yet kill your child.'

Chapter Eighteen

Fashion on the Ration to the New Look

All very charming, but I think it should fly away with all your money and your coupons!

British Movietone News

At the end of the Second World War Jewish refugees Max and Anne Bruh established a fashion business in London. In 1939 Max had been apprenticed to a Berlin fashion house, Friedlander & Zaduk, but fled to England. Anne had escaped captivity at Wuppertal. They met in England, fell in love and married in 1945. The pair chose to acquire an existing, almost defunct, clothing business using the name 'Frank Usher'. It sounded pleasingly traditional and very British. More importantly, it already possessed the textile trading coupons any business needed to operate. By the time clothes rationing ended, the firm was well enough established for the Bruhs to take advantage of a gap in the market for ready-to-wear clothing for the fashion-conscious at more affordable prices. As economic conditions eased, this would eventually place Frank Usher as a go-to brand for the middle classes attending university balls, golf club dances and the like. But, if early post-war period style and fashion was notable for anything, it was that even the smallest of changes, took the longest time to reach British wardrobes.

Clothes rationing began on 1 June 1941 and, like most rationing, did not reach its strictest level until peace was restored. The British war machine had placed enormous demand on textile production. Mass mobilisation meant that a quarter of the British population was entitled to wear a uniform as part of the armed forces, the women's auxiliary forces, or one of the many uniformed voluntary services. Raw materials and labour had been directed away from civilian production to keep up with uniform demands, as well as to produce essentials like tarpaulins and blankets.

Rationing and strict price controls were introduced to regulate supplies. Each item of clothing was given a points value, which was dependent on the amount of material used and how much work was involved in making it. In theory, every member of the population, be they a duke or a factory worker, was subject to the same privations. Whether you intended to wear your outfit to the opera, or a church hall dance made no difference. A man's shirt counted as eight points. Fustian or corduroy trousers as five points, other trousers as eight. A nightshirt or pair of pyjamas were also eight points, a pair of handkerchiefs was one point.

Women could expect to hand over eleven points for a short woollen dress and seven for one made in other fabrics. A long, lined coat was fourteen points, a skirt seven, a jumper five. Undergarments like petticoats, slips and cami-knickers 'cost' four points; others, like corsets, were three points; and a pair of stockings two points.

Every adult was given sixty-six clothing points each year. It was their choice how to use them. On the face of it, this might seem a reasonable total, but it effectively amounted only to one complete outfit per year. Children, whose clothes were obviously lower priced, were given an extra ten points to account for their continual and rapid growth. Otherwise, if an item became damaged, or worn, or even too small or too large – as some did when the effects of food rationing kicked in – replacements would have to be bought from the allocation, or alterations made. Thus, even more than usual, items were handed down to younger family members, and housewives became extremely adept at performing repairs, letting down hems and patching worn elbows and knees on existing clothes. Then, for an eight-month period between September 1945 and April 1946, the restrictions became even tighter and only twenty-four coupons were issued, effectively limiting shoppers to three coupons a month.

An even more pressing issue was the shortage of materials. There was no silk fabric for underwear, and under 'Make Do and Mend' guidelines housewives tried to use what was readily available. Some women fashioned their own underwear from butter muslin – a kitchen item akin to a finely woven cheesecloth and unrationed. Others even managed to make bridal or bridesmaid dresses from it.

In 1942 the Utility scheme, which the government had introduced to regulate furniture design, had been extended to clothing. It continued until well after the war ended. Its purpose had been to offer a range of well-designed, price-controlled affordable clothes made in approved fabrics that guaranteed good quality, longevity and, so, value both for money and for coupons. To save precious fabric, men's suits were to be single, not double, breasted with narrowed lapels. Their trousers, like women's 'slacks', were to have no turn-ups. Detailing was kept to a minimum. Ladies' dresses 'were to feature no more than two box-pleats, or four knife-pleats'. Buttons were restricted to five, and pockets to two. 'The amount of ruching and gauging are strictly limited; no braid, embroidery or lace is to be used'.

It became frowned upon to be seen in showy, overly elaborate designs. Even the high-end fashion designers, which the government had sensibly decided to involve in Utility design, had to abide by the same guidance. Having well-known names like Hardy Amies and Edward Molyneux – as well as Norman Hartnell, who was shown in *British Pathe News*' 'Modes for Million' at work on his own Utility mass-market designs – made what was essentially practical and low-cost at least seem 'special'. The problem was that such designs had the inevitable consequence of appearing rather similar. This was mitigated by what Pathe News informed viewers were 'ten different materials and twelve different colours – one hundred and twenty variations in all'. Certainly, as the newsreel claimed that 'in spite of restrictions, these dresses are most becoming'. Clothes may have been simple, but they remained well-proportioned with flattering, feminine shapes and gently nipped-in waists.

Utility clothes were hard-wearing, too. The relatively large number of 1940s clothing items bearing the distinctive CC41 mark and still in good condition is testament to the quality of production. By the time it came to an end in 1952 the Utility scheme had done much to encourage mass production of affordable fashion items.

Increasingly, there was more choice to be had but rationing still dominated. Anne Stewart, writing about the range on offer in Claridge (of Worthing) – the self-proclaimed 'Fashion House with Personal Attention', in a 'Woman's World' column of the *Worthing Herald* in June 1946, pointed out, 'One admired the neat styles, the new slants, the nice materials, and enjoyed the sensation of being once again at a crowded dress show with mannequins, flowers and refreshments, but one regretted the fearful frustration of being bound body-and-bank-balance by coupons.'

Shoppers could buy other items. the *Nelson Leader* of 18 April 1946 ran an advertisement for Lewis's department store in Manchester featuring a 'non-Utility' design by Berkertex – 'it looks like a suit … it's actually our very latest design featuring the flared peplum.'

Peplums, softer shoulders, increased skirt length and more fluid lines – named the 'London Line' by the American *Journal of Retailing* – began to appear even within the post-war Utility range in the autumn. In November 1946, the *Yorkshire Observer* reported on the latest styles in the London fashion salons on show with the following year in mind. Their 'Woman Correspondent' noted, 'Women's clothes are becoming more feminine, and spring is in the air. Coats are very full – either swagger or tightly belted at the waist – with drooping shoulders, and with wide sleeves inserted at deep armholes. Big sleeves and big pockets are the outstanding features.'

The newspaper was proud of the local companies that had provided material. J.J.L. & C. Peate of Guiseley supplied a brown-and-gold-check tweed and Walter Sykes of Huddersfield a fine, grey, horizontally-striped worsted. Salts, of Saltaire, made the fine wool used in a black, three-piece suit, while near-neighbour company, William Rogerson's, of Bradford, produced a crepe romain that was used in a number of dresses.

Clothes were surprisingly colourful, with fashion features in newspapers describing shades such as 'gold, amber, camel, beige, violet, and hunting pink' – the latter actually the deep scarlet shade of traditional hunting jackets. Others wrote of 'deep carnation red, sage, primrose, tropical blue, off-purple, aqua, luggage tan, shocking pink, shell pink and lilac'.

Then, in 1947, in France, Christian Dior released his 'Corolle' line. Coined the 'New Look', although it was really just an exaggeration of styles introduced before the war, it was characterised by softer, rounder shoulders, cinched-in waists and longer, fuller skirts, and tight pleating – all features that used copious amounts of fabric.

In Britain, where such things were still in great shortage, the designs were initially considered rather wasteful. They favoured style over practicality and certainly did not have the newly working British woman in mind. Nevertheless, the New Look remained an influence in fashion well into the 1950s even if, in Britain at least, it was in a somewhat diluted form. In part this was because high fashion was out of the price range of all but the very well-off. The country's economic situation meant that few Britons had the money to spend on anything but essential items.

On 15 March 1949 clothes rationing ended. But, as the *Birmingham Gazette* pointed out the following day, for some time rationing had already been unnecessary: 'Shopkeepers are confident they will be able to supply all the clothes most people can afford. Shortage of money – which retailers have long contended was a sufficient rationing factor in itself – prevented any abnormal buying yesterday.'

However, the change soon affected a number of local workers. Some thirty-five employees of the Board of Trade in Birmingham, tasked with dealing with clothing coupons, were expected to lose their jobs with immediate effect.

By 1950 it was, at last, becoming more acceptable for the fashion-conscious to embrace new and more elaborate clothes. At midsummer, the *Wiltshire Times* ran an advertisement for Button Clemoes of Trowbridge. Under the heading, 'Glamour Fashions', the advert promoted its 'Special display of inexpensive Models, Glamourous Summer Fashions, Bathing Wear, Millinery' and advertised 'Fashions by Famous Makers. Dresses by Dula Models, coats by Harella, suits by Linda Leigh, skirts by Slimma, Handbags by Tudor.'

But there were still shortages. And waiting lists. Particularly for much-valued items like the new Nylon stockings. Button Clemoes ran its own 'New Hosiery Register ... to enable us to make a fair distribution of our Nylon Hosiery Allocations.'

'Please register NOW your name and address at our HOSIERY SECTION. The first to register will be the first on the list for NYLONS from our next quota.'

It must have seemed worth the wait as Nylon was being hailed as the material of the future. *British Pathe News*, in its 1949 film 'Nylon Fashions', went as far as to call it 'science's greatest gift to women'.

At the very least, a little glamour was returning to daily life. Women, who had previously been advised to keep hair simply styled and under control with headscarves and the like, were now beginning to embrace bounteous waves and curls, or short feathered cuts. For evenings, faux chignons were fashioned from hair pieces, and decorated with pieces of velvet, flowers and even raffia.

Beauty products had never been rationed. The government, conscious of the effects that war, shortages and imminent danger might have on female morale, had elected to encourage women to take care of their appearances for the sake of themselves and those around them.

Towards the end of the war Yardley had run an advertisement that read, 'To work for victory is not to say goodbye to charm. For good looks and good morale are the closest of allies.'

That was all well and good – it was not easy to obtain products like face powder or mascara. While manufacture of cosmetic products continued throughout the war, many businesses had switched at least part of their production to helping the war effort in a more direct manner. The British arm of multinational Coty, for example, known for their face powder and fragrances, began to produce foot powder for the army and 'anti-gas' ointment.

Cyclax, one of the oldest cosmetic manufacturers in Britain, had produced both a burns cream and a camouflage cream as well as products to prevent sunburn in troops who had been posted to Africa and the Far East. Now peace had returned, Cyclax had resumed production of its popular range of perfumes, bath salts, shampoos and depilatories. This proved a slow process because its Tottenham Court Road factory had been destroyed during the Blitz of 1942, and its replacement, in Harlow, would not be completed until 1953. During the war one of Cyclax's most popular products had been a lipstick, designed specifically for 'Service Women' in a shade known as 'Auxiliary Red'. It was designed to flatter all women, whatever colour uniform they wore. It even formed part of a kit given to women serving their country. Cyclax's 'day lotion', a sort of foundation, came in range of colours with strange names like Peach, Light Rachel, Rachel, Deep Rachel, Dark Rachel, Sunburn No1 and Sunburn No2. However, British women were not quick to indulge in the newly available beauty products. Habit meant that such items were still regarded as luxury items. And a heavy purchase tax of 90 per cent, reduced to 60 per cent in 1958, ensured this would remain the case for years to come.

Chapter Nineteen

Britain Can Make It – But Britain Can't Have It

Life is going to be more fun. It is going to be lived in lovelier surroundings, with more colour, more convenience, and a torrent of new ideas pouring into the shops from British industries.

Janet Grey, *Daily Sketch*

On 26 September 1946 mounted police were deployed to control large crowds that had gathered outside London's Victoria and Albert Museum. Although the V&A had long been renowned as the world's leading art and design museum, the crowds were not flocking to see the centuries of beautiful design – most of the fine exhibits were still safely stowed away in their wartime evacuation spots in Wiltshire, Somerset, and Oxford. These crowds were there to see the future – via the government-sponsored 'Britain Can Make It' exhibition which had opened two days earlier.

The exhibition had been conceived by the Council of Industrial Design which was established at the end of 1944 by Hugh Dalton, President of the Board of Trade in the wartime government to 'promote, by all practicable means, the improvement of design in the products of British industry'. Six years of war had turned Britain into a military machine. Just about every manufacturing industry had either been downscaled dramatically or had been adapted towards producing the necessities for fighting a war and sustaining its people. If the country was to get back off its ecomomic knees, it was now essential that Britain be seen as a nation that could be trusted to bring modern, innovative and high-quality well-designed goods to the global market. Much effort had gone into ensuring 'Britain Can Make It' would provide the shop window to do just that.

At the official opening, King George VI had said:

> I believe that the many visitors from abroad who visit this exhibition will find in it much evidence of our power of recovery in the face of all difficulties and of our continued leadership in the arts of peace. I believe that our own people after the long years of strain and denial will draw encouragement from the sight of the things here which from now on will become available to them in increasing numbers.

The public were certainly keen to find out what they might soon be buying. To ensure that they turned up in their thousands, in the days prior to the opening members of the press, from national titles and local newspapers, up and down the country, had been invited to take preview tours. The publicity drive worked because, almost immediately, the exhibition attracted around 20,000 visitors a day, all paying one shilling (5p) for adults, and sixpence (2.5p) for children, many of whom had to queue for as long as two hours before they could even walk through the doors.

Visitors followed a fixed circulation route, a third of a mile in length, around the 2-acre site. They were shown products from more than 1,200 firms. They began with a section on the transformation of industry from wartime to peacetime.

According to the *Banbury Guardian*:

> Here the articles on show are lit by slim pencils of light against a background illustrating bomb-shattered London – a grim reminder of the days of blackout and nightly raids. Next comes 'Shop Window Street' a blaze of light and colour symbolic of the return to peace. Here is a display of what British industry is getting ready to produce.

Much was made of the advances that Britain's war machine had given peacetime production. Visitors were reminded that technology from Spitfire construction was being applied to improved kitchen equipment. A British Movietone newsreel noted 'out of the plastic used in gun turrets, they are now making shoes that look like Cinderella's slippers'. There were several educational displays that showcased raw materials, new materials, mass-production techniques and – something rather new to the public – design aspects like proportion, utility, colour, texture and decoration. One of the most striking displays in the 'What does Industrial Design Mean?' section was 'The Birth of an Egg Cup' which posed the question,

'Who does decide the shape of the egg cup?' and used a 12-foot (4-metre) high plaster egg, various illustrations and a machine capable of producing 3,000 egg cups a day to answer it.

To showcase British design and manufacturing in situ, a series of twenty-three furnished rooms, from homes, offices and schools was set up, each organised by a different designer and given a unique fictitious occupant with descriptions by John Betjeman and sketches by Nicolas Bentley. Among them were 'The Kitchen of a Cottage in a Modern Mining Village' by Edna Mosley; 'Kitchenette in a Small Flat' by Frederick Gibberd; 'Bedroom with Man's Dressing-room, and 'Bathroom in a Large House' by John Hill; 'Bed-sitting room in a Block of Flats' by Ursula Mercer; 'Dining Room in a Small Suburban Villa' by David Booth; 'Living Room in an Old Stone House in Scotland' by R. Mervyn Noad; 'Living Room in a Small House on a New Estate' by Elizabeth Denby. 'Secondary Schoolroom' by Denis Clarke Hall; Richard Sheppard's 'General Administrative Office'; Brian O'Rorke's 'Manager's Office'; and 'Technical Office' by Christopher Nicholson provided the non-domestic settings.

The *Yorkshire Post and Leeds Mercury* thought it likely that visitors would spend most time in these rooms 'where all the latest ideas in house, office and school design are displayed in an appropriate setting'. They were certain, too, that 'women will note with pleasure the work of many feminine architects'.

Much was made of the many firms from across the nation who had submitted examples of their wares to the organisers. One of these was Banbury's Messrs Henry Stone & Son Ltd, whose light oak finished dining-room furniture was a key feature of Booth's 'Suburban Dining Room'. Their local paper, the *Banbury Guardian*, however, was convinced that another section would prove the main draw: 'It will be hard to get the children away from the exhibit of toys displayed … under a revolving spiral roundabout, fourteen feet high in aluminium and green and scarlet felt and hung with glittering toys of the kind most children today have never seen.'

A bedroom with convenient bedside and overhead lighting and a modern dressing table, and a particularly decadent bathroom featuring an over-bath shower, hollow glass bricked walls and even a sun treatment area, might have might have seemed rather out of reach to the average visitor, but the aspirational exhibits certainly engaged at least one national journalist.

Janet Grey, women's editor of the *Daily Sketch*, appeared utterly won over by everything she saw:

> I now know exactly what I'll have in my next home because I've seen everything I want. My kitchen is going to have cupboards from wall to ceiling, and as many as possible of the fittings will be of stainless steel. The china and pottery will be gaily coloured – no more plain white for me – and all food storage jars will be glass so that I know what's in them.
>
> In the living room, I shall have a lamp which looks like a giant's table lamp. It's the same shape as an ordinary table lamp, stands on the floor by an armchair and gives just the right amount of light for reading. On other lamps I shall have shades that are made of two layers – Perspex over celluloid.

Elsewhere were innovative household items, all displayed in a modern and artistic manner. Kitchen gadgets 'floated' in mid-air, while dining tables topped with new materials like Wareite - a plastic laminate which was essentially a Swedish version of Formica – were printed with bold patterns. There were sections devoted to radio and television. Items here included a portable radio which was about the size of a handbag and hung from a strap, allowing it to be carried over the shoulder. For the first time new entertainment technology was being marketed towards a female demographic.

Women were, of course, also the target of most of the new kitchen appliances, and the area devoted to new fabrics and women's dress occupied more than a third of the exhibition space. It was spectacular, too, taking place beneath a gigantic silken tent.

As some manufacturers were keen to point out, many of the designs were not new at all. Most had either been on sale, or been about to go into production, before the war, but what was essentially a re-launch of many items was widely welcomed. While the public longed to see items that they could buy reach shop shelves, guided by the press, and several newsreels, they were also enthused by the more futuristic ideas. An electrical air-conditioned bed capsule caused some curiosity, not least with Her Majesty Queen Elizabeth who was given a 'guided tour' of its features.

But it was Benjamin Bowden's 'The Classic' bicycle which created the biggest stir. It was anything but classic and was lauded as the 'Bicycle of the Future'. A noted car designer, Bowden brought many elements of motor-car design to his version of the no longer humble pushbike. In fact, there was no need to push, at least uphill, for the stream-lined aluminium vehicle had an engine – a direct-drive hub dynamo that stored downhill energy which could be released to assist when going uphill. The bike also had a handlebar panel that featured light switches, and electric bell, a speedometer, and even a radio. The design – a concoction of aerodynamic swirls and curves – would not have looked out of place in a *Flash Gordon* comic strip. The press flocked around it, and King Farouk of Egypt immediately ordered six. Unfortunately, no single model was ever produced. Plans to produce the bikes in Wales in a factory employing former miners came to nothing, and Bowden moved to South Africa where he hoped to put his design into production, with government help. However, having given Bowden enough money to purchase materials from the UK, the South African government inexplicably changed tack, blocked all imports, and even confiscated the only working prototype. In the 1960s Bowden did release his design as the now engineless Bowden Spacelander, of which only 522 were ever made.

Back at the V & A, visitors were teased with a world of an even more science-fiction nature. The *Daily Herald* promised readers: 'Deserts will be made fertile, the Arctic continent made habitable, and trips to the Moon will take from two to five days – if British scientists' ideas for an atomic-powered "spaceship" are fulfilled.'

Although visitors to 'Britain Can Make It' were repeatedly shown all that was good and optimistic, not every newspaper in every part of the country was entirely won over. Because there was one rather large, and unavoidable, fly in the ointment – that of availability.

The *Broughty Ferry Guide and Carnoustie Gazette* made its readers aware:

> As a shop window the 'Britain Can Make It' exhibition … is not going to be very interesting for the British housewife. For a shilling she will be able to see something of the state of things to come in the way of household goods, but the prices, something every woman looks for, will not be shown. A potential trade buyer will be able to

obtain a confidential quotation, but it has been decided that it will be advisable for this information to be kept from everyone else. So the housewife may be spared a shock. Visitors ... will not miss the modern commentary that tags displayed on the goods will show not the price – but their availability.

British visitors were soon disabused of any notion of this being a shopping opportunity. Most of the exhibits were labelled 'available soon' or 'available later'. In fact, only around 30 per cent were available to purchase during the exhibition. And then only in very limited quantities. As the *Yorkshire Post* noted, 'Such non-Utility furniture as is seen is not likely to be on the market for some time.'

In truth, 'Britain Can Make It' was never targeted specifically at the British buyer, but at those from overseas whose orders of bright, new British-designed goods were going to prove essential in repairing the country's battered post-war economy. The nation was heavily in debt and more strictly rationed than ever before. It could not simply buy its way out of difficulty. It had been reported that British industry was losing orders from overseas, not because of high price or low quality, but because the heavy demand for its goods far outweighed the ability to supply. Much rested on 'Britain Can Make It's role in convincing a global market that the United Kingdom could create, and deliver, the type of innovative, world-class, high-quality goods that were worth the inevitable delays.

This is not to say that the domestic market was being entirely overlooked, just that the goods showcased there were not expected to go on general sale at home for some considerable time. The organisers, anticipating that the display of so many British designs and products would bring a sense of optimism and pride in the country's future, hoped that it would also promote a so-called 'design-consciousness' among the British public that might, one day, fire aspirational desire and so stimulate manufacturing and retail.

Although some newspapers gently mocked the exhibition, renaming it 'Britain Can't Have It', if visitors were disappointed to learn most of what they saw was out of reach, they did not seem too perturbed. The *Banbury Guardian* remarked 'It is well worth waiting a little longer before spending money on anything but essentials', while the *Daily's Sketch*'s Janet Grey was most admiring:

Britain Can Make It – But Britain Can't Have It

This is a state enterprise … . Never were so many new ideas gathered under one roof, never was an exhibition presented more brilliantly. You come away inspired by great draughts of colour and beauty. You know that now Britain can put on a show like this, things are looking up.

National recovery was still a long way off but, as the optimistic *Banbury Guardian* noted, 'Britain Can Make It' shows that the end of the austerity period is at least in sight.'

Chapter Twenty

Two Foreign Office Men are Missing

… there were two figures huddled in heavy coats with astrakhan collars and trilby hats pulled over their eyes waiting for them.

Sunday Mirror

On Thursday 7 June 1951, Britain's evening newspapers portrayed a range of national stories as their front-page leads. For the *Coventry Evening Telegraph* the main story was that Princess Elizabeth had that day deputised for her father, King George VI, at the Trooping the Colour ceremony on Horse Guards Parade. The *Nottingham Evening Post* led on the Test Match being played at Trent Bridge in the city, telling readers that 'South Africa's luck in toss continues'. However, they all carried the story that would come to echo down the years whenever the Cold War was examined. 'Two Foreign Office Men Missing – Went to France, Then Silence.'

The news agencies' story appeared in all the regionals, and that in the West Hartlepool-based *Northern Daily Mail* was typical:

> Two members of the Foreign Office, Mr G.F. de M. Burgess, and Mr D. Maclean, had been missing from their homes since Friday, 25 May, and nothing was known of their whereabouts since they went to France a few days earlier. They had been suspended with immediate effect from 1 June, and all possible enquiries were being made.

A Foreign Office official re-assured the public that there was no reason to believe that the men had taken any official papers with them. The passports of both men carried diplomatic visas, although that had little significance when it came to customs and other formalities. French Interior Ministry officials had told the Reuters news agency, 'Both men are known to be in Paris and our agents are looking for them.'

These were indeed nervous times, as the Cold War ground on. *The Guardian* commented:

> Following upon the cases of Professor Pontecorvo, Dr Fuchs, and others who either defected to the Russians or were caught and convicted of espionage on behalf of the Soviet Union, it was inevitable that the Foreign Office should have been asked by journalists today whether there was any suspicion that Mr Maclean and Mr Burgess have, for ideological reasons, made their way behind the Iron Curtain … .

Bruno Pontecorvo, an Italian nuclear physicist, had defected to the Soviets in 1950. During and after the Second World War, Klaus Fuchs, a German theoretical physicist, and naturalised British citizen, had supplied to the Russians information from the Manhattan Project that produced the first nuclear weapons. In March 1950 he received a nine-year prison sentence from a British court after being found guilty of four counts of breaking the Official Secrets Act by 'communicating information to a potential enemy'. In 1947 he had attended the same Combined Policy Committee conference as Donald Mclean.

As Britain's security services were wondering if the pair soon to be known simply as 'Burgess and Maclean' were heading for Russia, the Reverend W.C. Smalley, general secretary of the Baptist Union of Western Canada, had a different take on the Cold War, telling the Commonwealth Baptist Conference in London, 'What a difference it would make to the world today if Stalin had been brought up a Baptist … .'

The following morning, the *Daily Herald* reported that Scotland Yard and French police were checking the authenticity of two telegrams sent from Paris by the missing men. The messages – one to Maclean's widowed mother, Lady Maclean; the other to Burgess's home, Clifford Chambers at 10 New Bond Street in London's West End – were the first news of the men since they boarded the night ferry, the four-year-old SS *Falaise*, to St Malo in Brittany on 25 May. They had driven from London in an Austin A70 hired by Burgess, arrived with only a few minutes to spare and almost collided with a lorry driven by dockworker Sid Hampton. He later told reporters, 'I was about to tell them off for speeding in the docks when one of them threw a couple of bob on the ground and shouted, "Buy yourself a drink".' Hampton asked what about the car they had abandoned on the quayside. As they ran up the gangway, seconds before it was raised, Burgess yelled, 'I'm back on Monday … '.

The *Daily Herald*'s diplomatic correspondent, William Norman Ewer, wrote that there seemed to be no evidence to support the theory that this might have been a flight for political motives, 'or that, as has been hastily conjectured for political purposes, the two "may be on their way to Moscow".' Ewer was, himself, an interesting character. A writer for left-wing publications, he was a pacifist and conscientious objector during the First World War, had been accused of being a Russian agent from the early 1920s, left the Communist Party of Great Britain in the 1930s and by 1947 was disillusioned with the Soviet Union and became an anti-communist member of the Labour Party, writing articles critical of life in post-war Russia. His anti-Soviet work during the early years of the Cold War had apparently been funded by the Information Research Department, a propaganda arm of the British Foreign Office launched in 1948.

In his *Daily Herald* piece on 8 June 1951, Ewer wrote that friends and colleagues of Maclean assured him that it would be 'entirely alien to his character and record' to take political flight. Reports that highly confidential documents were missing from files in his charge were 'completely untrue'. Similarly, while Burgess had certainly held Communist views when he was at Cambridge twenty years earlier, there was no reason to suspect him of any Communist affiliation: 'he had always remained a close student of Marxist theory and Stalinist practice, yet none of his friends, including myself, has seen anything to suggest that he has, for years, been even a "fellow traveller"'.

Donald Maclean was the son of Sir Donald Maclean, a prominent Liberal politician, who died in 1932. At the University of Cambridge in the 1930s he was part of a group of well-off students who shared a fashionable contempt for capitalist democracy. Guy Burgess was a fellow member. After Cambridge Maclean entered the Civil Service, and in 1938 was appointed Third Secretary at the British Embassy in Paris. Then he worked in London before serving in Washington from 1944 to 1948. There he was promoted to First Secretary and then Head of Chancery before being posted to Cairo. A notoriously heavy drinker after recovering from 'a nervous breakdown caused by overstrain', he was back in London as head of the Foreign Office's North American Department. He had, it would transpire, been supplying the Soviet Union with highly-classified information (he gained the position of Combined Policy Committee on Atomic Development) and with other secret material relating to the formation of the North Atlantic Treaty Organisation (NATO). In 1949 FBI agents discovered that, between 1944 and 1946, a member of the British embassy staff was sending messages to the Russians. By a process of elimination, a short list of three or four individuals was drawn up. One of the names was Donald Maclean.

Guy Burgess, an Old Etonian who had worked for the BBC as a 'talks producer', had entered the Foreign Office in 1947, and from August 1950 until May 1951 had been working at the British Embassy in Washington as a Second Secretary. The *Daily Herald* reported that he had been recalled because, according to US officials, Governor John S. Battle of West Virginia had made a complaint against Burgess for speeding. In truth, Burgess's dissolute lifestyle – he was a heavy drinker and a promiscuous and indiscreet homosexual – made him particularly vulnerable, even if he had not sympathised with the Soviets. From 1944 to 1947 he had been a personal assistant to Britain's Deputy Foreign Minister, Hector McNeill, and, like Maclean, had been well placed to send top secret Foreign Office documents to the Soviets on a regular basis.

In May 1951, as British and American counter-intelligence closed in on them, the two men fled. It was Maclean's 38th birthday and, as he walked out of their ten-roomed home in the little Kent village of Tatsfield, without a word of explanation as to where he was going, he left behind the American wife – now heavily pregnant again – he had married in 1940 and their two young sons. A regular at the Old Ship Inn in the village told reporters, 'He usually kept himself to himself, had one or two pints of old and mild, and then went. About six weeks ago he came into the bar with a tall man who might have been Mr Burgess. They chatted for a few minutes, then left.'

The *Daily Herald* commented that Burgess, who was now 40, 'in contrast to Maclean' ... is the tall, handsome bachelor man-about-town'. Before Sid Hampton narrowly missed the two men on the dockside at Southampton, Burgess had been seen at the Reform Club in Pall Mall earlier that day. There he made a telephone call to friends at Sonning, near Reading, and left the club soon afterwards. The charge for the 3s 6d (17.5p) call was still posted on the club's notice board. Then, with two friends, he ate oysters and drank Chablis at a crowded Wheeler's in Old Compton Street in Soho, followed by lunch at a German restaurant near Oxford Street. He met up, for the second time that day, with a young American student friend, bought a suitcase, returned to his flat to collect some clothes, £300 in cash, and, after another drink at the Reform Club, set off to drive to Maclean's home, twenty-two miles away.

One of his friends told the newspaper, 'Guy was one of those chaps who is here today and gone tomorrow. When he strolled out, I never knew whether he was going to Washington, or for a walk in St James's Park.'

Until December 1950 Burgess's mother and stepfather had lived in a mansion with 17 acres of grounds in Berkshire. They sold the estate and moved into a flat in the West End. A friend of his mother said, 'She told me that she was sailing to America on 1 April, to see Guy, who was then in Washington. When his family lived here, Guy paid frequent visits, and for most of the time here he lived in a cottage on the estate. Guy cut quite a dash in our quiet village.'

So, Guy Burgess and Donald Mclean sailed on the SS *Falaise*, using tickets that Burgess had originally bought to use for himself and his young American friend. No further trace of the two men appeared until February 1956, two weeks after the Russian leader, Nikita Khrushchev, had denied Burgess and Maclean were in the USSR. The Tass news agency in Moscow summoned two foreign correspondents, both British, to a five-minute interview at Moscow's National Hotel for some 'very important' information. According to the *Sunday Mirror*, 'When the two Britons reached the door, there were two figures huddled in heavy coats with astrakhan collars and trilby hats pulled over their eyes waiting for them.'

In Room 101 Guy Burgess opened a brown briefcase and handed a 1,000-word statement to four journalists – Richard Hughes of the *Sunday Times*, Sidney Weiland from Reuters news agency and two Russian pressmen. It explained that the pair had gone to the USSR to 'work for the aim of better understanding between the Soviet Union and the West'.

'Both of us had become convinced from our official knowledge in our possession that neither the British nor, still more, the American Government was the seriously working for this aim.'

Neither Burgess nor Maclean were in the mood to answer questions. Burgess said, 'I have given out too many statements to the Press in my time not to know what I have just given you fellows. We just don't want to add to our statement.' Maclean did add that his family had joined him in Moscow. Burgess's mother said that during the exchange, her son had sent her his love. She said, 'Now I may get letters and may even be able to go and see my son.'

When the whole story eventually emerged, it was revealed that Burgess and Maclean had been part of a spy ring involving five men who had studied at Cambridge in the 1930s. Kim Philby, the leader of the group and the man who had tipped off Burgess and Maclean that they were about to be arrested, defected to the USSR shortly before he was about to be exposed in 1963. During his time in Moscow, Philby had an affair with Maclean's wife, Melinda, who had left her often violent, drunken husband for his fellow spy. The other members of the group, Anthony Blunt, and double-agent John Cairncross, confessed in the 1960s and were granted immunity from prosecution, although, after his treachery was made public knowledge in 1979, Blunt, a distinguished art historian – from 1945 to 1973 he was Surveyor of the King's/Queen's Pictures – was stripped of his knighthood. It was Blunt who had contacted Soviet agents to arrange for Burgess and Maclean to escape to Russia.

Guy Burgess was 52 when he died in Moscow in August 1963, suffering from arteriosclerosis and acute liver failure. Maclean delivered a eulogy before the cremation, describing his fellow defector as 'a gifted and courageous man who devoted his life to the cause of a better world'. Burgess's ashes were interred in the family plot at a Hampshire village church. Donald Maclean was 69 when he died in Moscow in March 1983, apparently at the comfortable apartment near the Moscow River where he had lived alone in recent years, according to colleagues at the Moscow institute where he had worked as an analyst of British affairs. At a brief funeral service at a crematorium attached to the sixteenth-century Donskoy Monastery, Maclean was eulogised as a 'faithful son and citizen' of the Soviet Union. His ashes were brought back to England by his son Fergus and buried by his parents' grave in a Buckinghamshire churchyard. The burial by the local vicar was conducted in comparative secrecy, to avoid publicity, with only a few family members present. According to the *New York Times*, MacLean's ashes were 'inside an urn decorated with a hammer and sickle'.

Chapter Twenty-One

By The Skin of Their Teeth

I have seen worse and had to face worse. I have no doubt that we shall come through ... we shall use the growing sense of the need to put Britain back in her place.

Winston Churchill

When Labour was elected in 1945, Britain was on her knees. The war had left industries bankrupt; more than two million homes had been either badly damaged or destroyed leaving millions of people homeless or living in slums, and rationing of food and fuel would, in some instances, soon become more severe than it had been during the conflict. By the time that the 1950s dawned the old wartime spirit, which had sustained people in the years after VJ Day, was fading fast. The hope of the brighter future promised by Clement Attlee had done for Winston Churchill. But, having delivered most of its manifesto, and also presided over the decolonisation of India, Pakistan, Ceylon, Burma and Jordan, and seen the creation of the state of Israel upon Britain's withdrawal from Palestine, Attlee's government now had no clear direction. It was running out of energy – and it was also losing some of its leading figures.

Aneurin Bevan, who, as Attlee's first Minster of Health, had overseen the setting up of the NHS. In 1951, he was named as Minister of Labour, but after two months in office he resigned from the re-elected Labour government when it proposed introducing prescription charges for dental and optical services and diverting money from the National Insurance Fund to pay for re-armament after Britain entered the Korean War. Harold Wilson, President of the Board of Trade, and John Freeman, who had held ministerial posts in both the War Office and the Ministry of Supply, also departed in protest.

Ernest Bevin, the Foreign Secretary, and Sir Stafford Cripps, the Chancellor of the Exchequer, both resigned from the Cabinet due to failing health. Only a month after leaving the Foreign Office, Bevin, who was 70, died from a heart attack. Cripps, who was suffering from stress-related colitis, also resigned as an MP. He died in April 1952; he was 62.

By the beginning of the new decade, the British people were becoming restless. The Second World War had ended five years earlier, but austerity continued. And in June 1950, when communist North Korea, backed by the Soviet Union and China, invaded South Korea, Britain sent troops to join the UN force in the first major conflict of the Cold War. Not only did this have a devastating impact on Britain's economy, it also meant that the country's young men were again going to war. UK soldiers, including a significant numbers of National Service personnel, were in the thick of the action during the war in Korea. More than 1,000 were killed in action, 2,674 were wounded, and 1,060 were reported as either missing or taken prisoner.

The Conservatives, meanwhile, had spent their time in opposition re-modelling their policies to accept a mixed economy and the welfare state. They also promised that, if returned to power, they would build 300,00 houses a year, something seen by Labour Party as 'pure electioneering'.

Overall, then, Labour was not best placed to contest the 1950 general election, the first held after a full-term Labour government, although it was also the first to be held after the abolition of plural voting where some people had more than one vote if, for instance, they owned property in one constituency but lived in another, something that might have been seen to favour the Conservatives. The university seats were also abolished. There were other changes, with eleven new English seats and more than 170 major boundary alterations across the country.

The turnout in 1950 was 83.9 per cent, the highest for a UK general election under universal suffrage, and the Conservatives enjoyed a 5.8 per cent national swing towards them, which saw them gain ninety seats. Labour lost seventy-eight seats, but it was not quite enough to lose them the election. They were returned to power, albeit with the highly vulnerable majority of only five seats, down from their 146 majority in 1945. The 1950 election brought some new faces into the House of Commons, including Edward Heath (Bexley), Enoch Powell (Wolverhampton South), Reginald Maudling (Barnet) for the Tories, and Jo Grimond (Orkney and Shetland) for the Liberals. The House said farewell to Willie Gallacher, its last Communist Party MP, who lost to

Labour the West Fife seat that he had held since 1935. It was also the first general election to be covered by BBC TV. The programme was hosted by Richard Dimbleby.

In the early autumn of 1951, with a balance of payments crisis, the fourth since the war, leading to speculation against sterling, Attlee called another general election, scheduled for 25 October. The snap election was a huge risk, and it was always going to be an uphill struggle for Labour, who entered the campaign facing a seven-point opinion polls deficit in favour of the Tories.

The Economist said that one conclusion to be drawn from the polls was that 'class war no longer wins votes'. The 'middle voter', it went on to say, was not so simple-minded as to believe that 'capitalist profiteers' were to blame for high prices. Most people seemed to see 'the better ways of living in lower Government expenditure, hard work and more more competition'. They now have little faith in controls and subsidies, still less in nationalisation'. According to *The Economist*, six years after the end of the Second World War, the British were still 'a people suffering from high prices of the necessaries of life, heavy taxes, an acute housing shortage, threats against profit-earners, and a prevailing feeling of uneasiness'. In fact, although small pockets of a new prosperity were beginning to emerge, Britain was still riven by social and economic inequalities, and the class divide was still flourishing.

The campaign had a particularly nasty edge to it. The *Liverpool Echo* commented:

> One of the most deplorable aspects of the recent Labour Party policy statement is its efforts to make war and peace a party issue. There is no party in Britain, unless it be the Communist, that does not want peace. Most reasonable people will therefore welcome the Archbishop of York's sentiments when he says, 'It would be nothing less than a calamity if, in preparation for a General Election, attempts were made to divide the country into those who want peace and those who want war.' We all want peace. The nation, as the archbishop says, is united in the determination to seek peace and to have partisan charges of warmongering thus condemned. Such charges are false and dangerous.

It was an issue that was soon to be revisited, On 21 September 1951 the *Daily Mirror* said:

> Mr Attlee has shown courage and great good sense. Belaboured by the Tories and undermined by his own splinter group, he has challenged them and the nation to a showdown. The cards are on the table. There are only two: a world economic situation which presents Britain with an unceasing struggle to make a living; an international political situation of cold war, fraught with dangers to world peace. Both situations require firm handling by a strong Government. Only the electors can provide that. What needs to be done can only be done by a government with a decisive majority.

On election day itself Churchill issued a writ for libel against the *Daily Mirror*, claiming 'damages for libel contained on page one of the issue of the *Daily Mirror* newspaper dated October 25, 1951'. The front page in question had shown a drawing of hand holding a cocked revolver with the words 'Big issues of 1951' written on the barrel, and the headline 'Whose Finger?' Then, 'Today your finger is on the trigger. See you defend peace with security and progress with fair shares. Vote for the party you can really trust,' accompanied by photographs of Attlee and Churchill. The *Daily Mirror* had used the phrase 'Whose finger is on the trigger" earlier in the election campaign, and it was inferred by many to be accusing Churchill of warmongering. Two days before election day, in a speech winding up the Tories' campaign, Churchill had vigorously denied the accusations:

> This is a cruel and ungrateful accusation. It is the opposite of the truth. If I remain in public life at this juncture, it is because, rightly or wrongly but sincerely, I believe that I may be able to make an important contribution to the prevention of a third world war, and to bringing nearer that lasting peace settlement which the masses of the people of every race and in every land fervently desire.

Undaunted, the *Daily Mirror* went ahead with its headline. The writ also included the names of the newspaper's chairman, Harry Guy Bartholomew, and its editor, Silvester Bolam, who in 1949 had been sentenced to three months' imprisonment after being found guilty of publishing material that might have prejudiced the trial of John George

Haigh, the serial killer known as 'the Acid Bath Murderer'. Bolam had allowed Haigh, who was eventually hanged for his crimes, to be described as a murderer while trial was still under way.

In May 1952 Churchill would withdraw the writ, accepting an apology from the *Daily Mirror*, which also agreed to pay his legal costs and contribute to a charity. In a statement the newspaper said that it had:

> never intended to suggest that Mr Churchill did not dislike war and the possibility of it as much as the defendants. They had never the slightest intention of making any such imputation and accordingly desire to express their regret that the publication of such statements and pictures might have conveyed this impression.

In the days before the 1951 election, the Tories minds, though, were focused on other matters. In a speech at Tyneside, David Eccles, who had won the Chippenham seat for the Conservatives in a 1943 by-election, and who was 'a rising hope' for the Tories, said:

> Good housekeeping is unspectacular work but, my word, what results you get when mother is an efficient manager. Does not a man like Lord Woolton [Britain's wartime Minister of Food], look to you like the spitting image of a first-rate national housekeeper? Can't you see Lord Woolton, who fed us so well during the war, sending our traders bustling round the world's shops and getting us something good to put on the table? A chop or a steak? My first claim, therefore, is that a Conservative Government will get you better value for the money you are earning now.

The 1951 general election was the first to feature televised party election broadcasts. The first was on 15 October when Viscount Samuel, for the Liberal Party, spoke for fifteen minutes but still ran out of time. He was followed by Sir Hartley Shawcross for the Labour Party and Anthony Eden for the Conservatives, both of whom used an interview format. On election night, the results programme was televised from the Lime Grove Studios in London. Psephologists David Butler and H.G. Nicholas gave their expert analysis from 10.15pm until 4.00am. Live coverage was provided in three locations – Birmingham, Salford, and Fulham – with Richard Dimbleby covering the Salford result.

On election day thick fog blanketed many towns and cities in northern England, but voters were still out early, braving the choking conditions that were exacerbated by the smoke from tens of thousands of domestic coal fires and factory chimneys. Elsewhere the sun shone, but the turnout was slightly down on 1950, at 82.6 per cent.

There was a hiccup at the count for the Cardiff West constituency. When ballot boxes were taken to the College of Technology for counting, one was found to be missing a key for its padlock. The presiding officer responsible had inadvertently dropped it inside the box before securing the self-locking padlock. The returning officer Mr W.G, Hopkins, who was the deputy town clerk, arranged for the lock to be sawn off. To preserve the secrecy of the ballot until the declaration was made by the lord mayor outside the City Hall, the candidates were ushered through an underground passageway to the City Hall, emerging into a boiler house to await the announcement.

It was Labour who polled the highest share of the vote at the 1951 General Election – 13.9 million, 200,000 more than the Conservatives, and higher than their landslide victory of 1945. But it was the Conservatives who took the election with 321 seats to Labour's 295, Churchill returning to the post of prime minister for the first time in peacetime, and at the age of 77. It gave Conservatives an overall majority of seventeen seats. Due to a lack of funds, and the fact that, this time, they could not get insurance against the loss of deposits, the Liberals could field only 109 candidates – compared to the 475 they had put up only twenty months earlier – and took only six seats. In 1950, 319 of them lost their deposits; in 1951, sixty-six did so. One of the biggest election casualties was Lady Megan Lloyd George, the youngest child of Britain's leader in the First World War, David Lloyd George. Lady Meghan, the Deputy Leader of the Liberal Party, lost the Anglesey seat that she had held for twenty-two years.

'Tories by the skin of the skin of their teeth,' was the *Daily Mirror*'s front-page headline. There were those who felt that Attlee had badly timed calling a snap election. Both Herbert Morrison, the Deputy Prime Minister, and Hugh Gaitskell, Stafford Cripps's successor as Chancellor of the Exchequer, doubtful of Labour's chances following its loss of so many seats in 1950, wanted to wait, in the hope that the economy would improve sufficiently for Labour to regain its popularity. Attlee, however, had listened to the concerns of King George VI, who, considering Labour's slim majority, saw the possibility of a change of government while the monarch was out of the country for six months on the planned Commonwealth tour in 1952. Attlee wanted the political uncertainty resolved before the royal tour, albeit in the event the King was too ill to undertake the trip. It was resolved, but not in the way that Attlee wanted.

Winston Churchill, meanwhile, echoed his own words of May 1945, when he told Parliament, 'Let us not forget the toils and efforts that lie ahead.' This time he warned, 'A difficult and a hard time lies before us all ... .'

Chapter Twenty-Two

Britain in Colour

It is the most mentally-mobile exhibition in history – a brilliant conception carefully carried out and constructed

Robert G. Tarran

In the midsummer of 1951 an excited group of some seventy people boarded a train at the Midlands brewing town of Burton upon Trent. Employees of two local newspapers, the *Burton Daily Mail* and the *Burton Observer*, they were bound for London's South Bank and the spectacular Festival of Britain. What an impact it had on them – an apparently just-landed spaceship, a slender cigar-shaped object seemingly hovering in mid-air, the new Royal Festival Hall in all its concrete, steel and glass futuristic glory, and twenty further freestanding pavilions – each designed to reflect all that was good about Britain, its history and its people, and all that it, and they, hoped to achieve.

Intended to revitalise a run-down nation and bring joy to a post-war population, the Festival of Britain ran between May and September 1951. The creation of Clement Attlee's Labour government, it cost the national purse an estimated £12 million (£402 million at today's values). Dissenting voices, particularly from the political right – Winston Churchill, and Lord Beaverbrook among them, claimed that it was a frivolous expense. The government argued that it was vital to the nation's future. Unlike its predecessor and inspiration, the Great Exhibition of 1851, the Festival of Britain would be no world's fair, but a celebration of British achievements in science, technology, design and the arts. And it would encompass the entire country. The Festival of Britain would turn the nation into Festival Britain.

London, of course, was the cultural heart. The main site was south of the Thames, in Lambeth where some twenty-seven acres of disused and bomb-damaged factories and low-value Victorian housing, between Waterloo Bridge and County Hall, stood ripe for redevelopment.

Gerald Barry, former editor of the *News Chronicle*, was appointed director-general of the Festival organising committee. In line with its innovative approach, most of the committee members were forward-thinking individuals like 38-year-old Hugh Casson, its director of architecture, whose young team themed the Festival in an International Modernist style. Gordon Russell who, during the war, had led the design panel for Utility furniture, oversaw how industrial design was to be represented. In charge of captions for the Exhibition was Laurie Lee, yet to write *Cider with Rosie*, who had worked with the GPO and Crown Film Units. Huw Wheldon, later to work as a BBC broadcaster and executive, represented the Arts Council, while Ian Cox, a senior BBC science producer, became director of science and technology. Abram Games, designer of posters for the War Office, and postage stamps for the 1948 London Olympics, won the competition to design the emblem for the Festival with his strikingly modern, yet oh-so-British, red-white-and-blue work that bore the head of Britannia, the points of a compass and patriotic bunting.

Construction began at a pace, while careful attention was paid to landscaping with mature trees, plants and wildflowers, as well as boulders brought in to reflect the natural environment of Britain. Large sculptures by Barbara Hepworth and Henry Moore were carefully placed on the site. Every detail of design was planned with care, right down to each stick of furniture. Indeed, if a single item summed up the ethos, it was Ernest Race's Antelope chair. A modern take on the classic Windsor, it was fashioned from plywood and enamelled steel and was used right across the site. Stylish and comfortable, it was robustly constructed with wide-set legs that made it easily stackable. Drainage holes in the seat made it suitable for indoor and outdoor use. Painted in the Festival colours of yellow, blue, red or grey, and featuring atom-like balled feet, it became an instant classic.

On 3 May the Festival of Britain was officially opened by the King. The following morning the first of eight million visitors entered. From across London and from farther afield they came. Into mainline rail stations, or coach parks at Regent's Park and Clapham Common. By London Underground into Waterloo and Charing Cross, across the Thames via the purpose-built Royal Engineers' Bailey Bridge, using buses, trams, and even boats which docked at Nelson and Rodney piers. Visitors came in their tens of thousands each day – from across the capital and all corners of the country. Some for the day, others for the weekend, on family trips, educational visits and workers' outings – like the 'two bus-loads' who travelled from the Derbyshire coalfield at Denby, the jam makers of T.W. Beach & Sons of Evesham, brewers from Tetley's in Leeds, and members of the Runcorn Mothers' Union.

The first sight for those arriving by boat was the Skylon – a 90-metre (295ft) high, thin metal sculpture that appeared to float 50 metres (164ft) above the ground. In fact, it was a tensegrity structure held vertically in place by three cables at each of its ends, and designed by Hidalgo Moya, Philip Powell and Felix Samuely. The hum it made as wind rushed between its aluminium louvres only increased its otherworldly air. The 100-page official guide, which featured plenty of images, maps and advertisements, many of them in colour, could be purchased for half a crown –2s 6d (12.5p) in the coinage of the day. The most useful section was *The Way To Go Round* which informed visitors, 'The Exhibition, which tells a continuous story, will make most sense if the pavilions are visited in the order shown ... .'

For navigation purposes, the South Bank site was divided into two halves, relating to the flow of the Thames. Upstream (to the west) concerned the 'Land', and Downstream (to the east), the 'People'. The Upstream pavilions began with *The Land of Britain* which promised to enlighten visitors on 'how the natural wealth of the British Isles came into being'; the *Natural Scene* pavilion discussed 'the rich and varied life that inhabits these islands'. Nearby were *The Country* – with its livestock displays of some 5,000 animals, including bulls and ducks as well as agriculture and rural crafts, and *Minerals of the Land, Power & Production, Sea and Ships* and *Transport*.

The spectacular *Dome of Discovery* – at the time the largest dome in the world – was the work of architect Ralph Tubbs and resembled a flying saucer. There visitors learned 'British initiative in exploration and discovery is as strong today as ever it was'. Areas devoted to the *Earth* led to a polar section where demonstrations were held in the special *Polar Theatre*: the *Sea*, the *Sky* – featuring weather forecasting and meteorological research – *Outer Space, The Physical World* and the *Natural World* – which promised to tell the 'secrets of life' – completed the Dome.

The Downstream Circuit began with the *The People of Britain* while the *Lion and the Unicorn* pavilion was concerned with their character. Traditionally, the lion and unicorn represented England and Scotland, but here they stood for 'action' and 'imagination'. Noted the guidebook, 'We are a people of mixed ancestry and now a blend of many different qualities ... compositions of various particular habits, attitudes, instincts, qualities and characteristic moods.'

Sections on *Language* and *Literature* showed both how the English language had grown to be spoken so widely and how works of English literature had contributed to its spread. *Eccentricities and Humours* discussed the British love of the unconventional. *Skill of Hand and Eye* showcased traditional craftsmanship. *Instinct of Liberty* considered the British attitude to freedom. In considering *The Indefinable Character*, the guidebook acknowledged the difficulty of summing up what it meant to be British. It suggested that although visitors might remain 'not much the wiser about British national character, it may console [them] to know that British people are themselves still very much in the dark about it.'

At the *Homes and Gardens* pavilion visitors were given six solutions to the problem of being 'many people on a small island'. *New Schools* pavilion considered education, the *Health* pavilion all things biological and medical and *Sport* looked at active life from favourite sports like association football – named here 'soccer' – rugby, cricket and golf, but also cycling and even sailing. The *Seaside* pavilion displayed what it called the three types of British seaside – the working ports, the tourist resorts and the wild coastline.

There were displays devoted to specific subjects, like *Television* where, for the first time, many people who didn't even own a set could learn about a production control room and the different types of programming broadcast by the BBC. The neighbouring *Telecinema* – 'the first cinema in the world to be designed and built for the showing of both films and television' – featured a futuristic large screen television and introduced Stereophonic Sound.

The *1851 Centenary* pavilion brought back to life the Great Exhibition in model, and 'peep-show' form, a Victorian-era shot tower – survivor of the clearance – had a much-vaunted radio beacon, and the *Design Review*, located under seven arches of the approach to Waterloo Bridge, showcased the very latest in industrial design.

Some thirteen full restaurants, cafes, self-service canteens and bars were spread across the site. Some were operated by large companies like Messrs Charles Hagenback of Wakefield, others by independent franchisees like Susan Throssel who, in normal life, owned a café on the Marina at Bexhill-on-Sea. The concessionaire for both the Rocket and the Turntable Café, J.S. Richards of Southsea, had advertised a vacancy for a bought ledger clerk to work in central London until the end of September.

The only permanent aspect of the South Bank, the Royal Festival Hall, was designed by Leslie Martin, Peter Moro and Robert Matthews of London County Council's architecture department. Described as an 'egg in a box', its layers of foyers, terraces and bars, ensured that even sounds from the nearby railway viaduct did not penetrate to the curving auditorium. Robin Day designed every piece of furniture in the Hall. Audience seats were made from pressed and cast steel elements, materials borrowed from the automotive industry, which proved so comfortable and hard-wearing that they are still in use today. The Hall was modernity at its most beautiful. Journalist Bernard Levin wrote about his first impressions of the building: 'I was overwhelmed by a shock of breathless delight at the originality and beauty of the interior. It felt as if I had been instantly transported far into the future and that I was on another planet.'

The nostalgic fun of the Festival Gardens at Battersea Park was another popular location. Transportation from the South Bank site was easy – either by regular shuttle buses, or river craft –but there is no doubt that its biggest fans were Londoners, who embraced its entertainments and convenience. Much of the funding came from appropriate sponsorships like that of Nestle's who presented the Playland, Schweppes with the Grotto, and Sharp's Kreemy Toffee who supported the Punch and Judy shows. There was a whimsical clock sponsored by Guinness, and beauty manufacturer Leichner hosted the Ladies Powder Room, where advice was free and expert make-up application could be had for a 'small charge'. The Dance Pavilion was, apparently, the largest in Europe. Inside, an oak dance floor – large enough for 400 dancing couples – was surrounded by red carpet. Large sections of paned-glass walls allowed natural light to stream in and at night a large chandelier glittered. At the Festival Children's Zoo, sponsored by London Zoo, 'hundreds of mice perform their antics all day long' in 'Mousetown'. And two bear cubs, named Ruff and Scruff, lion cubs, wallabies, a racoon named Sally, a cage of monkeys, a llama, goats, sheep, rabbits, guinea pigs, hamsters and tropical fish, and even a reindeer named Rudolph, made up the menagerie.

A two-faced stage was built so that performances could take place in the open air or, in the event of rain, under cover. The Riverside Theatre was built to resemble a small Victorian auditorium complete with stalls, promenade circle and a small gallery. It held six shows a day – mornings devoted to vintage cinema, and the evenings to variety theatre, often in the form of *Mr Sachs's Song Saloon* featuring Leonard Sachs and his recreations of traditional music hall, later so familiar to television viewers of the *Good Old Days*.

The Far Tottering and Oyster Creek Branch Railway proved one of the most popular elements, particularly with children. Known almost universally as the 'Emmet Railway', it was billed as 'Britain's most eccentric'. Designed by cartoonist, and later sculptor of kinetic art, Rowland Emmet, it eventually carried a remarkable number of two million passengers. Emmet oversaw the design and construction of every quirky element, from stations and signals to tunnels and trains. Three engines were each designed to appear as if made from an old vehicle. Passengers, seated in wagons three or four abreast, squealed with delight as they travelled between stations. Others preferred the thrill of the American fairground rides. Three Abreast Gallopers was a traditional carousel; the Lighthouse Clip, a huge helter-skelter; and the Leaping Lena, a circular ride with jeep-like 'cars' that bumped up and down eccentrically. There was the Rotor – a German-designed cylinder that spun so fast that, as the floor retracted, riders remained airborne, pressed back by centrifugal force into the wall of the cylinder. Many a female rider regretted her wardrobe decision as she battled to keep her rising skirt in place. The 'star' ride was the wooden roller-coaster known as the Big Dipper. According to a newsreel, riders could expect to complete the '55-mile-an-hour journey with your hearts in your mouth and your stomach trying to catch up'.

One of the least recognised, but undoubtedly most admirable, components of the Festival of Britain was the Live Architecture Exhibition in Poplar, where the new Lansbury Estate showed a modern way of town planning that concentrated on community and human needs. Centred on Chrisp Street Market – the first purpose-built pedestrianised shopping area in Britain – it featured low-rise flats and maisonettes that were blessed with indoor bathrooms and plenty of outside space. Visitors could tour examples of the housing, walk around several of the streets, examine a small school and visit two restored churches. Priority for the new homes was given to existing Poplar residents and although only ten per cent of the number of anticipated visitors came to the area, the Lansbury Estate has proved the most long-lasting element of the entire Festival.

Some of those living outside London found the cost of visiting prohibitive. The *Formby Times* of 24 February had reported that the County Secondary School was re-thinking plans to take its pupils due to the 'divergent arrangements of the Festival officials and the British Railways'. Schoolmaster, and councillor, Edwin M. Melrose, complained:

> The railway authorities say they cannot let us leave Formby before 10 am unless we pay full fare. If we go at 10 o'clock it means we are not likely to reach the Festival site before 3 pm. The Festival ruling is that no organised parties are allowed in at the cheap rates after 3 o'clock. I have written, but neither ... will budge from their rulings.

Formby Women's Conservatives group had already cancelled after not enough members wanted to travel to persuade British Railways to lay on a special train.

For those unwilling, or unable, to travel to the capital, many aspects of the Festival travelled to them. The former Royal Navy ship *Campania* was refitted to house the Sea Travelling Exhibition and travelled the coast, docking at Southampton, Dundee, Newcastle, Hull, Plymouth, Bristol, Cardiff, Belfast, Birkenhead and Glasgow. The Land Travelling Exhibition – at the time the biggest transportable exhibition ever created – ferried its 5,000 exhibits to four cities – Manchester, Leeds, Birmingham and Nottingham. And several major static exhibitions were staged across the nation, at places like Belfast, Stratford, Llangollen, Aberdeen, Oxford and York.

Then there were the locally organised events in thousands of communities. One of the most ambitious took place in Clitheroe where 150 cast members performed Edward German's comic opera *Merrie England* in the grounds of the ruined Clitheroe Castle for 3,000 spectators. Produced by Laurence Hardy, a stalwart of local carnivals, it was quite the spectacular. Weekly rehearsal schedules had been published in the *Clitheroe Advertiser and Times*.

With the bandstand stage 'transformed into a perfect setting by scenery which blends delightfully with the natural surroundings' the local newspaper called it 'one of the most memorable undertakings of its type in the history of the town'.

The weather was not so easily organised. Less than an hour before curtain-up, a chilly wind kicked up and rain began to pour. 'Even the most optimistic heart must have expected the performance would be called off. Water cascaded from the roof of the stage to transform the sylvan setting into a bedraggled cavern of gloom,' the paper noted.

Yet, just minutes later,

> A silver-lining edged the clouds and when, five minutes later, the first patches of blue sky came into view the crowds descended upon the Castle. The turnstiles began their merry clatter, and on the stage, workmen brushed and mopped ... at 2.30 precisely, when the first strains of Edward German's lovely music echoed through the Castle. Nature's own overture had come only just in time.

The performance was declared a triumph and received a standing ovation at its conclusion.

Another community that embraced the Festival was Eardisland in Herefordshire. In late July, Eardisland School celebrated the end of the academic year with a Festival of Britain theme over two days. On the first day, parents and friends were treated to a show performed by the children. Poems and nursery rhymes were recited, children's tunes were played and folk songs sung. On the second day there was an exhibition of children's work on different themes including 'places we have visited shown on a map with labels bearing short descriptions' and even 'history of a loaf'.

Over in the Lincolnshire fenland town of Boston, residents ran their own mini-Festival in June and July. There were many and varied events, most of which were attended by the Festival Queen, who had been crowned at the Festival Pageant. The Boston Aero Club held a Festival Air Display to which attendees were taken by special buses of the Lincolnshire Road Car Company. Boston Parish Church of St Botolph's, better known as 'Boston Stump', played host to Mr Stanley Hildebrand's production of T.S. Eliot's *Murder in the Cathedral*, and there was even a Festival Regatta.

The Oxfordshire town of Banbury really went to town. The theatrical performances by groups like the Banbury Cross Players, the King's Sutton Women's Institute Drama Group, and the Charlton, Adderbury and Old Banburians Dramatic Societies were just part of a busy arts programme that also included dances, competitions and art exhibitions. An 'Old Time' cricket match, an athletics meeting, a swimming gala, a horse fair, the British Legion rally and the Sweet Pea Society's annual exhibition were held alongside more unusual events like the Elocution and Miming Festival. In July the National Union of Railwaymen's Women's Guild hosted Miss Betty E. Chester, the Railway Queen who was received at the railway station by the stationmaster, followed by a 'welcome at Banbury Cross by a lady on a white horse' and by the mayor at the town hall.

Events took many forms. In Lancashire the *Barnoldswick and Earby Times* carried advertisements for a Lancashire Health Services Exhibition at the Baptist School in Nelson. Perhaps aware that it was not a natural crowd-puller, organisers offered free admission, 'valuable prizes, competitions, and films'. In Burnley an Ideal Home and Trades Exhibition was held at the Mechanics' Institute, promising 'everything for the homeowner' including fashion parades and performances from Jack Wafer, 'the world-famous hypnotist'. In Tynemouth there was a Festival of Britain flower show. The *Ripley and Heanor News* in Derbyshire reported on a Festival of Britain football tournament run by the local branch of the British Legion where local schools, from surrounding communities like Codnor, Marlpool, Langley Mill and Smalley competed for the William Gregg VC Trophy.

It would, however, be wrong to suggest the Festival of Britain was universally embraced. In East Anglia, as early as January, there had been disquiet. H.S. Houlsham, chairman of Harleston Parish Council, had asked whether there would be any benefit to the nation at large, pointing out, 'Quite a lot of money is being spent south of the Thames. Some of the money would be better spent providing houses for the people.' He accepted tourists might be drawn to places like Norwich but doubted that they would come to their neck of the woods. A.K.J. Wharton did think it worth making some effort but agreed that 'there was little to rejoice about', and that the town should certainly not make 'a binge' of it.

Robert Saunders thought the community should do something to benefit local children. 'Must they go to Norwich to see other people enjoying themselves?', he asked.

The people of Cockermouth in Cumberland seemed plainly disinterested. 'Public apathy and poor attendance' led to the resolution: 'Owing to lack of support, no further action to be taken.'

Even a full month into the Festival, some communities remained unhappy. Owners of hotels and boarding houses in Morecambe complained that holiday bookings in the town had reduced dramatically. They believed that the heavy promotion of the Festival of Britain, particularly its London-based attractions, was negatively affecting interest in seaside holidays. Mrs F. Newton, a former vice-president of the local Association of Hotel and Boarding Establishments, said: 'We are becoming too London-minded. The Festival of Britain can become the "Chaos of Britain" because it strikes of the life blood of many of us.'

For most, though, the Festival was an entirely positive experience with which businesses strove to achieve a connection, however minor. Businesses like Chas Wilson, 'television, radio and amplifier specialist', which ran advertisements in the *Luton Pictorial* for its latest in-stock item, the Ambassador Television, which, it noted, had been 'chosen for the Festival of Britain'.

The Festival of Britain came to an official end on 30 September 1951, with a thanksgiving service held at the Royal Festival Hall, although several elements, including the Battersea Pleasure Gardens, remained open a little longer. The Festival infrastructure had not been designed to last beyond the five months of the exhibition. Indeed, when the October general election returned the Conservatives, that put paid to any ideas of extending it. Churchill's first act as prime minister was to order the immediate demolition of most of the South Bank site. Down came the pavilions and walkways, the *Dome of Discovery* and the Skylon, pieces of which were fashioned into souvenir paper knives. But, in many ways, it had served its purpose. Defunct industrial sites and poor-quality housing had been cleared. Local cultural scenes had been rejuvenated. And an estimated one-third of the population had attended a Festival event. The national spirit had certainly been revived. As writer Harry Hopkins later noted, Festival Style 'caught hold quickly and spread first across London and then across England ... . In an island hitherto largely given up to gravy browns and dull greens, [it] boldly espoused strong primary colours'.

In early 1951, Gerald Barry had promised that the Festival of Britain would 'afford us all the opportunity ... for some harmless jollification'. He said, 'After more than a decade of voluntarily imposed austerity, we deserve it, and it will do us good.' And so it proved. Modern Britain had begun.

Chapter Twenty-Three

Joyous Event ... Greatest Sorrow

This is a happy day ... but it is also one that brings serious thoughts, thoughts of life looming ahead with all its challenges ...
Princess Elizabeth

At half-past ten on the morning of Thursday 20 November 1947, 25-year-old Dorothy Ormston made the short walk up the aisle of Jesmond Parish Church on the arm of her father. Waiting at the altar was John McCabe, an eleven-year veteran of the Royal Navy.

As the couple married in a suburb of Newcastle upon Tyne, some 300 miles away, in Central London, another bride walked up an altogether longer aisle to marry her naval hero sweetheart. The McCabes took time out of their celebrations to send the other newly-weds a congratulatory telegram. But the two couples' futures were certain to be markedly different.

While family and friends watched on as Dorothy and John said their vows, a worldwide radio audience of 200 million listened in as 21-year-old Princess Elizabeth married the newly titled Duke of Edinburgh at Westminster Abbey. It was the first truly global royal event, and it came at the end of a busy year for the Princess.

In February, she had joined her parents and sister on a three-month royal tour of South Africa, Southern Rhodesia, Swaziland, Basutoland and the Bechuanaland Protectorate. The first overseas tour since before the war, it was designed to reinforce the links between Britain and her far-flung dominions. It mattered little that domestic newspapers carried only minimal coverage of the royal visit. It mattered a great deal that widespread coverage was given to the radio broadcast given by Princess Elizabeth from Cape Town on her 21st birthday.

The speech was written by Dermot Morrah, a journalist sent to cover the tour for *The Times*. The King's private secretary, Sir Alan Lascelles, told Morrah that his words had moved the Princess to tears, perfectly capturing the sense of duty she wished to convey. It remains one of the most quoted speeches of the twentieth century. Speaking to 'all the people of the British Commonwealth and Empire, wherever they live, whatever race they come from, and whatever language they speak', she told them, 'This is a happy day ... but it is also one that brings serious thoughts, thoughts of life looming ahead with all its challenges and with all its opportunity.'

She added, 'I am 6,000 miles from the country where I was born. But I am certainly not 6,000 miles from home ... my parents, my sister and I have been ... made to feel that we are just as much at home here.'

She then spoke to her own generation:

> If we all go forward together with an unwavering faith, a high courage, and a quiet heart, we shall be able to make of this ancient commonwealth, which we all love so dearly, an even grander thing – more free, more prosperous, more happy and a more powerful influence for good in the world – than it has been in the greatest days of our forefathers.

And then she made a promise:

> Through the inventions of science I can ... make my solemn act of dedication with a whole Empire listening ... I declare before you all that my whole life whether it be long or short shall be devoted to your service and the service of our great imperial family to which we all belong ... God help me to make good my vow, and God bless all of you who are willing to share in it.

What she did not reveal, was that she was about to marry.

Princess Elizabeth and Prince Philip of Greece and Denmark first met as children, but their friendship had begun in the summer of 1939, when the dashing 18-year-old naval cadet had been chosen to keep 13-year-old Elizabeth, and her sister, company while their parents visited the Royal Naval College. After war broke out, with Prince Philip serving in the Royal Navy, the pair began writing to one another and a romance gently developed. They became engaged in 1946 but her father requested that they not make it public until after Elizabeth's coming of age. There had been 'talk' about the relationship – what the *Faversham Advertiser* called 'speculations and rumours' although, by modern standards, press coverage was very restrained. There were just enough clues for readers to understand that their princess was involved in a serious romance. By September, when Philip joined the Royal Family at Balmoral, some newspapers declared that an engagement between the two was 'impending'. On behalf of Buckingham Palace, Lascelles gave an unequivocal denial: 'Princess Elizabeth is not engaged to be married. The report is incorrect.'

On 18 September, *The Sketch* featured a photograph of the 'Greek Sailor Prince' with a brief biography. Then, while the Royal Family were in Southern Africa, Philip was granted British naturalisation, relinquished his Greek titles, and took the surname 'Mountbatten'. It seemed only a matter of time before an announcement was made. It came, via a court circular, just after midnight on 10 July 1947, timed so that all corners of the Commonwealth could be informed at once:

> It is with the greatest pleasure that the King and Queen announce the betrothal of their dearly beloved daughter, the Princess Elizabeth, to Lieutenant Philip Mountbatten, RN, son of the late Prince Andrew of Greece and Princess Andrew (Princess Alice of Battenburg), to which union the King has gladly given his consent.

British newspapers covered every aspect of the forthcoming nuptials, from Philip's intention to remain in the Royal Navy, to the platinum and diamond engagement ring made from stones taken from a tiara belonging to Philip's mother.

The Kirriemuir Free Press & Angus Advertiser, which covered the area of the Queen's ancestral home concentrated on local connections: 'The betrothal of Princess Elizabeth to Lieutenant Philip Mountbatten will be of considerable interest to everyone in Angus and Glamis in particular. The Princess was well known and extremely popular in the county which she visited regularly in her early childhood during holidays at Glamis.'

In the four months between engagement and wedding, British newspaper readers were treated to all manner of quirky stories, like the one that appeared in the *Sunday Post* in early November. It reported that 23-year-old Isabel Lamont of Stirling was such a lookalike for the princess that people often stopped and stared at her in the street. 'Almost every day strangers stop her just to remark on the likeness.' Just like Princess Elizabeth, Miss Lamont had, until recently, served in the Auxiliary

Territorial Service (ATS) and her colleagues had nicknamed her 'Our Princess'. Miss Lamont told the newspaper, 'I saw the Princess at Stirling Castle when she received the freedom of Stirling and I'm proud to be thought like her.'

Royal wedding or not, in common with every young couple planning their wedding day in those early post-war years, Elizabeth and Philip were subject to certain restrictions and Buckingham Palace had to return hundreds of donated clothing coupons, because to use them would have been illegal.

Winston Churchill had declared, 'Millions will welcome this joyous event as a flash of colour on the hard road we have to travel.'

The *Buckingham Advertiser* predicted that, rather than decked out in austerity-friendly khaki, 'London will, after all, go gay for the Royal Wedding', describing how the Quartermaster General at the War Office was examining stores so that members of the Household Cavalry could wear 'full blue and scarlet dress, plumed helmets, gleaming breastplates, swords and white pantaloons'. In addition, the Fuel Ministry had decided that Buckingham Palace could be 'dim-lit'. The possibility of the rest of austerity Britain remaining grey and dull abided. J.J. White, the mayor of Ramsgate, wrote to the *Thanet Advertiser & Echo* to request that local businesses 'be-flag their premises for that day'.

On the day itself, according to the *Daily Mail*, 'The people thronged to the route by train, by bus, by car, on foot. They edged and manoeuvred their way to any and every vantage point, sometimes to be summoned away from this tree, that railing, the other corner by the ubiquitous police.'

Some 6,750 police officers, reinforced by 300 City of London constables, 600 specials and 450 plain-clothes officers kept the streets of the capital safe. Among the crowds were twenty-nine members of North Shields Watch Ashore, an organisation that provided support and friendship to partners and families of Merchant Navy personnel. Its members had travelled to London three days earlier, and would return, as the London *Evening News* would report, late on Friday, 'tired, but full of excitement'.

That morning, Prince Philip waited at the Abbey, as two large blue Daimlers containing eight bridesmaids and two pages, among them Princesses Margaret and Alexandra, and Princes William of Gloucester and Michael of Kent. They were followed by the Household Cavalry and, finally, by the Princess herself, accompanied by her father. According to the *Daily Mail*, 'Joy radiated out of the slim figure, white-dressed, white-veiled, in its fairy coach.'

The Princess, whose Norman Hartnell dress was made from duchesse satin from Dunfermline, carried a bouquet of white orchids and a sprig of myrtle taken from a bush grown from Queen Victoria's own bouquet. With the bride inside the ancient church, the streets fell quiet as those unable to follow the service on the BBC waited. Then came a celebratory peal, and the newly-weds emerged from the Abbey, and a colourful, joyful and noisy procession took them back to Buckingham Palace.

There the crowds gathered outside, looking up impatiently to the balcony. They did not shout for the King, but for the bride, and, according to the *Daily Mail*, it was 'urgent, imperative, irresistible, the sound beat against the front of the palace like a great wind ... . But even when they broke the bounds and the cordons, this crowd was a British crowd: good-humoured, considerate of humanity and human decency, even in its headlong, instinctive rush.'

Then 'Naval officer and Princess, Duke and Duchess, future Queen, and Consort, stood together on the balcony. The King, the Queen, Princess Margaret, the other bridesmaids, the majestic figure of Queen Mary — all appeared. But it was only the two that caught the eye and, with it, the heart of that mass of happy humanity.'

When it came to announcing pregnancies, the royals did things a little differently from the rest of Britain. The first hint the British public had that a new prince or princess was due came on 5 June 1948 when Buckingham Palace issued a simple statement: 'Her Royal Highness, The Princess Elizabeth, Duchess of Edinburgh, will undertake no public engagements after the end of June.' Just in case, the message had been too subtle for its readers, the *Londonderry Sentinel* noted that 'royal births in recent years have been preceded by announcements couched in similar terms'. The newspaper helpfully suggested that 'the event will probably take place in the second half of October'.

As the supposed date grew nearer, and eventually passed, people began to gather outside Buckingham Palace. When, in mid-November, it was announced that, instead of their usual practice of spending the weekend at Windsor, the King and Queen would remain in central London, the crowd grew to more than 1,000. As dusk fell, the onlookers left for home and so, on the evening of 13 November, as the Princess's gynaecologist,

Sir William Gillatt arrived at the Palace, only 100 hardy souls were there to see him. The following morning the *Sunday Dispatch* reported that the physician had elected to remain at the Palace overnight. Whilst there was no question of a respectable newspaper declaring that Elizabeth was in labour, the *Sunday Post* alerted readers that 'today, or tomorrow are the days on which the birth is expected'. They also noted the significance that the Home Secretary, Chuter Ede, had 'left a list of his movements with the Court Post Office, so as to be available at any time for the telephone call which will inform him of the royal birth'.

It was his duty to announce the news by having a bulletin fixed to the door of the Home Office. It was a small price to pay for the politician – this royal baby would be the first born without the presence of a serving Home Secretary in the delivery room.

While the nation waited, the *Sunday Pictorial* published an article in which its readers had provided their own choices for the new prince or princess. Elizabeth was the most popular choice for a girl, followed by Mary. Philip was the favourite boys' name, with George in second place. Among less popular suggestions were Anne and Andrew, something for the royal couple to keep in mind, perhaps?

For now, broadcasters, bellringers and the nation at large waited. Finally, late on the evening of 14 November, newsreader John Snagge told the nation:

> This is the BBC Home Service. It has just been announced from Buckingham Palace that Her Royal Highness Princess Elizabeth, the Duchess of Edinburgh, was safely delivered of a prince at 9.14pm, and that her Royal Highness and her son are both doing well.
>
> Listeners will want to offer their royal congratulations to Princess Elizabeth and the Royal Family on this happy occasion. We play the *National Anthem* in honour of the prince.

Snagge did not go into details. The labour had lasted thirty hours and the delivery had been by caesarean section. The *Liverpool Echo* noted, 'This weight [7lb 6oz] is very nearly the ideal which modern gynaecologists hope for in the case of boy babies.'

It would be almost a month before the baby's name – Charles Philip Arthur George – would be announced. In the meantime, the feeling of national joy came to a sudden end when it was announced that, due to the ill-health of the King, the royal tour of Australia and New Zealand, which had been scheduled for early 1949, had been indefinitely postponed. Even as the crowds continued to gather outside the Palace for baby news, a team of five doctors had been treating their ailing monarch for a 'defective blood supply to the right foot' and had decided that 'it would be hazardous for his majesty to embark upon a long journey which might delay his recovery, and which might involve serious risk to a limb'.

As the *Belfast Telegraph* said:

> The people have become so used to the regular comings and goings of the Royal Family that the announcement that His Majesty will carry out no public engagements for six months, or even more, is a severe shock and is bound to cause widespread concern ... it is a marvellous thing how four simple words 'the King is ill' can move millions to real concern.

It was a reminder that George VI, who had restored a sense of calm after the abdication of his brother, Edward VIII, and guided them through the war with such dignity, was just as vulnerable to human physical frailty as were they.

When Elizabeth and Philip's second child, Princess Anne, came into the world, on 15 August 1950, there was almost as much excitement. Police had to hold back large crowds that had gathered outside Clarence House, where the young family were living while renovations took place at Buckingham Palace. Spectators at the Test Match between England and the West Indies at The Oval were told, through the loudspeakers, 'Ladies and gentlemen, we have a new baby princess.'

When the King attended Princess Anne's christening that autumn, he appeared in reasonable health once more. But there would be more concerning news. Like many of his people, the king was a lifelong heavy smoker, and, in September 1951, he underwent the removal of his left lung for what was officially called 'structural abnormalities', in fact a form of lung cancer. The public were kept up to date with his progress with bulletins such as 'the King has gained strength during the day'. Again, his recovery was slow, but steady, and seemed to be continuing. In late January 1952, on the eve of Princess Elizabeth and the Duke of Edinburgh's departure for a tour of Africa, the King joined his family in the royal box at the Theatre Royal, Drury Lane, to see Mary Martin in *South Pacific*. It was his first visit to the theatre since his operation, and an audience of almost 3,000 gave him a standing ovation of several minutes as he arrived. It was a jolly occasion that the King clearly enjoyed. According to the *Northern Whig*, he was seen 'applauding generously, and periodically rocking backwards and forwards with laughter'. A member of theatre staff told newspapers, 'I have never seen a man enjoy it more.'

The following day the King stood on a bleakly cold tarmac of London Airport to wave off Philip and Elizabeth, insisting on waiting until the plane disappeared into the distance. All had seemed well.

One week later, on Tuesday 6 February 1952, George VI's valet, James MacDonald, tapped on the King's Sandringham bedroom door, carrying his morning cup of tea. Receiving no response, he let himself in and found the King apparently asleep. 'He called softly to his master', the *Daily Mirror* reported. There was no response. The alarm was raised, officials summoned, and the Queen and Princess Margaret awoken. When it became clear there was nothing, medically speaking, to be done, the wider family were informed, and the wheels set in motion for the well-rehearsed plan – codenamed 'Hyde Park Corner' – of informing the nation.

At 11.15 that morning, as classes of seven- and eight-year-olds across Britain were sitting cross-legged on the floor enjoying their special schools programme of *Music and Movement*, the broadcast was interrupted by the voice of newsreader John Snagge.

'This is London,' he began. 'It is with the greatest sorrow that we make the following announcement: It was announced from Sandringham at 10.45 today, February 6, 1952, that the King, who retired to rest last night in his usual health, passed peacefully away in his sleep earlier this morning.' The BBC then closed down its usual programming for the remainder of the day, broadcasting only news bulletins and summaries.

Six thousand miles away, Princess Elizabeth, had yet to learn of her father's death. A telegram sent to Government House in Nairobi could not be decoded. At lunchtime the princess's secretary, Martin Charteris, was called by a newspaper editor enquiring whether the news coming through on the teleprinter wires was true. Once confirmation had come, Charteris told the Duke of Edinburgh who, in turn, informed his young wife that she was now Queen and head of the Commonwealth. Plans were made to return as soon as possible.

The following morning, a grieving nation turned to front pages for the latest news. The *Daily Mirror* informed readers: 'In a dramatic homeward dash to her sorrowing people, Queen Elizabeth the Second – as she was proclaimed yesterday – was last night flying through the darkness with her consort.'

At London Airport the new queen was met by her uncle, the Duke of Gloucester, the Lord Chancellor, Prime Minister Winston Churchill, Leader of the Opposition Clement Attlee, Anthony Eden, and Lord Woolton. *British Pathe News* told viewers, 'No queen had ever such counsellors so pre-determined to give of their best, no queen had ever such a people so devoted.'

George VI's body lay in state at Westminster Hall. Over the next few days, more than 300,000 people, waited in a queue, six deep, stretching along the banks of the Thames, in two loops, between Lambeth and Westminster Bridges.

Richard Dimbleby's BBC radio commentary set the scene for those unable to attend:

> How real the tears of those who pass by and see it, and come out again, as they do at this moment in unbroken stream, to the cold, dark night, and a little privacy for their thoughts ... . Never safer, better guarded, lay a sleeping king than this, with a golden candlelight to warm his resting place, and the muffled footsteps of his devoted subjects to keep him company.

On the morning of the funeral the King's coffin was taken the one mile to Paddington Station and then to St George's Chapel at Windsor Castle. More than a hundred London streets were closed to traffic. The processional route was lined with troops and, standing behind them, several rows deep, were everyday Britons, many of whom had slept out on the streets to ensure their place. Flags flew at half-mast, windows were draped in purple and Big Ben tolled fifty-six times – one for each year of the king's life. In a carriage, came the Queen, the Queen Mother, Princess Margaret and the Princess Royal. From the window of Marlborough House, the frail Queen Mary watched her son's coffin pass by. Behind them walked the Duke of Edinburgh with other royal dukes, Windsor, Gloucester and Kent. followed by seven reigning sovereigns, three heads of state, three crown princes and seven foreign princes.

In towns and villages across Britain, church services were held to coincide with the funeral, a two-minute silence was observed and dozens of local newspapers remembered their king. The *Lynn News & Advertiser*, whose readers included Sandringham residents, described the late king as 'a man of Norfolk ... the gentleman we knew'.

Yet, even as the nation mourned, it also began to look forward to a coronation and what was proclaimed a 'new Elizabethan Age'.

Chapter Twenty-Four

A Crowning Glory

In the Mall several of the crowd's cheerleaders called for three cheers for the British Everest Expedition and the general comment was, 'What a Coronation Day gift for the Queen'.

Yorkshire Post

Arm-in-hand, hand-in-hand, they poured off buses, trains, the Underground. Some wore earmuffs like Everest conquerors. Some had Coronation hair ribbons and vast bow ties which almost engulfed their wearers. There were two yellow-turbaned Indians from Camden Town, and, among the Wolf Cubs and Sea Cadets, a sprinkling of Cinema Club Minors darted about like rainbow fish in their paper jockey caps of red, white, and blue.

So Laurence Thompson of the *News Chronicle* described the 'invasion of the Embankment by 33,000 schoolchildren from London and the Home Counties' on the morning of 2 June 1953. It began just after 6.00am 'with a precision that the Earl Marshal would have envied'. Thompson felt sympathy for the thousands of parents who had their offspring ready and for the 600 volunteer teacher stewards who had undertaken to marshal the children inside ninety minutes. As London's clocks struck seven, the Thames steamer *Hurlingham*, 'plastic pennons flying, carrying 235 children from the Dockland, touched at Westminster Pier. Four minutes later, she was empty, her passengers trotting obediently to their places'.

Then the processions began: 'The Lord Mayor's coach was favourite until that gartered knight who is forever Winnie, until the Mounties, until the superb lancers riding like centaurs behind the Pakistani Prime Minister, until the inevitable blushing trooper of the Household Cavalry whose mount insisted on traversing the route backwards until …'

Thompson's golden prose – he was both distinguished journalist and acclaimed author – continued to describe the pageantry and tried to decide who was favourite. The Queen Mother and Princess Margaret received a special cheer, as did the mounted air marshals, 'clearly more used to jet planes than that dangerous beast, the horse'. The Yeoman of the Guard, 'even in the age of Spacemen, brought the house down'.

Then came the Queen herself, in her golden coach: 'There was a moment's hushed silence ahead of her, like the wall of air pushed forward by a supersonic plane, followed by crash after crash of cheering.'

The American columnist, Earl Wilson, said that 'it was just like watching a football game' as he and his wife had their umbrellas up and down half a dozen times while they waited for the Queen to leave for Westminster Abbey. For all the splendour on display, however, it was 'a plumpish red-haired girl in her twenties' who got his cheers. She climbed up a gate and then shinned up a 20-foot-high stone lamppost where she 'precariously succeeded in eluding a bobby who went up after her'. Later, as they walked through a wet Hyde Park to their flat in Berkeley Square, the Wilsons were 'amazed to see people sleeping on sidewalks, face up to the rain, though it was midday'. In a pub on Down Street a man told them that he had seen four people collapse on one corner of Piccadilly. 'He, himself, wasn't taking any chances on that happening to him. He had left some other men in charge of his spot on the pavement where he was waiting and was getting strength and fortitude with a few drinks there at the bar.'

George H. Johnston of the *Sydney Sun* was prepared to bet that the 3 million Australians who would, in the next few weeks, see the colour-film of Queen Elizabeth's crowning, would not really believe it all:

> They will blame the shortcomings of colour photography and the ineradicable memory of all those Cecil B. de Mille epics for the apparent major weakness of the film – its overwhelming improbability. But the film cannot possibly exaggerate. For man has not yet perfected a technique capable of coping with the rich improbable dreamlike splendour.

On the eve of the Coronation of Queen Elizabeth II there was also news of the triumphant ending of a great adventure story. New Zealander Edmund Hillary and Sherpa Tenzing Norgay of Nepal had become the first people to stand atop the world's tallest mountain, Mount Everest standing more than 29,000 feet high. The *Daily Herald* described it as a feat of 'superb bravery, endurance and skill' which 'epitomised not only the effort of hundreds who contributed to their ascent, but the triumphant spirit of the entire Commonwealth in this splendid hour'.

The *Daily Herald* took the view that as Mount Everest stood partly in Nepal, partly in Tibet, 'thus it is nobody's national property'. It had been named by the British after Sir George Everest, the surveyor-general of India when, in 1832, it was first discovered by triangulation to be the world's highest mountain. Locals called it 'Chomolungma', which means 'Goddess Mother of the Snow'. The newspaper suggested that 'because of the happy timing of its conquest, it might now with propriety be renamed Mount Elizabeth'. Because three reconnaissances involving the exploration of hundreds of miles of unknown territory – and included that of 1951 which pioneered the eventual route to the top – were all British affairs, the *Daily Herald* suggested that 'no race has a better claim to write into the history books a wonderful success story under the chapter heading of Mount Elizabeth'. The paper thought that 'all the Western world ... would surely applaud such a change'.

In 1953, never mind renaming Mount Everest, many Britons, were more interested in the news that, on 27 July, a final agreement to end combat was made at Panmunjom on the 38th parallel. The Korean War was finally over. Well, if not officially over – because no formal treaty has ever been signed – at least halted by the armistice. South Korea objected to the continued division of Korea and did not sign a formal peace treaty and so the war never technically ended, but the fighting that had cost more than 1,000 British lives did.

One year later Britain celebrated the end of fourteen years of food rationing. Restrictions had gradually been lifted, starting with flour on 25 July 1948, followed by clothes on 15 March 1949. On 19 May 1950 rationing ended for canned and dried fruit, chocolate biscuits, treacle, syrup, jellies and mincemeat. Petrol rationing ended in May 1950 and soap came off ration in September 1950. In 1953 sales of sugar were off ration and in May 1954, butter rationing ended. Now, on 4 July 1954, the final restrictions – on the sale of meat and bacon – were lifted.

A new Queen, our boys coming home from Korea, and now as much food as you could afford – Britain's grey post-war years were surely finally over.

Acknowledgements

Sources consulted for this book were HistoricEngland.org; *Forced Immigration Review* (article by Agata Blaszcyk); the following newspapers:

Banbury Guardian
Birmingham Daily Gazette
Birmingham Daily Post
Bedfordshire Times and Independent
Belfast Telegraph
Bellshill Speaker
Bradford Observer
British Medical Journal
Broughty Ferry Guide and Carnoustie Gazette
Cape Times
Cheltenham Chronicle and Gloucestershire Graphic
Coventry Evening Telegraph
Daily Express
Daily Herald
Daily Mail
Daily Mirror
Daily Sketch
Daily Worker
Derby Evening Telegraph
Detroit Free Press
Economist
Evening News (London)
Glamorgan Advertiser
Gloucestershire Echo
Hull Daily Mail
Liverpool Echo
London Gazette
Londonderry Sentinel
Luton Pictorial
Lynn News & Advertiser
Manchester Guardian

Melton Mowbray Times
Motherwell Times
New York Daily
New York Times
News Chronicle
Northern Daily Mail
Northern Whig
Nottingham Evening Post
Official Report of the Organising Committee for the XIV Olympiad
Orzel Bialy
Picture Post
Pontypridd Observer
Portsmouth Evening News
Radio Times
Rochdale Observer
Sidney Morning Herald
Staffordshire Sentinel
Stars and Stripes
Straits Times
Sunday Pictorial
Sunderland Echo and Shipping Gazette
Sussex Agricultural Express
The Daily Gleaner
The People
The Spectator
Washington Evening Star
Washington Post
Yorkshire Post

Index

Adam, Adjutant-General Sir Ronald, 42-43
Agar, Lieutenant Commander Herbert, 38
Alanbrooke, Viscount, 4
Alexander, Viscount, 4
Amery, John, xi
Amery, Leo, x, xi, xii
Amies, Hardy, 133
Amnine, Michael, 34-36
Ardagh, Robin, 130
Attlee, Clement, viii, ix, x, 4, 12, 19, 44, 46, 52, 61, 72, 150, 152-153, 155-157, 176
Attlee, Tom, ix
Attwood, Leading Aircraftman Arthur, 46
Austin, Herschel, 78

Baker White, Major John, xv, xvi
Balcon, Michael, 127-128
Barker, Geoffrey, 14
Barlow, Sir Anderson, 30
Barratt, Detective Superintendent Tom, 92
Barry, Gerald, 158, 167
Bartholomew, Harry Guy, 153
Beales, W.L.B., 50
Beaverbrook, Lord, 157
Brees, Pauline, 97
Beckwith, Reginald, 3
Bennett, Air Vice-Marshall Donald, 51
Bentley, Nicolas, 139
Bellinger, Frederick, 47, 49
Bernhardt, Sarah, viii

Betjeman, John, 139
Bevan, Aneurin, 58-59, 60-61, 77, 150
Beveridge, William, viii, 57
Bevin, Ernest, 80, 150-151
Birch, Richard, 130
Blankers-Koen, Fanny, 121
Blankers-Koen, Jan, 121
Bligh, Jasmine, 123, 126
Blunt, Anthony, 149
Bolam, Silvester, 153-154
Bonn, Issy, 125
Booth, David, 139
Bose, Amalendu, 115
Bossom Alfred, 29
Bowden, Benjamin, 141
Bracken, Brendan, x, xi
Braddock, Bessie, 22
Bradman, Don, 118
Brice, Leading Aircraftman Dennis George, 98
Brough, Peter, 125
Bruh, Anne, 131
Bruh, Max, 131
Burgess, Guy, 144-149
Burgess. Major John, 39
Burke, Anthony, 14
Burghley, Lord, 120
Butler, David, 154
Butler, Robert Austin ('Rab'), 63
Butlin, Billy, 120, 129
Byrne Christopher, 14

Callaghan, James, xii
Campbell, Sir Edward, xii
Campbell, John J., 80

Capper, Jannet Maud, 102
Carr, Air Vice Marshal Sir Roderick, 44
Castle, Barbara, xii
Casson, Hugh, 158
Caswell, Joshua, 90, 94-96
Chamberlain, Neville, ix, 22, 30
Charteris, Martin, 175
Chester, Betty E., 165
Chubb, A.E., 71
Churchill, Winston, vii, viii, ix, xi, xii, xvi, 4, 22, 57, 63, 76, 101, 150, 153-157, 166, 171, 176
Clark, Petula, 128
Clarke Hall, Denis, 139
Clifford, Andrew, 17
Compton, Denis, 116
Cowell, Elizabeth, 126
Cox, Ian, 158
Cracknell, Vera, 36
Crimmin, Flying-Officer William John
Creech, Arthur, 98-99
Crippen, Hawley Harvey, 102
Cripps, Sir Stafford, 150-151, 155
Cunningham, Viscount, 4
Cymbalist, Leading Aircraftsman Norris, 46-47

Dain, Dr Guy, 58
Dalton, Hugh, 137
Dawson, Seaman John, 130
Day, Robin, 161
de Mille, Cecil B., 179
Denby, Elizabeth, 139
Dickens, Charles, 31-32, 60, 64
Diggory, George, 61
Diggory, Sylvia (née Beckingham), 61
Dimbleby, Richard, 152, 154, 176
Dior, Christian, 134
Dobbs, Alfred, xii
Dorman, Kate, 61
Dors, Diana, 128
Drennan, Gwen, 34, 36

Dresser, Lieutenant-Colonel H. Bruce, 99
Duke of Windsor, 176
Dutton, George, 112
Dyer, Daphne, 35

Eccles, David, 154
Ede, James Chuter, 79, 99, 173
Eden, Anthony, xii, 23, 154, 176
Eisenhower, General Dwight D., 124
Elsplid, Lieutenant Haldor, 2
Eliot, T.S., 165
Emmet, Rowland, 162
Evans, Dame Commander Edith, 4
Evans, Kathleen, 93
Everest, Sir George, 180
Ewer, William Norman, 146

Fell, Irvine, 106
Fellbrich, Heinz, 74
Fellbrich, June (née Tull), 74
Ferguson, Mr J.E., 117
Fonteyn, Margot, 126
Foot, Michael, xii
Forbes, Ann Kathleen, 36
Forbes, Mrs Ian, 34, 36-37
Formby, George, 127
France, Emily, 38
Frandsen, Flying Officer Roy Viggo Gordon, 98
Fraser, Peter, xii
Freeman, John, 150
Fuchs, Klaus, 145

Gaitskell, Hugh, xii, 155
Gallacher, Willie, 151
Games, Abram, 158
Garbett, Cyril, Archbishop of York, 152
Gardner, Margery Aimee, 91
George, Edward Alfred,
German, Edward, 99
Gibberd, Frederick, 139
Gillatt, Sir William, 173

Glattes, Kapitänleutnant Gerhard, 71
Glitz, F.C.W., 77
Gloucester, Duke of, 14, 176
Goldie, Sir Noel B., 107
Goodlad, Douglas, 128
Granger, Stewart, 127
Grant, Julian, 66
Greene, Graham, 128
Greenwood, Arthur, ix
Greenwood, Joan, 127
Gregory, E.H., 28
Gregory, Frank, 107
Grey, Janet, 137, 140, 142
Grieve, George William, 98
Grimond, Joe, 151
Grove, J.W., 80
Groves, Henry, 27
Groves, Mrs N., 27-28
Gruzinski, Anselm, 81
Guaricci, Sergeant Donato, 40-41
Guaricci, Eileen Marian, 40-41
Guthrie, Mary Sylvia, 51
Guttmann, Professor Sir Ludwig, 122
Guy, Stanley, 66

Haigh, John George, 102, 154
Halifax, Lord, ix
Halliburton, Horace, 83, 87
Hammond, Wally, 116
Hampton, Sidney, 145, 147
Handley, Tommy, 125-126
Hardy, Laurence, 163
Harris, Brian, 117
Harrison, Kathleen, 128
Hartnell, Norman, 133, 172
Hay, Will, 127
Healey, Denis, xii
Heath, Edward, 151
Heath, Elizabeth, 94
Heath, Neville George Clevely, 91-97
Henn, Colonel William, 107
Hepworth, Barbara, 158
Herod, Dennis, 110

Hewitt Cecil Rolph (aka C.H. Rolph), 100
Hildebrand, Stanley, 164
Hill, John, 139
Hillary, Edmund, 179
Hitler, Adolf, ix, 70, 75-76, 90, 96, 130
Hopkins, Mr W.G., 155
Hopkins, Harry, 166
Houlsham, H.S., 165
Houseman, Mr A., 115
Howells, Winston, 85
Hubert, William Henry Duval, 95
Hudson, Robert Spear, 22
Hughes, Ronw Moelwyn, 113
Hulbert, Wing Commander Norman, 46
Humphrey, Travers, 102
Humphreys, Mr Justice, 102
Hutton Len, 65, 116

Innes, Isabel, 26, 30
Isaacs, George, 85

Jacobs, W.W., 125
James, Gilbert, 106
Jewel, Jimmy, 125
Johnson, Amy, 129
Johnson, Alderman Thomas, 115
Johnson, William, 108
Johnson, Reginald, 99
Johnston, George H., 179
Jowitt, Sir William
Joyce, William, 102

Karas, Anton, 128
Kajdy, Major Julian, 80
Karvells, William, 39
Karvells, Peggy, 39
Kavanagh, Ted, 125
Kendall, J.R., 115
Kennedy, Charles G., 50
Kershaw, Sarah, 41
Keynes, John Maynard, xiii

King Farouk, 141
King George VI, 4, 114, 117, 120,
    137-138, 144, 156, 158, 168, 170,
    172, 174-177
King Edward VIII, 174
Knowles, Christopher, 23
Koziol, Bronislaw, 81

Lamont, Isabel, 170-171
Lascelles, Sir Alan, 168-170
Laski, Neville, 107
Law, Michael, 128
Lawson, Jack, 67, 78
Leather, Flight-Lieutenant Albert, 98
Lee, Laurie, 158
Leopold, Mr F.B., 16-18
Levin, Bernard, 161
Lewis, David North, 130
Lie, Trygve, 120
Ling, Alec, 28
Lipton, Lieutenant-Colonel Marcus,
    102
Long, Sergeant Charles, 36
Low, David, 126
Lowe, Police Constable, 112
Lowrey, Tommy, 117
Luly, Warrant Officer John Roy, 98
Luszcki, Revd Father Lucien, 82
Lyle, Colonel Floyd, 35

McCabe, Dorothy (née Ormston),
    168
McCabe, John, 168
MacDonald, James, 175
MacDonald, Ramsay, ix
McFarlane, Private John, 43
McGovern, John, 46
Maclean, Donald, 144-149
Maclean, Sir Donald, 146
Maclean, Fergus, 149
Maclean, Lady Gwendoline, 145
Maclean, Melinda, 149
McCluskey, Bridget, 40
Macmillan, Harold, xii

McNeill, Hector, 80, 147
Malcolm, Major S.F., 67, 72
Marshall, Doreen Margaret, 93-94,
    97
Marshall, Elsie, xii
Martin, Leslie, 161
Martin, Mary, 174
Massingham, Richard, 128
Maschke, Erich, 74-75
Mason-MacFarlane, Sir Frank Noel,
    xi
Matthews, Stanley, 111
Matthews, Robert, 161
Mathias, Bob, 122
Maudling, Reginald, 151
Melrose, Edwin M., 163
Menzies, Robert, xii
Mercer, Ursula, 139
Miller, Glenn, 60
Mitchell, Leslie, 126
Edward Molyneux, 133
Montgomery, Viscount, 4
Moore, Henry, 158
Morison, Hamish, 53
Morrison, Herbert, 19, 60, 155
Mosely, Edna, 139
Mountbatten, Lady Edwina, 120
Mountbatten, Lord Louis, 120
Mussolini, Benito, ix, 71
Moro, Peter, 161
Morrah, Dermot, 168-169
Moya, Hidalgo, 159

Nathan, Henry, 90
Newton, Mrs F., 166
Noad, R. Mervyn, 139
Noble, B.R.C, 98
Nicholson, Christopher, 139
Nicolson, Harold, 67, 72
Noel-Baker, Philip, 70

O'Connor, Terry, 119-122
O'Flanagan, Dr Kevin, 116
O'Rorke, Brian, 139

O'Toole, Edward, 14
Oakes, John, 42
Oliver, Jason, 130

Park, Air Vice Marshall Sir Keith, 44-45
Pataudi, Nawab of, 116
Petre, Captain Bobby, 117
Phelps, Jim, xvi
Philby, Kim, 149
Pierrepoint, Albert, 95
Pontecorvo, Bruno, 145
Pontin, Fred, 129
Portal, Lord, 4
Powell, Enoch, 151
Powell, Philip, 159
Prince Andrew of Greece, 170
Princes Charles, 173
Prince Philip, Duke of Edinburgh, 169-171, 174-175
Prince Michael of Kent, 171
Prince William of Gloucester, 171
Princess Alexandra, 171
Princess Alice of Battenburg, 170
Princess Ann, 174
Princess Elizabeth, 114, 144, 168-175
Princess Margaret, 114, 120, 171-172, 175-176, 179
Princess Royal, 176
Pym, Leslie, xii

Queen Elizabeth II, 32, 176, 178-179, 180
Queen Elizabeth (Queen Mother), 114, 120, 140, 170, 172, 175, 176
Queen Mary, 172, 176
Queen Victoria, 172

Rank, J. Arthur, 127
Reed, Carol,
Reed, Roy, 65
Reith, Baron, 31
Rhodes, Frances (née Henson), 38
Rooms, Florence, 30

Rooms, Lance Bombardier Walter, 30
Roosevelt, Franklin D., 76
Ros, Edmundo, 125
Russell, Gordon, 158

Samuel, Viscount, 154
Samuely, Felix, 159
Sandys, Duncan, 29-30
Shah of Persia, 120
Shawcross, Sir Hartley, 154
Sherpa Tenzing Norgay, 179-180
Sheppard, Alderman Frank, 106
Sheppard, Richard, 139
Shinwell, Emanuel, 9, 12, 78
Shumer, Percy, xi
Sikorski, Władysław, 76
Silkin, Lewis, 32
Simpson, Keith, 92
Sinclair, Sir Archibald, ix, xi
Slee, Air Commodore, 44
Smalley, Reverend W.C.. 145
Smith, Sir Ben, 18-20
Smith, Eddie, 114
Smith, J.W., 49
Snagge, John, 173, 175
Spooner, Detective Inspector Reg, 94
Stalin, Joseph, 76, 145-146
Stanley, Bob, 64
Stewart, Anne, 133
Stokes, Richard Rapier, 67-69, 72, 80
Storey, C.H., 21
Strachey, John, 18, 20, 22-23, 25, 43
Swaby, Frank, 104, 108
Swindell, G.H., 24
Symonds, Yvonne, 92

Tarran, Robert G., 28-30, 157
Tedder, Arthur, 1st Baron, 4
Thurtle, Ernest, 124
Thompson, Laurence, 178
Thompson, Lieutenant, 2
Topham, Mirabel, 116-117
Tompkins, Mr A.F., 18

Trautmann, Bernhard Carl ('Bert'), 75
Trinder, Tommy, 127
Truman, Harry, vii, 19
Tubbs, Ralph, 159
Turner, Bert, 114

Usher, Frank, 131

Van der Elst, Jean Julien Romain, 90
Van der Elst, Pieter. 90
Van der Elst, Violet (née Dodge), 90-91, 97
Vernon, Ernest, 107

Wafer, Jack, 165
Walters, Russell, 128
Waring, Peggy, 96
Warner, Jack, 1213, 128
Warriss, Ben, 125
Washbrook, Cyril, 116

Waters, Frank, 40
Wavell, Lord, 47
Webb, Clifford, 121
Welles, Orson, 128
Werner, Morris, xiv
Wharton, A.K.J., 165
Wheldon, Huw, 158
Wilcock, Group Captain Clifford, 27
Wilson, Earl, 179
Wilson, Harold, xii, 150
Withers, Googie, 127
Woolton, Lord, 154, 176
Wyatt, Alice, 92
Wyatt, Major Woodrow, 44

Xavier, Asquith, 88-89

Young, Miss O.M., 62

Zayne, Doreen, 84
Zayne, Herbert, 84